PREFACE BOOKS

General Editor: JOHN PURKIS

'A description of what the *Preface Books* were intended to be was included in the first volume and has appeared unchanged at the front of every succeeding title: "A series of scholary and critical studies of major writers intended for those needing modern and authoritative guidance through the characteristic difficulties of their work to reach an intelligent understanding and enjoyment of it." This may seem modest enough but a moment's reflection will reveal what a considerable claim it actually is. It is much to the credit of Longman and to their (founding) editor Maurice Hussey and his authors that these words have come to seem no more than a plain statement of fact.'

NATE NEWS

Graham Greene in 1939

A PREFACE TO

GREENE

CEDRIC WATTS

An imprint of **Pearson Education**

Harlow, England · London · New York · Reading, Massachusetts · San Francisco
Toronto · Don Mills, Ontario · Sydney · Tokyo · Singapore · Hong Kong · Seoul
Taipei · Cape Town · Madrid · Mexico City · Amsterdam · Munich · Paris · Milan

Pearson Education Limited
Edinburgh Gate
Harlow
Essex CM20 2JE
England

and Associated Companies throughout the world

Visit us on the World Wide Web at:
www.pearsoneduc.com

First published 1997

ISBN 0 582 43769 5 PPR

British Library Cataloguing-in-Publication Data
A catalogue record for this book can be obtained from the British
Library

Library of Congress Cataloging-in-Publication Data
A catalog record for this book can be obtained from the Library of
Congress

10 9 8 7 6 5 4 3 2 1
04 03 02 01

Set in 10/11pt Baskerville MT
Produced by Pearson Education Asia Pte Ltd.,
Printed in Singapore

Contents

Contents

List of illustrations

Editorial notes and acknowledgements

Unless otherwise specified, quotations from Greene's novels are taken from the British first editions listed in the bibliography. Frequently, they differ significantly in punctuation and phrasing from the US first editions and some later editions. For example, the first US edition of *Brighton Rock* (published by Viking) has a character called 'Drewitt' and lacks some of the Jewish allusions of the first British edition (Heinemann); and that Viking hardback version is the ancestor of the Viking, early Penguin and Bantam paperbacks. The Heinemann version (in which that character is called 'Prewitt') is the ancestor of the British Uniform and Library editions. For the Collected Edition (Heinemann and Bodley Head, 1970), Greene revised the text; among many other changes, he removed various Jewish allusions. Later Penguin texts follow the Collected Edition text.

Quotations from the tales are taken from *Collected Stories* (London: Bodley Head and Heinemann, 1972) or, in the case of tales not included in *Collected Stories*, from the first British collections in which the items appeared. Quotations from the essays are from *Collected Essays* (London: Bodley Head, 1969) unless otherwise indicated. Quotations from the plays are from the editions listed in the bibliography.

In any quotation, a row of three points (...) indicates an ellipsis already present in the cited text, whereas a row of five points indicates an omission I have made. I have corrected the accentuation of some foreign names. Any other changes to quotations are enclosed in square brackets.

During the preparation of this book, I was greatly helped by Norman Sherry's *The Life of Graham Greene*, Vols I and II. Michael Shelden's *Graham Greene: The Man Within* was also useful. For advice on various details, I am indebted to Professors David Leon Higdon, John Röhl, Michael Shelden, Norman Sherry and Norman Vance. Professor Hugh Drake deserves my particular gratitude for his extensive help, advice and encouragement.

Publisher's acknowledgements

We are grateful to the following for permission to reproduce copyright material:

Faber & Faber Ltd for extracts from T. S. Eliot: *Selected Essays* (1951); the author's agents on behalf of the Graham Greene Estate for extracts from his *The Name of Action, Rumour at Nightfall, Stamboul Train, A Gun for Sale, Brighton Rock, The Confidential Agent, The Power and the Glory, The Ministry of Fear, The Heart of the Matter, 'The Third Man' and 'The Fallen Idol', The Quiet American, Our Man in Havana, A Burnt-Out Case* (all published by Heinemann: 1930, 1931, 1932, 1936, 1938, 1939, 1940, 1943, 1948, 1950, 1955, 1958, 1961); *In Search of a Character, A Sense of Reality, Carving a Statue, Collected Essays, A Sort of Life, The Honorary Consul, Ways of Escape, The Other Man* (all published by the Bodley Head: 1961, 1963, 1964, 1969, 1971, 1973, 1980, 1983); *Why Do I Write?* (published by Marshall, 1948); *Reflections* (published by Reinhardt, 1990); *The Pleasure-Dome* (published by Secker, 1972); *The Lawless Roads* (published by Longmans, Green, 1939); extracts from an article on Graham Greene in *The Sunday Times Magazine,* 17 September 1995, and an interview with Graham Greene in *The Sunday Times,* 1 April 1984; Random House Ltd for extracts from *The Life of Graham Greene,* Vols I and II, by Norman Sherry (published by Cape, 1989 and 1994).

We are grateful to the following for permission to reproduce photographs, illustrations or maps:

The National Portrait Gallery (frontispiece and p. 16); from the Greene family collection (p. 18)*; Heinemann (London), p. 34; Longmans, Green (p. 42); from the collection of Bonte Durán, portrait by Harlip (p. 54)*; Verdant SA, courtesy of David Higham Associates Ltd (p. 56); Islay Lyons (p. 61); Brighton Borough Council Environmental Health Department (p. 170); UGC UK Ltd (p. 175 and p. 190).

*The publishers have been unable to trace copyright holders for these illustrations and would be grateful for any information that helps them to do so.

Abbreviations

CE   Graham Greene: *Collected Essays* (London: Bodley Head, 1969).

CCE   *Graham Greene: A Collection of Critical Essays*, ed. Samuel Hynes (Englewood Cliffs, N.J.: Prentice-Hall, 1973).

CS   Graham Greene: *Collected Stories* (London: Bodley Head and Heinemann, 1972).

GGFR   *The Graham Greene Film Reader: Mornings in the Dark*, ed. David Parkinson (Manchester: Carcanet Press, 1993).

IS   *In Search of a Character: Two African Journals* (London: Bodley Head, 1961).

Life   Norman Sherry: *The Life of Graham Greene* (London: Cape; Vol. I, 1989; Vol. II, 1994).

MW   Michael Shelden: *Graham Greene: The Man Within* (London: Heinemann, 1994).

OM   *The Other Man: Conversations with Graham Greene*, ed. Marie-Françoise Allain (London: Bodley Head, 1983).

PD   Graham Greene: *The Pleasure-Dome: The Collected Film Criticism 1935–1940*, ed. John Russell Taylor (London: Secker & Warburg, 1972).

PG   Graham Greene: *The Power and the Glory* (London: Heinemann, 1940).

R   Graham Greene: *Reflections* (London: Reinhardt, 1990).

SL   Graham Greene: *A Sort of Life* (London: Bodley Head, 1971).

WE   Graham Greene: *Ways of Escape* (London: Bodley Head, 1980).

Part One
The Writer and His Setting

Chronological table

1926	Becomes Roman Catholic. Joins *The Times*.	General Strike.
1927	Marries Vivien.	Lindbergh flies Atlantic.
1928	Visits Lewes.	Kellogg (anti-war) Pact.
1929	*The Man Within* successful. Resigns from *The Times*. Mediterranean cruise.	Labour Ministry in UK. Wall Street Crash.
1930	*The Name of Action.*	D. H. Lawrence dies.
1931	*Rumour at Nightfall.*	Economic slump develops.
1932	*Stamboul Train*: large sales.	F. D. Roosevelt becomes President of USA.
1933	Visits Norway and Sweden.	Hitler now Chancellor.
1934	*It's a Battlefield.* In Paris. Travels to Baltic states.	Hindenburg dies. Hitler becomes Führer.
1935	*England Made Me*; *The Bear Fell Free*; *The Basement Room.* Travels through Liberia with Barbara Greene.	Russian 'show trials'. Baldwin becomes Premier. Italy invades Abyssinia.
1936	*Journey without Maps*; *A Gun for Sale.*	Hitler reoccupies Rhineland. Spanish Civil War (until 1939).
1937	Literary editor of *Night and Day*.	Chamberlain becomes Prime Minister.
1938	*Brighton Rock.* Visits Mexico and France. Shirley Temple lawsuit.	Hitler seizes Austria. Munich agreement.
1939	*The Lawless Roads*; *The Confidential Agent.* Flies in bomber. Liaison with Dorothy Glover develops.	Molotov-Ribbentrop Pact. Poland invaded. Second World War commences.

1940	*The Power and the Glory*: large sales, wins Hawthornden Prize. Literary editor of *Spectator*. Works for Ministry of Information. In ARP during Blitz.	Churchill becomes Premier. Dunkirk evacuation. Battle of Britain.
1941	Joins SIS; agent in Sierra Leone.	Nazis invade USSR.
1942	*British Dramatists.*	Battle of El Alamein.
1943	*The Ministry of Fear.* Works for Kim Philby.	Battle of Stalingrad ends. Fall of Mussolini. Italy surrenders.
1944	Leaves SIS; works at propaganda centre.	D-Day.
1945	Managing director of Eyre & Spottiswoode (until 1948).	Atomic bombs dropped. Second World War ends.
1946	*The Little Train.*	UNO assembles.
1947	*Nineteen Stories.* Becomes lover of Mrs Walston.	Transistor invented. GATT established.
1948	*The Heart of the Matter* (best-seller); *Why Do I Write?*. *The Fallen Idol* (film). To Belgium, Austria, Czechoslovakia, Capri.	Israel founded. NHS begins. Berlin blockaded.
1949	Success of *The Third Man* (film). To Italy and Africa.	Communists rule China.
1950	*'The Third Man' and 'The Fallen Idol'*; *The Little Fire Engine.* In Malaya.	Korean War starts. Chinese take Pyongyang.
1951	*The Lost Childhood*; *The End of the Affair.* In Malaya and French Indo-China. Meets Jocelyn Rickards.	Colombo Plan. Festival of Britain.

1952	*The Little Horse Bus.* Receives Catholic Literary Award. Tours Vietnam; on bombing raid.	Uprisings in Kenya (until 1956). Hydrogen bomb tested.
1953	*The Living Room*; *The Little Steamroller. Essais Catholiques.* Visits Kenya.	Korean War ends. Death of Stalin. Mt Everest climbed.
1954	*Twenty-One Stories.* Visits Vietnam and Haiti.	French defeated in Indo-China.
1955	*Loser Takes All*; *The Quiet American.* Meets Ho Chi Minh. Liaison with Anita Björk begins.	Vietnam War (until 1973). Churchill resigns. Eden becomes Prime Minister.
1956	Visits Poland.	Hungarian uprising. Egypt invaded.
1957	Visits China and Cuba.	USSR launches Sputnik.
1958	*The Potting Shed*; *Our Man in Havana.* Director, Bodley Head (until 1968).	Verwoerd becomes Premier of South Africa.
1959	*The Complaisant Lover.* Visits Congo.	Castro defeats Batista.
1960	Visits Tahiti.	Sharpeville massacre. Kennedy elected President.
1961	*A Burnt-Out Case*; *In Search of a Character.* Liaison with Yvonne Cloetta develops. In Moscow; pneumonia.	Gagarin orbits earth. Bay of Pigs invasion.
1962	*Introductions to Three Novels.*	Cuban missile crisis.
1963	*A Sense of Reality.* To East Germany. In Jamaica. Revisits Haiti and Cuba.	Traitor Philby defects. Kennedy assassinated.
1964	*Carving a Statue.* Visits Goa. Meets Castro in Cuba.	Wilson becomes Prime Minister.

1965	Financial setback: investments lost by 'tax expert'.	Churchill dies. US Marines in Vietnam.
1966	*The Comedians.* Moves to Antibes. Becomes Companion of Honour. Revisits Cuba.	Verwoerd assassinated. Labour wins UK election.
1967	*May We Borrow Your Husband?* Visits Israel.	Six-Day War.
1968	In Paraguay.	USSR invades Czechoslovakia.
1969	*Collected Essays*; *Travels with My Aunt.* In Czechoslovakia. In Hamburg for Shakespeare Prize.	Unrest in Northern Ireland. Armstrong and Aldrin walk on moon.
1971	*A Sort of Life.* Meets Allende in Chile. Dorothy Glover dies.	Indo-Pakistan War. Bangladesh founded.
1972	*Collected Stories*; *The Pleasure-Dome.*	Growing unrest in Northern Ireland.
1973	*The Honorary Consul.*	Arab–Israeli War. Coup in Chile: Allende dies.
1974	*Lord Rochester's Monkey.* Says he is 'not a Catholic'.	IRA bombs in London.
1975	Edits *An Impossible Woman. The Return of A. J. Raffles.*	North Vietnamese army enters Saigon.
1976	Befriended by General Torrijos.	Mao Zedong dies.
1977	Visits Washington.	Panama Treaty signed.
1978	*The Human Factor* (best-seller). Catherine Walston dies. Greene apparently 'a Catholic atheist'.	Martial law in Nicaragua.

1979	Operation for intestinal cancer.	Thatcher becomes Prime Minister.
1980	*Dr Fischer of Geneva; Ways of Escape.* In Panama. Dos Passos Prize.	Iran–Iraq War. Reagan elected US President.
1981	*The Great Jowett.* Jerusalem Prize.	Coup in Grenada.
1982	*Monsignor Quixote; J'Accuse.*	Falklands War.
1983	*'Yes and No' and 'For Whom the Bell Chimes'.*	US troops invade Grenada.
1984	*Getting to Know the General.*	Mrs Gandhi killed.
1985	*The Tenth Man.* In Panama.	Gorbachev heads USSR; Cold War dwindles.
1986	Appointed member of the Order of Merit.	Chernobyl disaster.
1986–8	Visits Philby in Moscow.	US Iran-Contra scandal.
1987	In Nicaragua and Panama. Meets Noriega.	
1988	*The Captain and the Enemy.* Moscow doctorate.	Panama crisis.
1989	*Yours, Etc..* In Ireland. Collapses; needs transfusions.	Marxist dictatorships overthrown in Eastern Europe. Beijing revolt crushed.
1990	*The Last Word; Reflections.*	Mandela freed from jail.
1991	Dies at Vevey in Switzerland.	USSR defunct: CIS formed.

1 The life of a writer

The early years

1904–24

'Heaven lies about us in our infancy!', declares Wordsworth's 'Immortality Ode'; Greene's *Brighton Rock* says of Pinkie: 'Hell lay about him in his infancy.' One of the distinctive features of Greene's life was his readiness to seek and find the ominous and the dangerous, sometimes the hellish amid the ordinary, the horrific within the mundane. His recollections of his own childhood provide striking illustrations of this capacity, even though, ostensibly, Greene was exceptionally favoured by the circumstances of his birth. He entered an upper-middle-class family that was prosperous, large and well-connected, living in a pleasant part of England.

Graham Greene (baptised Henry Graham Greene) was born on 2 October 1904. His father, Charles, was second master at Berkhamsted, a private school in Hertfordshire; his mother, Marion, was a cousin of Robert Louis Stevenson, the novelist. One uncle was William Graham Greene, Admiralty Secretary and a founder of Naval Intelligence: he would be knighted in 1911. A great-uncle owned the Greene King brewery at Bury St Edmunds, a continuing source of wealth; another uncle, Edward, had been a highly successful businessman in Brazil; and another relative, Benjamin Buck Greene (1808–92), had been Governor of the Bank of England. In the little town of Berkhamsted, thirty miles north-west of central London, there were two connected families of Greenes ('seventeen . . . . . resident in one small place', 'the rich Greenes and . . . . . the intellectual Greenes'), each with its extensive retinue of nurses, maidservants and handymen. Graham belonged to the 'intellectual' Greenes; yet even that branch was amply rich by most people's standards. He and his five siblings lived in a household served by 'a nanny, a nursemaid, a gardener, a fat and cheerful cook, a beloved head-housemaid, a platoon of assistant maids'. He said that he had a general impression of happiness in his childhood; yet the early pages of his memoirs offer glimpses of the strange, disgusting and horrific:

> The first thing I remember is sitting in a pram at the top of a hill with a dead dog lying at my feet . . . . .
>
> There was a crowd outside one of the little houses and a man broke away and ran into the house. I was told that he was going to cut his throat . . . . .
>
> [M]y mother gained in my eyes great dignity from her superintendence of the linen-cupboard, where a frightening witch lurked . . . . .
>
> An unpleasant memory of those years is of a tin jerry full of blood: I was feeling horribly sick, for I had just had my adenoids out and my tonsils cut.
>
> (*SL*, pp. 14, 16, 17, 17)

If his recollections are accurate, they show the bases of some almost obsessional features of his eventual writings. That incident, for example, of the desperate man who runs into a house, perhaps to cut his throat, would recur in 'Analysis of a Journey', 'The Innocent', *Journey without Maps* and *The Lawless Roads*. Generally, he would be fascinated by combinations of the mundane and the horrific. Later preoccupations probably influenced his scansion of memory, so that he selected and heightened some grim elements of the early years. For his readers, Berkhamsted, however attractive its reality, would become permanently associated with a sombre canal, a humpbacked bridge, ugly almshouses and an attempted suicide. Childhood fears – of darkness, birds, bats, 'the witch in the linen-cupboard' – far outnumber childhood joys in those later works. Yet his mother, Marion, who seems to have been reasonably caring, recorded times when Graham appeared very happy, whether on an outing to primrose-filled woods or at a birthday party with his cousins. Certainly he was shy and sensitive; he recalled his mother as a remote figure of 'cool puritan beauty'. He felt early resentment towards his father, who seemed 'even more distant than our aloof mother'; and only after many years did he exhume 'a buried love' for this man who was 'liberal in politics and gently conservative in morals'.

A green baize door separated domestic life and the world of formal education. Greene entered Berkhamsted School at the age of seven, and three years later moved from the Preparatory to the Junior School there. In the holidays he browsed among the thousands of books in its library (and stole other works from the local W. H. Smith shop). He later recalled, with affectionate relish, the pleasures of his early reading: of Stanley Weyman, G. A. Henty and Rider Haggard, for instance.

[W]ithout a knowledge of Rider Haggard would I have been drawn later to Liberia? . . . . . And surely it must have been [Haggard's] *Montezuma's Daughter* and the story of the disastrous night of Cortez' retreat which lured me twenty years after to Mexico.

(*SL*, p. 53)

Like Conrad, whose early enjoyment of works of travel and exploration had led him to a maritime career and to the heart of Africa, Greene's itinerant life and dramatic narratives were being shaped by the magical impress of those books on the boy's imagination.

Prompted by his memoirs, biographers trace the eventual novelist's interest in espionage, betrayal and duplicity to his schooldays. At thirteen, Greene was a boarder in the school where his father was now the headmaster. And it was in those years as a boarder that his deepest misery developed. Thin, self-conscious and clumsy, he was poor at most sports; and the school's atmosphere seemed often foul and oppressive: he detested 'the smell of sweat and stale clothes', and 'no moment of the night was free from noise, a cough, a snore, a fart'. Worse still, he was bullied by two other boys, Lionel Carter and A. H. Wheeler. He portrays Carter as attractive but indefatigably resourceful in the infliction of mainly psychological torments; while Wheeler, at first a friend, had betrayed him by siding with Carter.

I had left civilization behind and entered a savage country of strange customs and inexplicable cruelties: a country in which I was a foreigner and a suspect, quite literally a hunted creature, known to have dubious associates. Was my father not the headmaster? I was like the son of a quisling in a country under occupation . . . . . I was surrounded by the forces of the resistance, and yet I couldn't join them without betraying my father and my brother.

(*SL*, p. 72)

His elder brother, Raymond, was a school prefect, while his father was a disciplinarian headmaster concerned to seek and punish real or imagined vices (particularly masturbation and homosexuality) amongst the pupils; he ensured that there were no locks on the lavatory doors. If the young Greene sided with his father by informing on the pupils, he was betraying his peers; if he sided with the other lads in rule-breaking, he was betraying his father. If he tried to please both sides, he was learning the wiles of a double agent. This division was eventually to prove a fruitful basis for many of the novels: so often his major works display sympathy with double agents of various kinds and with the protagonist whose loyalty to one principle or person entails treachery to another; so often he depicts a symbiosis between hunter and hunted. As a schoolboy, Graham attempted to resolve the division by repeated acts of truancy and by somewhat incompetent attempts at suicide (drinking hypo and hay-fever drops, eating deadly nightshade, swimming while stupefied by an overdose of aspirins). As for the bullying by Carter aided by the treacherous friend Wheeler, this gave him a lingering desire for revenge, 'alive like a creature under a stone'; and the revenge would take a variety of fictional forms. He would associate his adolescent experiences with evil and the hellish: repeatedly Greene later mined his schoolday recollections for infernal imagery, whether the ostensible subject were Africa (in *Journey without Maps*) or Mexico (in *The Lawless Roads*). One of Greene's grandfathers had been manic-depressive, and Greene's memoirs suggest strongly that he himself had inherited that trait. 'A manic-depressive, like my grandfather – that would be the verdict on me today', he wrote in 1971.

After an episode of truancy, Greene, now sixteen years old, was released from school for a while to be treated by a psychiatrist, Kenneth Richmond, a Jungian and spiritualist who encouraged him in the recording and analysis of his dreams. This was to be a lifelong preoccupation ('two novels and several short stories have emerged from my dreams'), and cryptic dreams were to figure prominently within his works too. Both Freudians and Jungians stress the covert personal significance of dreams, but Jungians (more mystical and less materialistic) place far less emphasis on the discovery of sexual repression than on the therapeutic value of a descent via the personal unconscious towards the collective unconscious and its sustaining myths. Richmond's conviction that messages could be received from the spiritual world may also have influenced Greene's belief in precognitive dreams. Socially, Kenneth Richmond and his wife Zoë introduced Greene to a relaxed and permissive lifestyle, and fostered his literary ambitions. The treatment seems to have been reasonably successful for a time: on his return to school, Greene now made friends easily (Eric Guest, Claud Cockburn, Peter Quennell) and, encouraged by a sympathetic classics master, continued to write fiction. A short story, 'The Tick of the Clock', for the school magazine (*The Berkhamstedian*), had been published in the *Star*, an evening newspaper (and would eventually reappear in *The Heart of the Matter*); 'The Creation of

Beauty', a tale in which God explains that the creation, with all its woes, is redeemed by 'the beauty of woman', appeared in the *Weekly Westminster Gazette*; and the typescript of a play went to drama societies but was never performed. Meantime, there were the throes of adolescence: 'Lust and boredom and senti-mentality, a frightened longing for the prostitute in Jermyn Street'; and, as enduring sustenance, the sensuality, sophistry and defiant romanticism of Browning's poetry: 'Better sin the whole sin, sure that God observes.'

In 1922 Greene failed to win a scholarship to Oxford University, but his father's money purchased entrance for the son. Greene read history at Balliol, was often drunk, and sent love-letters to a governess who was already engaged. He co-edited *Oxford Outlook*, predictably deeming his own poetry worthy of inclusion in this magazine. Other verses appeared in *Weekly Westminster*, the *Cherwell*, the *Oxford Chronicle* and the *Decachord*, and he organised a poetry broadcast for the BBC. Meanwhile, he defeated depression and boredom by playing Russian roulette with a 'small ladylike' revolver loaded with one cartridge. So he often claimed. In 1978, however, he reflected that the cartridges 'might have been harmless'. One biographer, Michael Shelden, speculates that the gun may only have been a starting pistol and the cartridge a blank, so that he risked merely a singed ear; but that is not how Greene usually portrayed the episode, and two of his Oxford friends regarded the danger as real. Greene recalled:

> The discovery that it was possible to enjoy again the visible world by risking its total loss was one that I was bound to make sooner or later.
> ..... A kind of Russian roulette remained too a factor in my later life, so that without previous experience of Africa I went on an absurd and reckless trek through Liberia; it was the fear of boredom which took me to Tabasco during the religious persecution, to a *léproserie* in the Congo, to the Kikuyu reserve during the Mau-Mau insurrection, to the emergency in Malaya and to the French war in Vietnam.
>
> (*SL*, pp. 128, 130–1)

He experienced boredom intensely, as a terrifying 'pressure inside the skull'; but his phrase 'the fear of boredom' simplifies a mixture of motives. One motive was romantic: emulation of the heroes he had read about in childhood, such as Rider Haggard's Allan Quatermain and the heroes of Captain Charles Gilson's *The Lost Column* and *The Pirate Aeroplane*. Another was emulation of Conrad, the voyager-novelist. Another motive was the search for source-materials for fiction. And another was his astute recognition that a travelling writer might be paid at least thrice in succession – first for pieces of reportage in newspapers or magazines, secondly for the re-publication of such journalism in book form, and thirdly for the emergent novels. A fascination by espionage, whether amateur or professional, played its part.

There was related astuteness when he joined the Communist Party branch at Oxford: he hoped that it might lead to 'a free trip to Moscow and Leningrad'; though, instead, it gained him access to the Party's headquarters at Paris and a tedious meeting there which provided material for a later novel, *It's a Battlefield*. A similar urge to obtain subsidised travel, excitement and entry to the world of intrigue led him to offer his services as a propagandist-cum-agent to the German Embassy. The harsh treatment of Germans in the French-occupied Rhineland (in the region of Trier) had, he said, aroused his indignation. Funded by the German Embassy, he went on a tour of the region with Claud Cockburn; and, though they failed to discover any atrocities, Greene used the experience as the basis of some articles and for (eventually) *The Name of Action*. 'I was ready to be a mercenary in any cause so long as I was repaid with excitement and a little risk. I suppose too that every novelist has something in common with a spy', he commented later. He even claimed that in 1923, in Dublin, he had offered to serve as an agent in Northern Ireland. The Irish journey was funded by the *Weekly Westminster Gazette*, which published his consequent 'Impressions of Dublin'.

By autumn 1924 Greene was leading what he himself called 'an odd schizophrenic life' at Oxford: attending tutorials on English history, watching debates at the Union, getting drunk, working on a never-published novel, and writing love-letters to Gwen Howell. She worked as a nanny to his sister Elisabeth, was ten years older than Greene and was already engaged; but, in talk, letters and love-poems, tormented by desire and jealousy, he sought in vain to lure her from her fiancé. Her marriage took place in February 1925. Some of the amatory poems appeared in *Babbling April*, a volume published two months later which attracted (and deserved) little attention; the planned printing of 500 copies was reduced to 300, and only 62 were sold in the first year. The *Times Literary Supplement* was dismissive. The Oxford aesthete, Harold Acton, reviewing the book in the *Cherwell*, deemed the poet homesick, sentimental, and modest 'in spite of the multitude of his egos'; a poem describing an episode of Russian roulette ('The Gamble') made Acton wish 'to throw down the book in disgust, to cry aloud: "For God's sake, be a man!" ' Greene responded in the *Cherwell* by scorning 'Mr Acton as a professor of Manliness'. To his mother, he said that this was 'All grist to the mill of advertisement'. For many years to come, Greene would be energetic, resourceful and astute in his quest for publicity, fame and commercial success as a writer.

By now he was a passably handsome but gangling young man: tall (6 feet 1 inch, he stated), thin, somewhat awkward, with large ears and prominent pale blue eyes. His accent was that of the English upper middle class, rendering 'bad' and 'sad' as 'bed' and 'sed'; his voice had a somewhat growly intonation, and the 'r' sounds were gutturalised in a Gallic manner. He wore spectacles but removed them for photographs. Evidence would accumulate that women often found fascinating his combination of the imposing and the diffident, the intense and the vulnerable.

Meanwhile, in addition to maintaining contact with the German authorities, Greene offered to be the Trier correspondent of an extreme right-wing paper, *The Patriot*, which supported the French, and solicited introductions from the French Embassy. This ingenious scheme to become a double agent was, he says, defeated mainly by the Dawes Plan, which helped Germany to meet her treaty obligations and resolved the crisis in Trier. In a variety of ways, however, Greene was to be a 'double agent' in his future life, whether as lover, political traveller or fiction-writer. Whatever his avowed religion, his tutelary deity was often Janus, the two-faced god who looks both ways at once.

1925–29

Greene, now aged twenty, graduated from Oxford with a second-class BA in History. He entered employment with the British–American Tobacco Company, but resigned after a few weeks and became a private tutor to an eight-year-old boy in Derbyshire. He then turned to journalism, and worked as an unpaid writer for the *Nottingham Journal*: unpaid, because he hoped that after serving an apprenticeship there he might be accepted by a London paper. Once again, his father supplied funds. Subsequently, on becoming a sub-editor of *The Times*, he was very happy to leave industrial Nottingham (which would feature in *Stamboul Train*, *A Gun for Sale* and *The Confidential Agent*) for the manifold attractions of London. It was while living in Nottingham that he took instruction in Roman Catholicism from a local priest, George Trollope, who was 'very tall and very fat . . . . . with big smooth jowls which looked as though they never needed a razor'. The reason for the instruction was that he was engaged to marry a Catholic.

Greene as a young man

Vivienne Dayrell-Browning (who later preferred to abbreviate her Christian name to Vivien) had written to Greene in 1925, when he was at Balliol, to correct the religious terminology in a film review he had published: she objected that Catholics did not 'worship' the Virgin Mary but offered veneration or 'hyperdulia'. The letter led to meetings and, after considerable reluctance on her part, to a love-relationship. Vivien, then twenty, worked as a secretary for Basil Blackwell, the publisher. Two years previously, she had become a Catholic convert. She wrote romantic poetry, some of which had appeared in *Poetry Review* and in a collection, *The Little Wings*. Greene, immediately impressed by her prettiness, rapidly declared himself 'frantically in love'. Put on his mettle by awareness that he had rivals, he sent her letters that were variously adoring, passionate, sensual, sentimental, whimsical, witty and facetious. In October 1925 he wrote:

> This is to certify that whereas the aforesaid Graham Greene has on this day, October 2nd, attained his legal majority & has thus become legal master of himself & his actions, the aforesaid Graham Greene herewith states & declares that he surrenders himself entire, with no reservation, to be the property sole & freehold, of Miss Vivienne Dayrell, to do with as she may at any time think fit.
>
> Signed:- Graham Greene.
> Witness: Paddy [dog] – his mark.
> (*Life* I, p. 230)

In these letters, Vivien is termed 'a saint', a 'miracle worker' who has 'given . . . . . the sun a gold it's never had before'; she holds 'all beauty and all mystery and all wonder'. He promised that for her sake he would become the 'youngest Conservative Prime Minister since Pitt, or Mr Graham Greene, O.M.[,] the successor of Thomas Hardy'. (He was to enter the Order of Merit in 1986.) Initially, she had declined his offer of marriage, one objection being that he was a sceptic whereas she was devout; but Graham persevered and succeeded, becoming a convert in the process. His friend Claud Cockburn recalled telling him:

> 'Go right ahead – take instruction or whatever balderdash they want you to go through, if you need this for your fuck, go ahead and do it, and as we both know, the whole thing is bloody nonsense.'
>
> (*Life* I, p. 193)

Greene's fervour increased: another letter to Vivien says:

> Will you be affectionate in spite of the cold weather? Will you be brazen? I shall be. Will you be scandalous? I shall be. Will you be shocking? I shall be. Gooja Gooja . . . . .
>
> (*Life* I, p. 20)

Father Trollope, a former actor who was to become a Redemptorist monk, prevailed in argument against Greene's atheism, and Greene became a communicant of the Roman

Vivien Greene

Catholic Church in February 1926, 'convinced of the probable existence of something we call God'. He insisted that his faith had a rational rather than an emotional basis. The marriage to Vivien took place at St Mary's Church in Holly Place, London NW3, on 15 October, 1927, and was followed by an idyllic honeymoon in France, during which the couple went sightseeing in Paris and swam naked in the Mediterranean. On the return, there ensued (Greene recalled) a particularly happy phase of his life: newly married to the adorable Vivien, writing a novel (his third attempt) in the mornings, and working for *The Times* from 4 p.m. to midnight.

His initial salary at *The Times* was £250 a year, with the prospect that it might soon double if his work were satisfactory. At that time, a doctor could earn around £600 per annum, an electrician £150; a new three-bedroom house might cost £500. Greene said that the period of sub-editing had literary value, for it taught him to eliminate linguistic clichés and superfluities; also gave him the excitements of being a strike-breaker, helping to produce and distribute the newspaper during the General

Strike. (He even served as a special constable, guarding the Establishment from the militant workers.) Eventually, in 1928, Charles Evans, the chairman of William Heinemann Ltd, accepted his novel, *The Man Within*, on generous terms: a £50 advance on a royalty starting at 12½ per cent. At Evans's office, Greene felt that he had joined the legendary company of Heinemann authors: Galsworthy, Masefield, Somerset Maugham, George Moore – and Conrad, whose 'bearded ghost . . . . . rumbled on the rooftops with the rain'. For a first novel, *The Man Within* sold very well: after the initial printing of 2,000 copies, rapid reprints took sales beyond 12,000 (*MW*, pp. 138–9).

In retrospect, Greene found himself baffled by the success of *The Man Within*, which seemed a 'very young and very sentimental' novel. Its action is set (rather vaguely) in the early nineteenth century. The protagonist, Francis Andrews, is described as 'a sort of Judas'. One of a band of smugglers, he has betrayed them to the authorities. His motives are mixed, but include a desire to prove his own importance to the smugglers who had derided him; he also feels a jealous admiration for their leader, Captain Carlyon. A beautiful and virtuous young woman, Elizabeth, persuades Andrews to walk from Shoreham across the South Downs to Lewes to testify at the trial of the arrested smugglers; and he does indeed appear in court, but largely because he has met a promiscuous woman, Lucy, who agrees to copulate with him only if he testifies. He returns to Elizabeth and they agree to marry; yet, in an act of cowardice, he deserts her when vengeful smugglers arrive, and she, assaulted, commits suicide. Andrews, rapidly reconciled to Carlyon, helps him to escape and lets himself be arrested for Elizabeth's death. As the novel ends, Andrews prepares to kill himself.

This is a strange, murky, implausible novel which seems largely to be an act of psychological self-purgation by Greene. Although the setting is the early nineteenth century, the characters' emotions and some of the dialogue seem to belong rather to the 1920s. There are numerous technical implausibilities; coincidental meetings abound. The plotting has remote echoes of Scott and Stevenson and of the Conrad–Hueffer novel, *Romance* (1903). In *Romance*, too, the hero is involved with smugglers, moves on a borderline between the guilty and the innocent, falls dangerously in love, and is the central figure in a trial. The protagonist of Marjorie Bowen's *The Viper of Milan*, which fascinated Greene, betrays his followers in vain and loses the woman he loves. For readers today, the main interest of *The Man Within* probably lies in its anticipations (variously vague, unfocused and naïve) of characters, situations and themes which were to be developed with far more acuity and sophistication in later works by Greene.

The central character is divided and often self-hating, capable of good actions but also of Judas-like treachery and cowardice; he recognises love and virtue but is led by lust into betrayal of the virtuous woman; and he has a strange love–hate relationship with a charismatic male who is both his admired rescuer and a second father-figure to be jealously defied. He is repeatedly drawn into ambush. In crude form there are anticipations of later self-condemning protagonists, including Scobie and Bendrix; of figures who try to assist the destruction of someone they admire (even the relationship between Martins and Lime is vaguely foreshadowed); of weary fugitives whose capture seems inevitable; and of those males who seem obliged to distrust and hurt the loving woman, like Bendrix in his relationship with Sarah in *The End of the Affair* or Brown with Martha in *The Comedians*.

Autobiographical pressures seem to distort the narrative. Andrews's resentful attitude to the jeering smugglers appears to derive from Greene's bitter recollections of the Berkhamsted schoolboys. The contrasting attractions of the saintly Elizabeth and the lustful Lucy may reflect Greene's division between marriage to Vivien and the appeal of illicit carnality (and reflects also the ancient misogynistic stereotype of woman as either virgin or whore). Andrews's harsh view of his father may derive partly from Greene's feelings of resentment towards his own father, who disliked the book when he read it. One of Greene's biographers speculates that the love–hate (or, as it proves, love–hate–love) relationship to the surrogate father, Carlyon, derives from a romantic friendship with Joseph Macleod. One connection is that Greene and Macleod, close friends and fellow-poets at Oxford, had watched a beautiful sunset together, as had Andrews and Carlyon. Macleod, who was to become a famous broadcaster, would be mentioned in *The Ministry of Fear*. The epigraph of *The Man Within* is Sir Thomas Browne's remark, 'There's another man within me that's angry with me'; and this might serve as epigraph not only to the long sequence of Greene's works featuring a divided, self-scorning protagonist, in whom goodness is at war with hatred and egotism, but also, indeed, to Greene's sense of himself, his psychology and his emotional allegiances. One symptom was his occasional employment of the pseudonym 'Hilary Trench', associated with a dark or vindictive aspect of his personality.

Features of the novel clearly result from direct research: Greene, like his protagonist, had walked over the Sussex downs from Hassocks to Lewes, and the description of the countryside and of Lewes High Street remains accurately evocative. (An early essay is 'A Walk on the Sussex Downs'.) Even where the novel is unconvincing, it has some of the memorability of dream or nightmare, an impression created partly by the stress on Andrews's subjective viewpoint and partly by the deliberately (if sometimes absurdly) poetic prose: claustrophobic warmth, chilly night, sinister fog are well conveyed. (A sample of the poetic prose: 'A sky curdled with dark, heavy clouds had forced the pace of night.') The nasty hero was, for the time, rather unconventional; and the treatment of the sexual encounter between Andrews and Lucy was, again for that time, frankly erotic. Greene had found, for marketing purposes, a convenient combination: some features of popular commercial fiction (picturesque location, dramatic action, love and lust) and some features to appeal to more intellectual readers (psychological introspection, ethical division, hints of religious allegory, mannered and even expressionistic prose). It was a combination which, handled more dextrously and given greater moral and social substance, would eventually help to ensure Greene's enduring success. And, like most of his other novels, *The Man Within* would be filmed: in 1947, with Michael Redgrave as Carlyon and Richard Attenborough as Andrews. (A 'shockingly bad' version, said Greene, recalling its scene of torture and 'its strong note of homosexuality'.)

The temporary success of *The Man Within* was indeed remarkable. From the start, the staff at Heinemann were enthusiastic: the manager of the trade department told his colleagues to buy a copy of the first edition ('it's sure to appreciate in value'), and lavish publicity was provided. Doubleday, Doran & Co. agreed to publish it in the USA. Two editions were sold before publication 'and within six months it went into six impressions and was translated into German, Dutch, Norwegian, Danish and Swedish' (*Life* 1, p. 366). The *Sphere*, hailing Greene as 'a new star', lauded this 'novel of extreme brilliance'; the New York *Outlook and Independence* called it 'probably the most original and possibly the strongest new talent of the year in English fiction, a remarkable study of the inward conflict of a dual nature'; to the *Nation* it was a 'perfect adventure story'; the *Sunday Times* praised 'this strangely fascinating book'; and the *Publisher's Circular* prophesied 'a big demand for this book – in style original and powerful'. Some reviewers compared it with work by Greene's relative, Robert Louis Stevenson. The novelist J. B. Priestley, at least, was not dazzled: he rightly thought the writing too mannered, the whole dreamlike and unconvincing. (In later works, Greene attempted to take revenge on Priestley; but the attempt would have a disastrous outcome.)

Elated by the reception of *The Man Within*, Greene resigned from *The Times* at the end of 1929 after securing a generous arrangement from Charles Evans: £650 a year for three years (half the money to be supplied by the American publisher, Doubleday, Doran & Co.), in return for three further novels. This sum, however, was an advance payment of royalties yet to be earned by those books. It proved to be an arrangement that the author would bitterly regret.

1930–32

His second published novel, *The Name of Action*, appeared in October 1930. It used the Trier location which Greene had visited years before; and it adapted political material from his unpublished Carlist novel, *The Episode*. The hero, a faithless 'hollow man', is a callow idealist who, while supporting a revolution against a puritanical dictator, Demassener, becomes infatuated by the dictator's beautiful wife. Eventually, however, after copulating with her, the disillusioned hero (Oliver Chant) accompanies the toppled (and sexually impotent) dictator back to England, while the beautiful wife is clearly destined to become the mistress of Kapper, the unsavoury leader of the victorious revolutionaries – a 'shifty-eyed, mean-bodied Jew'.

The plot of *The Name of Action* (like that of *The Man Within*) depends heavily on coincidental meetings; and the character of the hero again seems peculiarly weak in its basis: he is variously naïve, immature, and implausibly romantic. By the end, the novel has revealed a disturbing alliance of foes: the seductress, the Jew and the revolutionary; against them, the callow protagonist and his impotent father-figure. As in *The Man Within*, the hero's relationship to the older man changes from that of jealous betrayer to friend and rescuer. (Greene's Oedipal feelings seem to be at work.) Like its predecessor, this novel appears, at times, to be a means of psychological catharsis for its author. The narrative is more convincing in its treatment of locations and travel (particularly the cold river-journey by barge) than in its rendering of dialogue, emotional confrontation or social politics. The whole is an unconvincing *mélange* of Anthony Hope's Ruritania, Trier in the 1920s, Angelo's regime in *Measure for Measure*, the Grail legends of the impotent Fisher King, and expressionism. Yet, though unconvincing, it retains a memorability like that of a feverish dream. Such memorability is, indeed, characteristic of expressionistic works, in which the vista seems the expression of an abnormal state of mind.

Greene said that he had spent too long studying the

technique of 'the point of view' as analysed in Percy Lubbock's *The Craft of Fiction* and that he had neglected the art of rendering action vividly by means of economical language: the phrasing of *The Name of Action*, he justly felt, was too often self-conscious and self-indulgent. (A notorious example is: 'A revolver drooped like a parched flower to the pavement.')

Reviews of the novel were mixed but predominantly negative; Evelyn Waugh, for instance, gave it a mainly unfavourable account in the *Graphic*; the *New Statesman* was scathing: 'his story is half in Cloud-cuckoo land and half in Ruritania'. Greene recalled that sales were disastrous: only 2,000 copies. According to the publisher's records, cited by Shelden (*MW*, p. 156), the figure was 5,000; but this was still disappointing after the success of *The Man Within*.

In 1931, Greene and Vivien had moved to a cottage in Chipping Campden (a small rural market-town in Gloucestershire) in order to make the make the financial advance from the publishers go further. Rats and mice rustled in the thatched roof, but apples and lettuces grew in the garden. Greene, restlessly energetic, went on many rambles through the countryside, sometimes with his brother Hugh: he visited Tewkesbury, Stow-on-the-Wold and Gloucester. He and Vivien recalled this time as one of poverty (though they employed a maidservant and a gardener), discomfort, worry and love. Greene sometimes felt that his nerves were on edge; but he and his wife sent each other endearing love-letters even when they were both at home and only a few yards from each other. *The Man Within, The Name of Action* and *Stamboul Train* were all dedicated affectionately to Vivien. Nevertheless (as biographers note), Greene's diary shows that he secretly maintained relationships with two women in London, apparently prostitutes, Annette (or 'A') and 'O'. In *England Made Me*, Annette would become Anthony Sant's favourite prostitute. Greene's commitment to marital fidelity and his powers of sexual self-control were consistently weak; repeatedly, he betrayed and deceived his wife. His sexual anxieties were not so feeble as to be allayed by only one partner; nor was his Catholicism so inflexible as to deter him from a long sequence of adulteries.

Greene's father, a diabetic, had now retired from teaching and, with Marion, was living at Crowborough; there they were sometimes joined by Greene's brother Herbert, who was often unemployed. Raymond, a brother three years older than Graham, had commenced a distinguished career as a physician and gained fame as a mountaineer in the Himalayas: notably on the Kamet and Everest expeditions (1931, 1933). A sense of rivalry with Raymond was another of Graham's incentives to travel far and wide.

The literary career faltered again when *Rumour at Nightfall* was published by Heinemann in November 1931. This story of the Carlist rebellion, set in Spain, again drew material from the abortive *The Episode* – that misbegotten work prompted by Conrad's *The Arrow of Gold*. Actually, the Carlist material serves as mere backdrop for a novel of jealous love between two men, one of whom (Chase) is angered when his friend (Crane) falls in love with a beautiful Catholic woman. Crane hastily marries her, experiencing a miraculous or hallucinatory conversion; but, betrayed by Chase, he is killed by rebels, leaving his friend and widow to console each other. Once again, one male friend betrays another; once again, the woman is the fulcrum of jealousy. The ostensible subjects of his first three published novels may have been smuggling, revolution and Carlism respectively; the underlying subject seems to be Greene's difficulty in reconciling the claims of heterosexuality in the large adult world with recollections of adolescent and post-adolescent male friendships and enmities in the narrow world of the public school and the Oxford college.

Rumour at Nightfall is marred by pretentiously 'literary', sub-Conradian descriptive passages and by prolix, sub-Jamesian analyses of dialogue; generally, by romantic elaboration. Two instances:

> [Crane sees] shadows from house to house that lay like velvet carpets stretched for a reception or a dance, or like deep felt to deaden sound outside the dwelling of a dying man . . . . .
> She said with a quiet amusement that he felt would always fall like rain upon parched soil, like sunlight on a dripping hedge, like the moon on darkness bringing peace, 'You would be shriven too easily.'

> (pp. 221, 214–15)

Action freezes into tableaux; commentary suffocates dialogue.

The work's reception was utterly depressing for Greene. *Rumour at Nightfall* sold only 1,200 copies, he later recalled, though another 1,000 were sold by Doubleday in the USA. Heinemann recorded sales nearer 3,000, but still low. Reviews were generally hostile, deploring the theatrical, artificial features of the narration. The *New Republic* complained of the excessive mental analyses of the characters and noted 'atmosphere laid on heavily, like paint'; the *Spectator* said that Greene is 'one of those authors who have something to say but whose turgidity prevents them from saying it'. A scathing review by Frank Swinnerton persuaded Greene it was time to make a fresh conceptual start. Both this novel and *The Name of Action* were eventually suppressed by the author, excluded from the collected editions of his works and from his books' listings of his publications: a drastic act of self-criticism and penance.

Greene was in debt to the publishers; and he had rashly devoted time to a biography of the atheistic libertine poet, John Wilmot, Earl of Rochester, only to see it rejected by Heinemann. (It did not appear until 1974, as *Lord Rochester's Monkey*, by which time bawdy verse was welcomed rather than eschewed by publishers.) Greene sought, unsuccessfully, to return as a journalist to *The Times*, and was rejected by the *Catholic Herald*; he even solicited a lecturer's post at a university near Bangkok. Vivien was pregnant; the worries mounted. In August 1932 he reflected that he was effectively £30 in debt with no guarantee of any money or employment after that month. (The average income of an employed person was then £3 per week.) Like his great literary hero, Conrad, who had so often groaned under the burden of depression and debt, Greene experienced the anguish of having committed himself to the notoriously risky career of a novelist.

After these years of financial struggle, however, *Stamboul Train* was to provide an interval of success. This novel was well researched and was written with a new thematic richness, diversity of characterisation, liveliness of movement and sharpness of observation. He had turned away from nostalgic literary romanticism towards contemporary cinematic realism; away from the verbosity of *The Arrow of Gold* to the mobile montage of film.

Greene loved travel, but was somewhat reluctant to pay his own fares. Hence, in part, his flirtation (and later steady relationship) with secret service work. When researching *Stamboul Train*, he asked the French railway company to pay his return fare to Constantinople; the firm declined, so he was obliged to buy his own ticket – though then he travelled only as far as Cologne, taking copious notes. To save money on meals, he (like Coral Musker in the novel) took sandwiches on the journey. For descriptions of Istanbul, the setting of the end of the novel, be relied on memories of his 24-hour visit during a recent Hellenic cruise, on H. G. Dwight's *Constantinople*, on a Baedeker guide-book and probably on John Dos Passos's *Orient Express*. His memories of Nottingham blended with Coral's recollections. Coral herself was based partly on Anna Sten, star of the film *The Crime of Dmitri Karamazoff*.

Published in December 1932, the novel was at once declared a Book Society choice: this guaranteed large sales to the members, perhaps 10,000 copies. The choice was not entirely unexpected, since Greene had friends on the selection committee (he had met Clemence Dane at Oxford, and Edmund Blunden was a friend of the family); furthermore, the Society's secretary, Rupert Hart-Davis, had promised to use his influence. Heinemann soon printed around 13,000 copies. Doubleday (USA) sold initially another 4,000. (Sales mounted to 21,000 and 5,000 respectively: *MW*, p. 165.) A last-minute hitch occurred when J. B. Priestley threatened a libel action: he had seen an advance copy and quickly identified the character of the novelist Savory as a satiric portrayal of himself. Savory is a complacent, pipe-smoking popular author, a 'modern Dickens', and, it is hinted, a potential sex-offender. To reduce the likeness between Priestley and Savory, Greene was humiliatingly obliged to devise hasty textual changes which he sent by telephone to the publisher; he had to pay for the revisions. (In *Brighton Rock*, however, he would jeer at the popularity of *The Good Companions*.) A complication is that Savory's shrewd calculative watchfulness as a writer, exemplified in the following extract (pp. 143–4), seems almost identical to Greene's:

> [Savory] wondered what terms he could use to describe the night. It is all a question of choice and arrangement; I must show not all that I see but a few selected sharp points of vision. I must not mention the shadows across the snow, for their colour and shape are indefinite, but I may pick out the scarlet signal lamp shining against the white ground, the flame of the waiting-room fire in the country station, the bead of light on a barge beating back against the current . . . . . One thing the films had taught the eye, Savory thought, the beauty of landscape in motion, how a church tower moved behind and above the trees, how it dipped and soared with the uneven human stride . . . . . That sense of movement must be conveyed in prose . . . . .

That sense is vigorously conveyed in *Stamboul Train*. The description of the train's progress from Bruges (pp. 13–14) is a model of filmic montage:

> The fire-hole door opened and the blaze and the heat of the furnace for a moment emerged. The driver turned the regulator full open, and the footplate shook with the weight of the coaches. Presently the engine settled smoothly to its work, the driver brought the cut-off back, and the last of the sun came out as the train passed through Bruges, the regulator

closed, coasting with little steam. The sunset lit up tall dripping walls, alleys with stagnant water radiant for a moment with liquid light . . . . . The sparks from the express became visible, like hordes of scarlet beetles tempted into the air by night; they fell and smouldered by the track, touched leaves and twigs and cabbage stalks and turned to soot. A girl riding a carthorse lifted her face and laughed; on the bank beside the line a man and woman lay embraced. Then darkness fell outside, and passengers through the glass could see only the transparent reflection of their own features.

Sharp details, rapid momentum, a strong sense of light and colour: these help a narrative in which nimble shifts of viewpoint from one character to another accentuate the mounting suspense.

Reviews of *Stamboul Train* were generally very good. Furthermore, Twentieth-Century Fox bought the film rights for the (then) large sum of £1,738: Greene was ecstatic. He commented later:

> That year, 1931, for the first and last time in my life I deliberately set out to write a book to please, one which with luck might be made into a film. The devil looks after his own and in *Stamboul Train* I succeeded in both aims . . . . .
>
> (*WE*, p. 26)

With *Stamboul Train*, Greene reached maturity as a novelist. The callowness, dreaminess and analytic prolixity of the early works have gone. *Stamboul Train* is gripping, ruthless, powerfully atmospheric; it has a vivid gallery of characters and a dextrously interwoven thematic strucutre. It has the pace of a thriller, the compression and technical agility of an experimental novel, and it is, as Greene deliberately intended, superbly cinematic. That the work also happens to be deeply tainted by anti-Semitism makes a sad commentary on its times.

1933–39

The financial success of *Stamboul Train* brought new security. From 1933 Greene was also being paid for regular book reviewing in the *Spectator*; after 1935 he would be the magazine's film reviewer, too. Feeling affluent after their relatively austere phase, Graham and Vivien moved from the cottage at Chipping Campden to a luxurious new flat in Oxford; and in December 1933 their first child (Lucy Caroline) was born by Cæsarean section at the Radcliffe Infirmary. Vivien recalled:

> It was like a train running slowly into the buffers . . . . . It
> certainly did hurt . . . . . It had to be a caesarean and they
> were so brutal about the stitches. I remember that awful head
> nurse or sister coming to me and saying, 'Oh this room
> smells' and flinging open the window, and I said, 'I can't do
> anything about it – I can't get up.' And she came up and leant
> over me and said, 'Don't you talk to me like that!' It was
> terrifying.
>
> (*Life* I, p. 504)

Greene, a reluctant father, had become reconciled to the idea of
paternity, but the presence of the baby made him even less
domesticated; he continued to seize opportunities to travel to
London and farther afield. He had visited Norway and Sweden in
1933; in 1934 he made a mysterious journey to Berlin, Latvia and
Estonia, accompanied for part of the time by the British Consul
of Tallinn. Shelden (*MW*, p. 189) speculates that, in the Baltic,
Greene was 'working for a foreign power'.

Meanwhile, between September 1932 and August 1933, Greene
had written *It's a Battlefield*, which was published in February
1934. At the opening of this novel, a communist, Jim Drover, has
been sentenced to death after stabbing and killing a policeman
during a turbulent demonstration. Friends attempt to bring
about a reprieve for him. His brother, Conrad Drover, a mentally
disturbed clerk with an inferiority complex, undergoes a breakdown.
Finally, while attempting to assassinate a Police Commissioner,
Conrad is knocked down by a car and dies, unaware that, after
all, his brother has been reprieved – not as a result of any
petition but on the grounds of political expediency. The three
main female characters are Jim Drover's wife, Milly, her sister,
Kay, and a wealthy patroness, Caroline Bury. Milly is weak and
lonely, and sleeps with Conrad; Kay is frankly hedonistic and
promiscuous; Caroline Bury (based partly on Lady Ottoline
Morrell) is a friend of the arts and of liberal causes.

The work as a whole is evidence of Greene's study of
socialism: he had read, with admiration, G. D. H. Cole's *The
Intelligent Man's Guide through World Chaos*. In the novel, however,
the socialist case is implausibly compiled. Duplicative descriptions
establish a laboured, detailed and unlikely parallel between the
prison in which the condemned man languishes and the match
factory in which Kay works long hours. In both places, there are
Blocks A, B, and C; in both, people may advance from the
relatively poor conditions of Block A, via Block B, to the better
conditions of Block C; in both, Block C provides facilities for
singing, and food good enough to be eaten by the warders or

management as well as by the prisoners or workers. As preparation, Greene had visited two prisons (Wormwood Scrubs and Wandsworth) in London and the Moreland ('England's Glory') match factory at Gloucester: the novel makes much of the long hours, poor wages, and appallingly noisy conditions experienced by the factory women. (The author had joined the Independent Labour Party in August 1933.) But, although the story offers some broad support to the socialist case, the narrator looks with a jaundiced eye on a Communist Party meeting. There power is seized by force by a brutal demagogue who has no sympathy with Jim Drover. Another communist, Mr Surrogate (based on Middleton Murry), is depicted as a jaded, ageing, rather hypocritical figure; he lives in pampered luxury.

The novel is strongly indebted to Conrad's *The Secret Agent*: a matter discussed in Part Two of this book. Greene, in his depiction of London's topography, in the interweaving of characters representing a cross-section of the urban society, and in the representation of individual psychology (which often moves towards inner monologue or stream of consciousness), may also be indebted to Virginia Woolf's *Mrs Dalloway* (1925). The increasing derangement of Conrad Drover has some resemblances to that of Septimus Warren Smith. But the comparison with Woolf throws into relief Greene's interest in the depiction of squalor and of sordid sexuality: repeatedly, sexual encounters are shown to be disappointing, treacherous or insignificant; loving mutuality seems to evade the characters. Mr Surrogate quotes Thomas Hobbes, the sceptical philosopher; and Hobbes's claim that in the state of nature man's life is 'solitary, poor, nasty, brutish, and short' seems to apply all too well to numerous denizens of London in *It's a Battlefield*.

Compared with *Stamboul Train*, *It's a Battlefield* marks a regression: the narrative lacks the tight, purposeful organisation and the accelerating dramatic momentum of the earlier novel. Greene repeatedly revised the text: the 'Commissioner' of the first edition became the 'Assistant Commissioner', and in some later editions the 'mad murderer' scene and the Communist Party meeting have been cut. His next work, *England Made Me*, which appeared in June 1935, also has its disappointing features, but it illustrates well Greene's use of shock-tactics.

England Made Me features a close relationship between a pair of twins, Anthony and Kate Farrant. Kate has become the mistress of Erik Krogh, a Swedish millionaire who is both a financier and a manufacturer; and she has done so largely because she seeks to help her brother. Anthony Farrant is the first of many gentlemanly parasites or charming con-men in

Greene's fiction. He is from a minor public school, is a prolific liar (claiming to be a retired captain from the army), moves from job to job, repeatedly being sacked because of his dishonesty, and is outwardly charming but lazy and inveterately parasitical. His later fictional relatives include numerous raffish confidence-tricksters, ranging from Hands in 'The Other Side of the Border' and 'Captain' Jones in *The Comedians* to the Captain in *The Captain and the Enemy* and Visconti in *Travels with My Aunt*. He is based on 'the black sheep of the family', Herbert Greene, who similarly roamed the world, being unable to hold down a job, getting into scrapes, borrowing money that he never repaid, and becoming an alcoholic. In a letter to Vivien about him, Graham Greene wrote:

> Herbert's started again. Cables home that the Lloyd's job has 'come to an end' and money needed . . . . . I wish to goodness he'd shoot himself . . . . . I think my people are getting simply desperate about him. If I was my father, I should simply send him nothing and let him get something or starve. Only I suppose he'd borrow enough money from some fool and get home. Killing would be no murder in his case.
>
> (*Life* I, p. 497)

'Killing would be no murder': so, in *England Made Me*, by an easy act of psychological transference, the Herbert character, Anthony Farrant, is eventually murdered, pushed into the sea by Krogh's thuggish henchman. Like other members of this literary clan, Anthony is an engaging rogue, relatively innocent when his tricks are compared with the machinations of Krogh in the world of finance and industry; and, like those other members, too, Anthony does have a capacity for sympathy with the underdog: he tries in vain to help the pathetic son of a socialist who has been unjustly sacked.

In *Stamboul Train*, Greene had dealt frankly (if caustically) with lesbianism; in *England Made Me*, he boldly breached another taboo by dealing with incestuous love. Astutely, he invoked the precedent of Shakespeare, whose bizarre late romance, *Pericles, Prince of Tyre*, is repeatedly recalled. For example: a Swedish scholar obtains from Krogh the money to stage this play in his own translation, and drunken comedy ensues as the Professor attempts to enlist actresses for the *magnum opus*. *Pericles* includes not only sordid brothel scenes; it also reveals and denounces the incestuous passion between Antiochus and his daughter ('both like serpents are, who though they feed / On sweetest flowers, yet they poison breed'). The Shakespeare play thus provides an ominous ironic commentary on the sexual promiscuity of the women encountered by Anthony and particularly on the fact that his sister's attraction to him is not merely affectionate but actively sexual. Their culminating exchange is this:

'I love you . . . . . you're the only damned man in the world I love.'
'Brother and sister,' he jeered, with a sense again of a great waste . . . . .

Commenting later on these siblings (*WE*, p. 38), Greene implied that ideally they should have copulated:

Kate was nearer to knowledge than Anthony and both used their superficial sexual loves, Kate with Krogh and Anthony with Loo, to evade the real right thing. The cowardly evasions were not mine; they belonged to the doomed pair.

Perhaps Greene was recalling his early sexual attraction to his cousin Ave, who later said: 'Graham wanted to marry me. Then he said no, we're cousins, my father and mother wouldn't have it . . . . .'(*MW*, p. 106). He later took her sister, Barbara, on an African journey.

In *England Made Me*, the Stockholm area is depicted with sharp detail, reflecting Greene's visit in 1933, during which his female companion was the young woman who provided the model for Loo, the tourist who slaps Anthony's face when he suggests that she is a virgin. Details of Krogh derive from the tycoon Ivar Kreuger, the 'match king' and 'Napoleon of finance' who eventually committed suicide. In 1933 Greene had reviewed for the *Spectator* George Soloveytchik's biography of the financier. Looking back on *England Made Me*, Greene felt with pleasure that Minty, the seedy journalist, was a characterisation that had gained an independent life. Nevertheless, the novel is, on the whole, a hollow, unconvincing work; the characters generally seem to be artifical constructs rather than living entities; the central relationship is too egregious to be interesting; and the plotting is awkwardly contrived. Predictably, sales of both this novel and *It's a Battlefield* were disappointingly low. Greene remarked:

I had squandered my reserves by writing *It's a Battlefield* which in spite of the praise from Ezra Pound and V. S. Pritchett remained almost unread. Second to it in public indifference came *England Made Me*.

(*WE*, p. 68)

Nevertheless, 1935 was a productive year: it saw the publication of not only *England Made Me* but also *The Bear Fell Free* and *The Basement Room and Other Stories* (his first collection of tales). *The Bear Fell Free* is a collectors' item, having been published in a limited edition of 285 copies. This is a slim volume containing a tale told in a highly experimental manner: the time-sequence is hectically jumbled like a box of jigsaw pieces. Gradually the reader construes the story of a disastrous air-flight and sexual treachery. (The name of the hero, Anthony Farrell, indicates his kinship to the hero of *England Made Me*; his duplicitous friend is given the name, Carter, of Greene's tormentor at school; and his mascot, a teddy bear, was also Greene's.) The experiment seems rather specious, for the ironies resulting from the jumbling might have arisen more effectively from relatively conventional narration; but it may have helped Greene to greater dexterity in other works, and, as will be shown in a later section, it is a key to his interest in trans-chronological devices.

Anthony Farrell had turned back from a rash attempt to fly the Atlantic. Graham Greene soon set out on a rash journey, but saw it through. In 1936, when he was thirty-one years old, Greene embarked on an arduous African trek through Liberia, a republic governed by the descendants of freed American slaves. For four weeks he trekked 350 miles through terrain which was often dangerous, oppressive, unhealthy, squalid, tedious. Characteristically if thoughtlessly, he had invited an attractive young woman to accompany him: his cousin Barbara (who later became Countess Strachwitz). Headlines in the *News Chronicle* announced: 'Beauty of 23 Sets Out for Cannibal Land / Cousin as Only Companion / To Blaze White Trail in the Jungle / Slavery and Disease'. (She was actually twenty-eight, not twenty-three.)

Starting from Sierra Leone, they entered north-western Liberia and progressed through the deepest inland regions of the country, crossing briefly into French Guinea before heading to the coast at Grand Bassa. They were accompanied by numerous African carriers and servants: Graham, 'from the beginning, treated them exactly as if they were white men', Barbara noted. The trek tested Greene's courage and physique to breaking-point; yet the resultant travel book, *Journey without Maps*, makes remarkably few references to Barbara, even though her resources of spirit and stamina seem to have been ampler than his. She nursed him when he seemed close to death, and reflected that, if *she* were in danger, he might well be too absorbed in noting the situation to go to her aid. Given the book's stress on the oppressive features of the journey – rats, ants, jiggers (parasites that burrow under the toe-nails and up the leg), mosquitoes, cockroaches, tropical diseases, oppressive heat, squalid amenities – one might well wonder why Greene ever wished to go.

He was escaping domesticity, his wife and the baby; though by the end of the trip he was yearning to be home again. He hinted that a death-wish impelled him, but a dose of tropical fever soon induced 'a passionate interest in living'. His companion was apparently charming and considerate: Barbara said that during the journey she became very fond of Graham. In addition, his travelling costs were partly subsidised: an advance had been provided by his publisher. There was an element of the fashionable:

> It was a period when 'young authors' were inclined to make uncomfortable journeys in search of bizarre material – Peter Fleming to Brazil and Manchuria, Evelyn Waugh to British Guiana and Ethiopia.
>
> (*WE*, p. 45)

Again, there was romantic emulation of admired writers of the past: notably of Conrad. Joseph Conrad had trekked through the Congo Free State in 1890, and his masterpiece 'Heart of Darkness' had ensued. *Journey without Maps* occasionally cites that masterpiece (and quotes Conrad's related 'Congo Diary'). On his journey down the African coast, Marlow, Conrad's narrator, had observed such places as Little Popo and 'Gran' Bassam': the very Grand Bassa that was the terminus of Greene's purgatorial progress. Another motive may have been the practice of espionage, however amateurish. Greene admits, in the book, that his passport permitted him to visit only western Liberia and certain ports; but, instead, he trespassed far into the interior. Perhaps he was observing the region for the British Foreign Office; and probably he was reporting to the Anti-Slavery Society, for he had cultivated the friendship of Sir John Harris, the Society's Parliamentary Secretary. The political interest would lie in the investigation of claims that Colonel Davis, a black mercenary, had carried out a savage campaign against villagers in remote regions, and that the President himself had been exporting slaves. These matters had been aired in the House of Lords and in a parliamentary Blue Book. Greene actually secured interviews with both Davis and the President, and (poker-faced) he reports Davis's claims that, far from being a ruthless murderer, he had been a rescuer and benefactor of the villagers. To Greene, 'there was something attractive about the dictator of

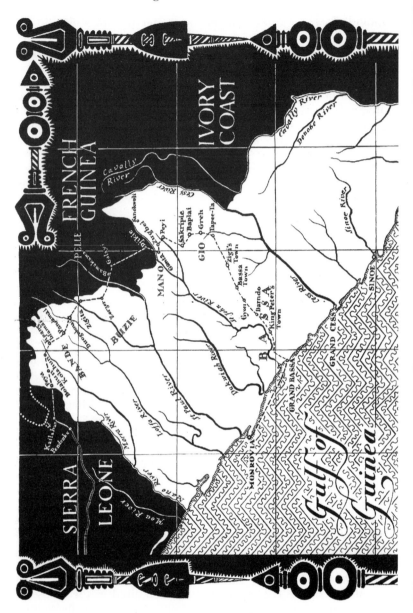

Map of Liberia: endpaper to Journey Without Maps *(1936)*

Grand Bassa'; he seemed to resemble Conrad's soldier of fortune, Captain J. K. Blunt. Another reason for the journey was cultural and psychological: an attempt to evaluate civilisation and human nature; a new endeavour to penetrate 'the heart of darkness'.

The eventual account, *Journey without Maps*, is variously interesting, perceptive, vivid, odd, and padded; it emerges as a confused attempt to vindicate a quixotic journey. Its best feature is probably the intense and discriminating interest that Greene took in the diversity of Africans whom he encountered, particularly in his considerate treatment of the various carriers and his compassionate concern for the sufferings he observed. Daily he dressed the sore of a carrier afflicted with venereal disease; and once he treated a leper:

> At Zigita a leprous man from the town came, with the sellers, to be healed, standing dumbly, holding out his rotting hands. Passive misery had been stamped on his face for a long while, but he had seen the carriers take medicine from me and one could tell that behind the misery a spark of belief had been struck in miracles. It was no good destroying hope and admitting there was nothing I could do. I gave him a few tablets of boric acid to dissolve and bathe his hands with.
>
> (p. 157)

Peter Fleming, reviewing the book in the *Spectator*, felt that Greene's 'unillusioned honesty' was preferable to the egotism displayed by Hemingway in *Green Hills of Africa*. One setback occurred when *Journey without Maps* was subject to a libel action by Dr P. D. Oakley, who believed that he had been misrepresented as the drunken 'Pa Oakley'; the book had to be withdrawn and was not reprinted for nearly a decade. Greene's satiric energies sometimes provoked a litigious response: first Priestley, then Oakley; later there would be the Shirley Temple case. Two literary by-products of the Liberian trek were 'A Chance for Mr Lever', a sardonic tale which has some resemblances to Conrad's 'An Outpost of Progress', and 'The Other Side of the Border' (the start of an unfinished novel), published eventually in *Nineteen Stories*.

After his return from Africa, Greene was busily productive, writing articles, books, tales, film reviews and book reviews. With the help of his literary agents – first Curtis Brown, then from 1935 Pearn, Pollinger and Higham – Greene was mastering the art of being paid several times for the same piece of work.

A good example is his long tale, 'The Basement Room', the

story of a boy's unintentional betrayal of Baines, the butler who has befriended him. Once again, as in *The Man Within*, the mentor is the victim of treachery. The viewpoint of the boy, variously beguiled and frightened by the machinations of adults, is well maintained, as is the irony that the betrayal will be a self-blighting one: 'The glowing morning thought, "This is life"[,] had become under Baines's tuition the repugnant memory, "That was life".' The tale was first commissioned for £50 as a serial by the *News Chronicle*. Then it became the first story in his first collection of tales, *The Basement Room*, of 1935. Next, it was serialised (for eighteen guineas) in *Argosy* magazine, and appeared in a further collection, *Nineteen Stories*. In 1948 it became a successful film, *The Fallen Idol*, for which Greene provided the screenplay. With his concurrence, the film made substantial changes to the story and its setting; yet, when re-published under the title 'The Fallen Idol' in the volume *'The Third Man' and 'The Fallen Idol'* (1950), the tale had reverted to its original form.

Throughout his career, Greene would be similarly resourceful in recycling his material: pieces of journalism would reappear in his travel books, prefaces would blend into his autobiographies, and autobiographical material would also be incorporated in tales and novels. He earned money in his sleep: he published his dreams. His film reviews were later reprinted in *Reflections, The Pleasure-Dome* and *The Graham Greene Film Reader*. There was some recycling of the materials of the novels: locations used in one novel would be re-used in another (Nottingham, Berkhamsted and Brighton, for example). Certain characters would recur under different guises; a character would even appear under the same name in two works. Repeatedly, as we have noted, Greene wrote his fiction with the cinema in mind, whether as a model for techniques or as one of the destinations of the text. 'The writer has become director and producer', remarked Evelyn Waugh (*CCE*, p. 97).

Greene's interest in the cinema was imaginative and professional. In the reviews which appeared in the *Spectator* (1935 to 1940) and in *Night and Day* (July to December 1937), he was lively and knowledgeable, radiating enthusiasm for the potentialities of film. Those reviews are variously witty, incisive, imaginative, constructive and cruel: no conventional courtesies sheathed his critical stiletto. He assailed sentimentality, priggishness and propaganda; he scorned the Hays Office censorship; and he applauded gritty realism, frank sensuality, wild comedy. He was quick to recognise the talents of Carol Reed, Fritz Lang and Luis Buñuel as directors, Humphrey Bogart and Jean Gabin as actors, Bette Davis and Ingrid Bergman as actresses; he delighted in the absurdities of the Marx Brothers and the pompous cynicism of W. C. Fields. Generous in praise and waspish in rebuke, he had the knack of making bad films sound so ludicrous as to be enjoyable. His cameos of some of the stars of the day are sharply memorable: Jean Harlow 'toted a breast like a man totes a gun'; Garbo is 'stiff, awkward, bony, rather grotesque'; Marlene Dietrich 'consents to pose' – as for acting, 'she leaves it to her servants'. Mae West has 'the Edwardian bust, the piled peroxided hair, the seductive and reeling motions reminiscent of an overfed python'.

He often assailed what he saw as the malign influence of Hollywood moguls, particularly 'the Mayers and the Goldwyns'. Sometimes the comments have an anti-Semitic edge: if Hollywood produces a film of value, that is perhaps 'when Jehovah is asleep'. There are also signs of an increasing bias against the United States: he complains repeatedly of what he sees as 'the eternal adolescence of the American mind', 'the same adolescent features, plump, smug, sentimental . . . . . Civilisation would shock them'. Among producers based in Britain, he repeatedly attacked a Jew from Hungary, Alexander Korda (formerly Sandor Kellner), whom he depicted as vulgar in outlook and alien to British culture:

> England, of course, has always been the home of the exiled; but one may at least express a wish that *émigrés* would set up trades in which their ignorance of our language and culture was less of a handicap: it would not grieve me to see Mr Alexander Korda seated before a cottage loom in an Eastern country, following an older and a better tradition. The Quota Act has played into foreign hands, and as far as I know, there is nothing to prevent an English film unit being completely staffed by technicians of foreign blood. We have saved the English film industry from American competition only to surrender it to a far more alien control.
>
> (*The Pleasure-Dome*, pp. 78–9)

Korda, head of London Films, generously responded by paying Greene extravagantly (£175 initially for a story, then £125 a week for collaboration which included script-writing). The magnate was to prove himself a particularly hospitable friend of Greene. He worked for the British security agency, SIS, as Greene was to do; so their collaboration extended from film work to modes of espionage. In the course of time, Korda paid Green £2,000 for the film rights of *The Power and the Glory*, £3,000 for writing *The Fallen Idol*, £4,000 for the rights of *The Heart of the Matter*, and £9,000 for *The Third Man*. Having condemned script-writers as virtual prostitutes, taking 'money for no thought', the author was happy enough to take the money. Typically, he mocked the tycoon obliquely in *Loser Takes All*. Korda, who owned the yacht *Elsewhere* (in which Greene and his lover would sail with the Oliviers), would be fictionalised as Herbert Dreuther, the imperious and impetuous tycoon who owns the yacht *Seagull*: 'For a month at a time he would disappear in his yacht with a cargo of writers and actresses and oddments . . . . .'

Greene himself, beginning to prosper, was diligently increasing his social circle. In 1935 he, Vivien and their young daughter had moved to 14 North Side, Clapham Common: a beautiful Queen Anne house overlooking the common, its pond and the church. It was to be destroyed during the Blitz, its devastation being commemorated both in the novel *The End of the Affair* and in the cynical story, 'The Destructors'. Here he entertained leading figures in the worlds of publishing and literature, among them Rupert Hart-Davis, Hamish Hamilton and Antonia White. Elsewhere, he met such notable figures as T. S. Eliot, Violet Hunt, Herbert Read, Rose Macaulay, H. E. Bates and A. L. Rowse. Greene's domestic responsibilities were growing: in September 1936 his son, Francis, was born, and Vivien recalled that at the time Graham was 'very supportive'. There were to be no more children; Vivien remarked that Graham took little interest in Francis and Lucy until the latter was about nineteen.

In July, Heinemann published *A Gun for Sale: An Entertainment*. The list of his works which appeared in the preliminary matter of this volume showed that Greene was now dividing his longer narrative works into the cateogories of 'Novels' (*The Man Within, It's a Battlefield, England Made Me*) and 'Entertainments' (*Stamboul Train* and *A Gun for Sale* itself). The two works he disowned, *Rumour at Nightfall* and *The Name of Action*, were excluded. He envisaged the 'novels' as relatively serious and subtle works, the 'entertainments' as relatively popular and commercial. Eventually, however, he rescinded this distinction (which sometimes seemed merely nominal), so that all were listed as novels.

A Gun for Sale is another cinematic thriller: William Plomer, reviewing it in the *Spectator*, said that it 'reads very much as a quick-firing gangster film looks and sounds'. Book sales were disappointing. In Britain, *It's a Battlefield* had sold about 7,500 copies, *England Made Me* 4,500; *A Gun for Sale* sold 5,000; US sales were about 2,000 in each case. On the other hand, Paramount had paid Greene (before publication) £2,500 for the film rights of *A Gun for Sale*: Alan Ladd and Veronica Lake would be the stars. His regular readers would have found some of the novel's material familiar, thanks to Greene's aptitude in recycling. The 'Nottwich' (Nottingham) of *Stamboul Train* is more fully depicted here; Coral Musker, the needy but honest showgirl of *Stamboul Train*, is reincarnated as the more robust and fortunate showgirl, Anne Crowder. Raven, the hare-lipped killer from a deprived background, anticipates in important respects the Pinkie of *Brighton Rock*: an isolated, callous figure, emerging from a sordid background and driven by hatred of the world at large. In Anne's sense of the division of her allegiance between Raven, whom she has befriended, and her fiancé Jimmy Mather, the detective sergeant devoted to law and order, there is a foretaste of Rose, whose loyalty to Pinkie leads to her defiance of Ida Arnold. The account of Kite's death in *A Gun for Sale* anticipates and partly explains the circumstances of Kite's death in *Brighton Rock*.

The plot of *A Gun for Sale* repeatedly depends on unlikely coincidences: for example, when Raven kidnaps Anne, he is unwittingly kidnapping the fiancée of the very police officer who is dedicated to pursuing him; and Davies, who is Raven's paymaster, happens also to be a financial backer of the very revue in which Anne is performing at Nottwich. The most unlikely incident comes when Anne, whom Davies thought he had killed, is found wedged up a chimney, bound and gagged but alive. (The finder is Raven.) Even though she has been trapped there for many hours, she soon becomes briskly active. Writing of *The Third Man*, Greene remarked: 'Reality, in fact, was only a background to a fairy tale'. So often in his novels we encounter the combination of a convincing, intensely-rendered setting and a highly-contrived plot-sequence. Finally, the most depressing feature of *A Gun for Sale* is that it presents with caricaturish clarity a stale anti-Semitic thesis. The villain, Sir Marcus, is at the centre of a conspiracy by wealthy Jews to profit by war and death. In *Stamboul Train* Greene had at least attempted to question anti-Semitic prejudice; here that prejudice is all too easily endorsed.

Soon, in December 1936, Greene was offered by Chatto & Windus the literary editorship of a new weekly magazine, *Night and Day* (modelled on the *New Yorker*), which first appeared in the following June. His salary was £600 per year, and Evelyn Waugh agreed to be a leading book reviewer at £6 per week. Other recruits included Elizabeth Bowen, John Betjeman, Christopher Isherwood, Herbert Read, Stevie Smith and William Empson. Despite the range of talented contributors, the magazine failed (its final issue was dated 23 December 1937).

Night and Day did not pay its way, and hopes of raising fresh capital to revive its fortunes were dashed by the Shirley Temple libel suit. When reviewing the child star's film *Wee Willie Winkie*, Greene alleged that the nine-year-old girl's 'well-developed rump', 'searching coquetry' and 'dimpled depravity' appealed to 'her antique audience [of] middle-aged men and clergymen'. One suspects that the reviewer, at any rate, found her provocative. Shirley Temple and Twentieth-Century Fox then sued the magazine, its publishers and printers, and Greene himself, for this 'beastly libel'. The case was heard in March 1938: the Lord Chief Justice deemed the review 'a gross outrage'. Damages of £3,500 were awarded to Twentieth-Century Fox; £500 to be paid by Greene (a sum roughly equivalent to £20,000 in 1996). Fifty years later, Shirley Temple, in her autobiography *Child Star* (p. 186), said:

> The whole event could be viewed as immensely fruitful. My punitive award was recycled immediately into 5 percent British War Loan Bonds to help arm sorely pressed England against a troubled Europe . . . . . [T]he saucy publicity tweaked British box-office interest, for *Wee Willie Winkie* prospered gloriously.

While reviewing, editing and travelling, between 1936 and 1938 Greene found time to write *Brighton Rock*. This, in several ways, is the most extreme of his texts. Here he goes deeper into Greeneland than ever before; and here he presents in most stark and appalling form the paradox of 'the virtue of evil'. This novel is partly a thriller, partly a detective story (with Ida as the detective), partly a satiric fantasy and partly a theological riddle. It is remorselessly cynical. It is ostentatiously stylised and expressionistic. Grotesque, jaundiced, sardonic, it can still (for all its implausiblities) leave in the mind an enduring aftertaste which is both foul and fascinating. This utterly distinctive minor masterpiece stages a bold conflict between the ethic of right and wrong and the ethic of good and evil; special pleading on behalf of the depraved Pinkie creates the bizarre sense that a callous, treacherous killer may, from a theological viewpoint, be superior to a decent, hedonistic, secular person like Ida.

Catholicism had figured significantly in some of his earlier novels (notably *Rumour at Nightfall* and *It's a Battlefield*), but in *Brighton Rock* the treatment is more radical and extensive. Norman Sherry remarks: '[I]ts religious theme, its examination of the Roman Catholic religion, makes it his first Catholic novel, his first enquiry into the ways of man and God' (*Life* I, p. 649). Rose Macaulay thought it 'horrifying'; Marghanita Laski said that the ending is 'the most painful any novelist has ever written'. Sales were slow initially: Heinemann took only £256 in the first nine months after publication. Gradually, however, it gained both large sales and high critical acclaim. In 1943 it was adapted as a stage play in a version which appalled the author: Hermione Baddeley seemed a grotesque Ida, and the theological conclusion was excised. (The play prospered after being transferred from Blackpool to the Garrick Theatre in London.) The film which appeared in 1948, however, was one of the more successful adaptations of a Greene novel; the young Richard Attenborough (who had taken the same rôle in the stage play) made a very effective Pinkie: a convincingly cold-blooded *enfant maudit.*

Greene had arranged further travels, which took place soon after the demise of *Night and Day* in December 1937. Viking Press of New York and Longman in England had agreed to commission a book by Greene on Mexico: a non-fictional work dealing with the persecution of the Catholic Church there. With Vivien he set off across the Atlantic on the *Normandie* in January 1938, and they travelled from New York to Washington and New Orleans. From there, Vivien returned disconsolately to England, while Greene proceeded to Mexico and made arduous journeys deep into regions where the Church had been suppressed by the atheistic authorities. Among the people, their plight and their localities, he found much to depress and disgust him. There resulted a travel book, *The Lawless Roads* (1939), and his finest novel, *The Power and the Glory* (1940). Together they offer a remarkable illustration of the transmutation of personal impressions into enduring art.

In the 1920s and 1930s, various British writers described Mexico. These included D. H. Lawrence, in *The Plumed Serpent* (1926) and *Mornings in Mexico* (1927), Aldous Huxley in *Beyond the Mexique Bay* (1934), and Evelyn Waugh in *Robbery under Law* (1939). In the late 1930s Malcolm Lowry wrote much of his *Under the Volcano* (1947). 'Since the depression', said Huxley, 'books on Mexico have been almost as numerous, I should guess, as books on Russia'. A travel-writer has no innocent eye but is usually concerned to test a prior schema against the evidence offered by the new region. So Lawrence's Mexico is a location of natural beauty and instinctual forces; he seeks and finds evidence of primæval vitality. Huxley, more detached, intellectual and sceptical in stance, moves rapidly from particular details to general reflections on history, psychology and philosophy, offering a lengthy criticism of Lawrence's primitivism. Greene's *The Lawless Roads* has remarkable similarities to *Journey without Maps.* As in the African travel book, the schema is predominantly

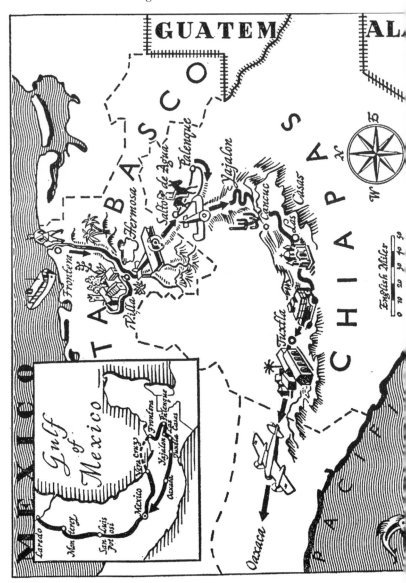

Map of Mexico: endpaper to The Lawless Roads *(1939)*

religious and entails personal reminiscences of upbringing in England. Greene opens with recollections of schooldays: the baize door separating home from school, the cruelties of 'Collifax' who practised torments with dividers, the smells, the lavatory doors without locks. Other people might not have been led to faith by such mundane features, but, according to Greene (p. 11), school provided evidence of Hell, and that leads to belief in Heaven: 'One began to believe in heaven because one believed in hell, but for a long while it was hell only one could picture with a certain intimacy . . . . .'

These early pages of *The Lawless Roads* have eerie echoes of *Brighton Rock*. Prewitt, echoing Marlowe, had said, 'Why this is hell, nor are we out of it'; *The Lawless Roads* quotes more closely: ' "Why, this is hell," Mephistopheles told Faustus, "nor am I out of it." ' That favourite Greenian inversion of Wordsworth, 'Hell lay about them in their infancy', recurs here. At the end of the novel, the old priest commends Charles Péguy, who challenged God in the name of the damned; in the travel book, Greene himself commends Péguy. The opening of *The Lawless Roads* serves not only to establish Greene's Catholic credentials for this book on the persecution of Catholics, but also to establish the religious criteria by which Mexico will be judged.

During his journey, Greene experienced some moments of contentment, ease, even bliss. But on the whole his impressions of Mexico were negative. The government was corrupt; religion was persecuted with varying degrees of rigour in the different states of the country; Greene was often regarded with hostility as a *gringo*, and he felt that many of the people seemed trapped in 'a cruel anarchic adolescence'. He regarded compassionately the partly superstitious, partly devout rituals maintained by the impoverished Indians, but repeatedly he found the Mexican *mestizos* untruthful and unreliable. Broadly, in a pattern similar to that of *Journey without Maps*, the poorest people of the interior often seemed better, in moral and religious terms, than the people of the cities. Mexico City, in particular, appalled him; he even came to share D. H. Lawrence's fierce and sweeping reaction:

> How right Lawrence was when he wrote: 'This city doesn't feel *right* – feels like a criminal plotting his next rather mean crime,' and again: 'I *really* feel cynical about these "patriots" and "socialists" down here . . . . . You know socialism is a dud. It makes just a mush of people: and especially of savages. And seventy per cent of these people are real savages, quite as much as they were three hundred years ago. The Spanish-

> Mexican population just rots on top of the black savage mass. And Socialism here is a farce of farces: except very dangerous.'
>
> (p. 115)

Actually, what Greene encountered was not socialism but tyrannical and exploitative government; but he had ample reason to feel depressed. In the states that he chose to explore, churches had been demolished or stood in ruins; atheistic indoctrination was provided in the schools; crass superstition flourished; squalor and poverty abounded. As always, Greene has a keen nose and eye for the squalid, and gives predictably detailed accounts of the poor sanitary arrangements (for example, the foul crusted lavatory on a steamboat; its door fell off in his hand) and of the pangs of his dysentery. Yet, in a typical paradox, he claims that with all its vileness, Mexico is preferable to the commercial civilisation of the USA:

> I loathed Mexico – but there were times when it seemed as if there were worse places . . . . . Here was idolatry and oppression, starvation and casual violence, but you lived under the shadow of religion – of God or the Devil. 'Rating for Dating' [an article in a US women's magazine] – it wasn't evil: it wasn't anything at all – it was just the drug-store and the Coca-Cola, the Hamburger, the graceless sinless empty chromium world.
>
> (p. 249)

The contrast is crudely schematic and rather self-indulgent: Greene denounces as 'Godless' a civilisation whose amenities he was sufficiently prosperous to enjoy at length. Certainly, in Mexico he displayed courage and tenacity in visiting some very remote, impoverished and unhealthy regions; but he was a visitor, a note-taking tourist, and could return to luxuries of the kind he so often denounced. 'The graceless sinless empty chromium world' of the USA was a world which was enriching him by publishing and filming his books. Like Conrad and Lawrence, Greene could bite tenaciously the hand that fed him. Nevertheless, *The Lawless Roads* demonstrates Greene's sharpness of vision, his thin-skinned sensitivity, and his disarming frankness when describing his own blunders and woes. There is some padding, but also a good range of evocative writing; and in *The Power and the Glory* the rancour and spleen of the travel book would be transmuted into a far more complex and prismatic rendering of Mexican life.

Greene returned to a Europe in which forebodings of a second world war were growing, and a forerunner of that conflict seemed to be the Spanish Civil War, fought between 1936 and 1939. Spanish army leaders, resenting the socialist and anticlerical tendencies of the Republican government, revolted; General Franco became leader of the rebellion, which was supported by nationalist, clerical and Fascist forces. The USSR helped the Republicans; Nazi Germany and Fascist Italy helped Franco. The eventual victory of Franco resulted partly from internecine strife on the Republican side, and partly from a change of policy in the USSR, which was moving towards an iniquitous pact with Hitler.

While the Spanish War was proceeding, many British writers felt obliged to take sides and to declare their support either for the Republican side (as did, for example, Auden, Spender and Day Lewis) or for the Fascist side (as did Roy Campbell and Edmund Blunden). Given that Greene was both left-wing and Catholic in sympathies, taking sides would be no easy matter: many of the Republicans were anti-clerical, while the Fascists had substantial backing from the Catholic hierarchy. In the event, he noted that the Basques of northern Spain fought on the Republican side (hoping for eventual autonomy) but did so with the blessing of their local priests; his sympathies therefore lay with them. (The bombing and strafing of the Basque city of Guernica by German aircraft was famously commemorated by Picasso.) Greene was commissioned, apparently by the BBC, to travel to Bilbao, which was being besieged by the Nationalists. He reached Toulouse, but no aircraft was readily available to take him further, so he returned empty-handed. His brother Herbert, in contrast, reached Spain and (to Ernest Hemingway's fury) was reputedly a spy for the Fascists. Herbert said that he initially supported Franco but later sympathised with the Republicans.

The Spanish Civil War is the lightly disguised background to *The Confidential Agent: An Entertainment*, which appeared in September 1939. In its plotting, this is one of the most blithely preposterous of Greene's works; plausibility is repeatedly sacrificed on the altar of dramatic incident and precipitate reversals. It is predominantly a popular, commercial thriller with more than a touch of fantasy; the political and ethical discussions are scarcely allowed to impede its hectic pace of action. Towards the end, the reader may not *suspend* disbelief so much as *expand* disbelief, relaxing into expectation of the increasingly implausible. The *Sunday Times* put the matter kindly in describing the work as 'an exciting fantasia', a 'kaleidoscopic affair' in which 'Mr Greene has few rivals'.

The novel's central character, 'D.', a scholarly widower, is the unlikely 'confidential agent' of a government which approximates to that of Republican Spain; repeatedly he is outwitted and thwarted by an aristocratic agent who serves 'the General' (Franco inevitably comes to mind). Although Greene makes brief attempts to veil the linkage with Spain, it is the Spanish conflict which fits most of the relevant political facts. The book's sympathies lie, on balance, with the Republicans, but it is quite a fine balance. '[M]y people commit atrocities like the others', remarks D.; and D. is betrayed by people who, though supposedly on his side, have sold out to the enemy. (His researches on *The Song of Roland* should have forewarned him.) D.'s idealism is wan, more weary and limited than that of Czinner, his literary relative in *Stamboul Train*. His mission ends in stalemate: he fails to gain a supply of coal, but at least prevents the other side from gaining it. Nevertheless, in an ending to gratify a film director with a taste for the commercially romantic, he succeeds in winning the love of a beautiful young woman who bravely (and to his surprise) joins him on the tramp-steamer for the return to his homeland. There, he may well be shot; in the meantime, they can enjoy a brief idyll.

> The light went by astern: ahead there was only the splash, the long withdrawal, and the dark. She said, 'You'll be dead very soon: you needn't tell me that, but *now . . .*'
> He felt no desire, and no claim: happiness was all about them on the small vibrating tramp. To the confidential agent trust seemed to be returning into the violent and suspicious world.

That's how the first British edition concluded. From later editions Greene excised the whole of that final paragraph, making the conclusion less conventionally affirmative.

One interesting development in *The Confidential Agent* is Greene's attempt to balance the anti-Semitic features of earlier novels by giving a predominantly sympathetic treatment to Mr Forbes (alias Furtstein), the businessman who is the fiancé of Rose, the novel's heroine. Admittedly, the holiday-camp that he owns is depicted by the narrator as a vulgar, alien importation. On the other hand, it is through Forbes's agency that D. is eventually rescued and put on that steamer heading home; and, in a gallantly romantic gesture, Forbes relinquishes his matrimonial claims on Rose (even though their marriage would be a financially astute move) so that she can join the man whom she really loves. Forbes is thus a positive counterpart, an altruistic complement, to the Myatt of *Stamboul Train*.

Another characteristic of *The Confidential Agent* is the presence of some private, personal allusions which would have eluded most of the original readers but which, in the light of subsequent biographical knowledge, are easily detectable. Greene's developing wry friendship with Alexander Korda, the film magnate who would be knighted in 1942, explains the text's repeated use of 'Korda' as a term in the international language 'Entranationo', an equivalent of Esperanto. Korda, we are told, is the synthetic language's term for 'the heart' (logically enough, recalling the Latin *cor, cordis*); in an Entranationo song, 'the word Korda, Korda came in a lot'. (The film producer was probably a model for Forbes.) The text also deploys repeatedly the name 'Glover'. A woman called Glover is the owner of a flat in which the hero takes refuge:

> He took it quickly in to the home-made water colours on the walls and the radio set by the dressing-table. It spoke to him of an unmarried ageing woman with few interests . . . . .
> It seemed hard luck on Glover – whoever she might be: . . . . . intrusion into a stranger's home was an act of lust.
>
> (pp. 147, 187)

England Made Me had been dedicated 'To Vivien / With Ten Years' Love / 1925–1935'; but *The Confidential Agent* eventually bore the dedication 'To Dorothy Craigie', and Dorothy Craigie was the *nom de plume* of Dorothy Glover, a book-illustrator (hence the water-colours noted above). Her sexual affair with Greene began in 1938 or 1939 and lasted through the war years, contributing some features to *The End of the Affair* (1951). Vivien described Dorothy (born in 1901) as 'a small stoutish woman in blue glasses'; to David Higham she was 'short and a bit stout (though not fat), stocky more than anything'. A photo confirms the impression that, compared with Greene's later partners, she was distinctly unglamorous. Initially their liaison was secret, but gradually Vivien became painfully aware of it. 'Graham said something about the most terrific sort of sexual thrill he had was seeing her sitting in a red dressing gown in front of a dressing table.' It is characteristic of Greene's use of private, personal material in his novels that Fowler in *The Quiet American* defines his 'deepest sexual experience' thus: 'Lying in bed early one morning and watching a woman in a red dressing-gown brush her hair.' Constituting an irony that must have been particularly painful to Vivien, Dorothy Glover collaborated with Greene by illustrating a series of story-books that he wrote for young children: *The Little Train* (1946), *The Little Fire Engine* (1950), *The Little Horse Bus* (1952) and *The Little Steamroller* (1953).

Derek Verschoyle, reviewing *The Confidential Agent*, said disparagingly: 'Mr Greene, with his eyes fatally fixed on Hollywood, has slapped his hero down against a merely formal background and handed out action neat.' Greene himself held a low opinion of this rushed 'entertainment', but he succeeded in his commercial aim. At first the book sold 5,000 copies in Britain, not as many as Greene might have expected; but Warner Brothers bought the rights, and the eventual film employed Charles Boyer as D., Peter Lorre as D.'s hapless victim, and Lauren Bacall as Rose. Bacall complained, with some reason, that the character was 'totally straight and dreary'.

The middle years

1939–45

On 23 August 1939 the Molotov-Ribbentrop pact was signed. This was the pact in which Stalin's communists agreed to cooperate with Hitler's Nazis. One rapid outcome was the conquest of Poland in the following month: the Nazis invaded Poland from one side, and the Russians invaded from the other. Britain and France, in support of the Poles, then declared war on Germany. The Second World War had begun.

The Molotov-Ribbentrop agreement made nonsense of many intellectuals' belief that communism was a bulwark against Fascism. Some of those intellectuals, and many of the well-to-do, followed W. H. Auden and Christopher Isherwood (a relative of Greene's) in seeking the sanctuary of the USA. Five thousand people departed for America in the first two days after the declaration of war.

To facilitate his writing and his private life, Greene had rented a studio in Mecklenburgh Square in Bloomsbury, away from his family. Dosing himself with benzedrine, he had worked on *The Confidential Agent* in the mornings and *The Power and the Glory* in the afternoons. He was still producing regular book and film reviews for the *Spectator*; in 1940 he became its literary editor.

As soon as the Molotov-Ribbentrop pact was announced, Greene evacuated his wife and children to his parents' home at Crowborough in Sussex. Vivien sent him many affectionate and pining letters, but Greene was secretly enjoying the company of Dorothy Glover. Touchingly, Vivien remarked reproachfully: 'Bizet wrote Carmen, Wagner wrote Lohengrin. Nobody writes me: Gee, I'm lonesome!' Eleven months later she and the children were moved again, this time to lodgings owned by Trinity College, Oxford; an old friend of hers was married to the College's President.

In late September 1939 Greene appeared before a military draft board and persuaded its members to postpone his conscription into the army until June 1940 so that he could finish *The Power and the Glory* – although, Norman Sherry notes, he had actually completed the writing of that novel (*Life* II, p. 30). He then eluded the army by taking a position at the Ministry of Information, even though he had previously criticised intellectuals who dash for Ministry posts. He spent six months there (with Dorothy Glover as his secretary), involved in plans for propaganda, before being sacked from an overstaffed office. Dorothy, however, remained. During these war years, Greene felt that he was in the position of 'loving two people [Vivien and Dorothy] as equally as makes no difference' (*Life* II, p. 145).

When *The Power and the Glory* appeared, it gained numerous excellent reviews. *The Times* said that it was 'beyond question his best novel. Nothing in his previous work has quite prepared us for the accomplishment'. Sir Hugh Walpole said: 'Greene's new novel proves that he is the finest English novelist of his generation. Simply magnificent.' Greene urged his agent (successfully) to press Heinemann to publicise the novel more extensively. Greene claimed that initial sales were only 3,500, but the print run was 12,600, and 5,000 copies were sold in the first five weeks. (After the war, the pocket edition of 1945 sold 18,650 copies, the uniform edition of 1949 23,450.) The sexual frankness of *The Power and the Glory* led to its denunciation by Cardinal Pizzardo of the Holy Office in Rome; Greene preferred to call him 'Cardinal Pissardo'. Pope Paul VI, long afterwards, told Greene to ignore those Catholics who took offence. This novel, too, was filmed: as *The Fugitive*, directed by John Ford: a work which, in the author's view, crudely simplified the issues.

During the Blitz on London, Greene worked as a fire-warden at nights (with Dorothy, a station-warden), reporting the location of explosions and fires, and helping to rescue people from bombed areas. Through the flames, smoke and debris, he worked courageously. He said later: 'In the blitz, one was very frightened to begin with but then one gave up the idea that one was going to survive and one wasn't frightened any more' (*Life* II, p. 57). He even experienced exhilaration, as landmark after landmark was erased during the nocturnal havoc.

Greene's sister Elisabeth worked in the Secret Intelligence Service (SIS, department MI6), and with her help he was appointed to a very well-paid post in MI6: the salary was about £1,000 a year, tax-free. Nominally a member of the CID Special Branch, in December 1941 he sailed from Liverpool for Freetown, aboard a cargo steamer. (During the perilous voyage, recalled in 'Convoy to West Africa', he wrote much of his critical book, *British Dramatists*, which includes particularly warm appreciations of Elizabethan and Jacobean playwrights.) At Freetown, Sierra Leone, he worked as a counter-espionage agent: among other tasks, he had to send information about Vichy airfields in French Guinea and to search ships for smuggled industrial diamonds. The search for contraband and the oppressively humid location later found their way into *The Heart of the Matter*; though Greene, unlike Scobie, was provided with 'a very nice piece & a good drinking companion', Doris Temple. Greene, like the agent Carter in the novel, also visited the primitive local brothel.

He was cheered by learning that *The Power and the Glory* had been awarded the Hawthornden Prize and that *A Gun for Sale* would be filmed by Paramount. He completed another 'entertainment', *The Ministry of Fear*, saying 'There's a good cinematic idea in it'; and his literary agent, Laurence Pollinger, sold that novel, also, to Paramount, for £3,250. *The Ministry of Fear* (published in 1943) has two aspects. Its plot is that of a mystery-thriller; a conspiracy of fifth-columnists in England is eventually exposed and destroyed. The plotting, as in some of his previous thrillers, is strained and implausible, dependent on coincidental meetings and ludicrously contrived intrigue; sometimes it is difficult to distinguish between the frequent dreams of its hero and the events around him, which are dreamlike, nightmarish or phantasmagoric in their unlikely concatenations. As a narrative, it seems to have been improvised with little overall planning. The second aspect, however, is quite different. As background to the tenuous sequence of the main events, Greene offers numerous vivid cameos of wartime London: the Blitz, the austerity, the drabness, the steady course of destruction, the ranks of sleepers on the smelly underground platforms, and the euphoria of survival in the morning.

[M]en and women were emerging from underground: neat elderly men carrying attaché-cases and rolled umbrellas appeared from public shelters. In Gower Street they were sweeping up glass, and a building smoked into the new day like a candle which some late reveller has forgotten to snuff . . . . . A notice turned them from their course, and on a rope strung across the road already flapped a few hand-written labels. 'Barclay's Bank. Please enquire at . . .' 'The Cornwallis Dairy. New address . . .' 'Marquis's Fish Saloon . . .' . . . . . He noticed the briskness, the cheerfulness of the faces: you got the impression that this was an early hour of a national holiday. It was simply, he supposed, the effect of finding oneself alive.

(pp. 200–1)

As so often in Greene, the detailed rendering of the location seems more truthful than the plot.

While Greene was in Africa, his father (who had retired from the headmastership of Berkhamsted in 1927) died after many years of diabetic illness. Greene said:

Suddenly, between the secret reports to be coded and decoded, I unexpectedly felt misery and remorse, remembering how as a young man I had deliberately set out to shock his ideas which had been unflinchingly liberal in politics and gently conservative in morals.

Charles Greene seemed to him 'a very good person in a way we don't seem able to produce in our generation' (*Life* II, p. 151).

Soon, after a row with his boss at Freetown, Greene was recalled from Africa to work at St Albans and London under Kim Philby, who would later be exposed as a traitor paid by Moscow. This phase of espionage would find its way eventually into *Our Man in Havana* and *The Human Factor*. In the summer of 1944, Greene suddenly resigned from MI6. Norman Sherry (*Life* II, p. 183) speculates that this was because he had realised that Philby was secretly working for the Russians. In London, Greene lived with Dorothy during the time of the raids by the Vls (the pilotless pulse-jet aircraft) and V2s (the appallingly destructive rockets): raids to be recalled in the novel *The End of the Affair*.

Greene then became a part-time editor for the publishing firm Eyre & Spottiswoode, and after the war stayed on as managing director until 1948. Initially lively and enthusiastic, he brought new authors (notably Mervyn Peake) to the firm's list; books by François Mauriac and R. K. Narayan were added, and one of his favourite novels, James's *The Wings of the Dove*, was reprinted in a new edition. Greene's boss at Eyre & Spottiswoode was Douglas Jerrold, a Catholic who had supported Franco in the Spanish Civil War. He perceptively observed that Greene was not 'a religious novelist' but one who was 'interested in religion', and whose works overemphasise sin and guilt while neglecting good works and salvation. To Jerrold, Greene was still an adolescent emotionally but an adult in business matters. At the office:

He would settle down to the serious business of the day, telephoning with rapid succession to his bank, to his stockbroker, to his insurance agent, to his literary agent, to a film company or two, and, if it was a really busy morning, to two or three editors. During these conversations the tortured conscience so frequently, and so movingly, on exhibition in his novels was notably absent.

(*Harper's*, August 1952, p. 52)

1945–55

In this post-war decade, Greene's fame and success rose to a zenith. He became internationally lauded and debated; his face appeared on the cover of *Time* magazine; his movements were followed by reporters. He became so prosperous that he was free to roam as he wished; he even bought a yacht, partly as a means of alleviating taxation. Greene could now mix on an equal footing with the wealthy and glamorous: among them Sir Alexander Korda, Laurence Olivier, Vivien Leigh, Margot Fonteyn and Noël Coward.

The Heart of the Matter (1948) is one of his major works; highly acclaimed, controversial, it became an enduring best-seller. Other important novels included *The End of the Affair* (1951), which boldly recruited God as a miracle-working character, and *The Quiet American* (1955), a partly prophetic account of the CIA's intervention in Vietnam. A minor novel was *Loser Takes All* (1955), a story of love and gambling with – for once – a happy ending. His tales appeared in two volumes overlapping in their contents: *Nineteen Stories* (1947) and *Twenty-One Stories* (1954). Non-fictional works included *The Lost Childhood* (1951) and his contribution to *Why Do I Write?* (1948). As a sign of his popularity and eminence, Heinemann began to produce the 'Uniform Edition' of his works. (A 'Collected Edition', by Heinemann and The Bodley Head, would appear in the 1970s, and he wrote a series of prefaces for it: another resemblance to his admired Conrad.)

In collaboration with Basil Dean, he adapted *The Heart of the Matter* for the stage; but the opening in Boston (1950) was disastrous, and the plans for the play to open in New York were aborted. (Doping himself with benzedrine was perhaps less helpful to his creativity than he imagined.) Nevertheless, he persevered with play-writing, and completed *The Living Room* in 1952. This is a predominantly realistic drama with theological debate and symbolic overtones. The basic plot is strong and simple: Rose, the heroine, has an affair with a married man; after meeting his distraught wife, she commits suicide as an altruistic act. There are hints that though, to Roman Catholics, suicide is a mortal sin, God may choose to be merciful. As Rose prepares to die, her *Pater Noster* veers into a childhood prayer whose poignant ending would have had particular resonance for Greene: 'Our Father . . . . . please God don't let school start again ever.'

The Living Room was an enormous success when it opened in London: Eric Portman (as Father Browne) and particularly the young Dorothy Tutin (as Rose) received accolades; on at least one occasion there were as many as fourteen curtain-calls. It ran at Wyndham's Theatre in London from 16 April 1953 until 9 January 1954. *The Times* said:

> All the men and women who matter in this play have a sense of sin; and their actions take on in consequence a momentousness all too rare on the stage . . . . .
>
> The play is beautifully acted, especially by Miss Dorothy Tutin as the young girl, and most effectively directed by Mr. Peter Glenville.
>
> (17 April 1953, p. 2)

Greene was now a significant dramatist as well as a major novelist. Yet, when making a curtain speech in response to cries of 'Author! Author!', he was predictably sombre:

> Do not call me a success. I have never known a successful man. Have you? A man who was a success to himself? Success is the point of self-deception. Failure is the point of self-knowledge.
>
> (*Life* II, p. 456)

His international fame was magnified by the prestige and popularity of two films: *The Fallen Idol* (1948) and *The Third Man* (1949). Both were directed finely by Carol Reed; both were admirably acted; and both succeeded greatly not only with the critics but with the general public. *The Third Man*, in which Orson Welles was at his best as the charismatic villain, Harry Lime, deservedly won the Grand Prix at the Cannes International Film Festival, and the theme music (by Anton Karas, the zither-player) became a best-selling record internationally. Thereafter, Greene sometimes found that musicians in night-clubs and hotels would play 'The *Third Man* Theme' when he entered. A less successful but still notable film was that of *The Heart of the Matter* (1953), in which Trevor Howard gained plaudits as Scobie.

Various works by Greene in this decade reflect, or comment on, his emotional entanglements, which became intensified in the post-war years. At the end of the war, he was seeing his wife, Vivien, at weekends while living with Dorothy Glover during the

Catherine Walston

week. Then, in 1946, he met the remarkable Catherine Walston. She was strikingly beautiful, intelligent, vivacious, seductive, uninhibited and wealthy. Her husband, Henry (known as Harry), was of Jewish ancestry (his father had changed his name from Waldstein to Walston), rich, agnostic, kind and tolerant. He stood as a Liberal candidate in 1945 and as a Labour candidate in a series of subsequent elections, eventually becoming a Life Peer nominated by Harold Wilson. He owned Newton Hall in Cambridgeshire, a huge farm at Thriplow nearby, a London flat in St James's Street, a flat in Dublin, a cottage on an island off the Irish coast, and a banana plantation on the Caribbean island of Santa Lucia.

Ironically (Vivien recalled), the relationship between Catherine Walston and Graham Greene was initiated when she asked him to be her godfather at her conversion to Catholicism. Vivien deputised for Graham, but at later meetings with his god-daughter he became entranced by Catherine and fell intensely, passionately, jealously in love. Their sexual relationship endured for a decade; they spent holidays together in Ireland, on Capri and at numerous other locations. (*The Living Room* was dedicated 'To Catherine with Love'.) While Vivien in Oxford did her best to cope with the austerity, rationing and shortages of post-war Britain, the Walstons at Thriplow lived in a land of milk and honey – or at least of 'grouse, partridges, ham, a leg of mutton and half a cold goose', as Evelyn Waugh reported. Greene took a flat next to Caroline's in St James's Street. Repeatedly he begged Caroline to leave Harry and marry him; but his infatuation was greater than hers, and very slowly, in spite of many idyllic and passionate reunions, the relationship cooled. The long-suffering Vivien knew of it: on one occasion the couple called on her unexpectedly in Oxford, and she was obliged to prepare a meal and overnight accommodation for them. Dorothy Glover, too, suffered; Greene sent her on an African cruise, hoping that during it she would transfer her affection to some other man. Only gradually and reluctantly, with many quarrels and reproaches, did Dorothy relinquish her hold.

Greene's attempts to reconcile adultery with Catholicism took ingenious forms. In one letter to Catherine, he said:

> Whenever we settled for any length of time, we would have two rooms *available*, so that at any time without ceasing to live together & love each other, you could go to Communion (we would break down again & again, but that's neither here nor there).
>
> (*Life* II, p. 324)

In another:

> [M]y prayer is always that God's will shall be in favour of our love. Don't be too sure that it may not be & who knows whether the peace we have so often got together has not been *with* him, instead of against him? I feel no wrong in this love for you . . . . .
>
> (*Life* II, p. 329)

Greene with troops in French Indo-China, 1951

He even assured her: 'I'm a much better Catholic in mortal sin!' (*Life* II, p. 257). After all, he had papal precedent: Pope Alexander VI had reconciled his conscience with extensive sexual activity. In *A Burnt-Out Case*, Parkinson puts a similar point in crude journalese: 'St Francis was the gayest spark in all the gay old city of Firenze.' Father Crompton, in *The End of the Affair*, says: 'There's nothing we can do some of the saints haven't done before us.' Catherine Walston's numerous lovers included Roman Catholic priests. Greene was increasingly displaying a voracious appetite for attractive young women: while assuring Catherine that he felt truly married to her, from 1951 he was also enjoying a sexual relationship with Jocelyn Rickards, a young artist from Australia who had hitherto been an inmate of the 'harem' of A. J. Ayer, the eminent sceptical philosopher. Rickards and Greene liked to fornicate in public places: a park at night, or the compartment of a train between Southend and London. With Graham she visited the music-hall at Islington Green, went to theatres, and met T. S. Eliot (who called her, aptly, 'Pixie'). Subsequently she became an adulterous lover of the playwright John Osborne.

Greene continued to travel far abroad to dangerous regions.

As usual, among other motives, he was impelled partly by a kind of death-wish, and partly by the related desire to let danger overcome his intense phases of boredom and depression. In 1950, commissioned by *Life* magazine, he explored Malaya during the crisis of insurgency by communist guerrillas, undertaking an arduous trek with Gurkhas. In the following year, he toured French Indo-China, where the French were fighting a losing battle against the Vietminh; there he came close to the battle-lines, flew with a bomber on its raids, and at Phat Diem perilously crossed a canal which was choked with corpses. The French authorities suspected him of being a British agent; and, in spite of his denials, they were correct in their suspicions, for Greene was sending reports to the SIS. Once again, his travels served multiple functions: he was writing articles for *Paris Match*, carrying out a form of espionage, and gathering material for a novel and an autobiographical work. As if he had not taken sufficient risks already, in August 1953 he toured Kenya during the Mau Mau insurgency, that campaign during which the Kikuyu rebels killed many white settlers and many more of the Kikuyu people. During this campaign, with its particularly atrocious slaughters, Greene's sympathies swung between the insurgents seeking liberation from colonialism and those settlers who, isolated and tense, remained on their farms at the risk of their lives.

The major novel of this decade, *The Heart of the Matter*, is characteristic of Greene in its blend of well-researched locations and highly personal experience. The setting is Freetown in Sierra Leone, where Greene had worked as a secret agent during the war. The locale is superbly evoked: the humidity (blotting-paper soaks sweat from Scobie's wrist as he writes), the tedium, the tropical diseases, the refuse; 'A dead pye-dog lay in the gutter with the rain running over its white swollen belly.' Scobie, the hero, is a scrupulous, sensitive police officer who is led gradually into corruption. It is easy to see analogies between Greene's relationship with Vivien and Scobie's pitying relationship with the wife, Louise, whom he no longer loves. (Louise's nickname for Scobie, 'Ticki', was also Vivien's for Greene.) To give her a holiday from the area that she finds oppressive, Scobie accepts a bribe to turn a blind eye to smuggling. Next, he commits adultery with Helen Rolt, a woman young enough to be his daughter, and is consequently blackmailed, so that he himself becomes a smuggler. A devout Catholic, he yet takes Mass in a state of mortal sin, being unable to repent his adultery. Next, he arranges for his servant (who knows too much of his corruption) to be 'silenced' – actually murdered. Finally, he commits suicide, an extreme mortal sin for a Catholic, attempting to disguise this as a heart attack. The suicide, we are led to believe, he undertakes partly out of pity for his wife and Helen, and partly out of pity for Christ, who (he imagines) would repeatedly be wounded by Scobie's protracted impenitence if he lived:

> He had a sudden picture before his eyes of a bleeding face, of eyes closed by the continuous shower of blows: the punch-drunk head of God reeling sideways . . . . .
> He thought, 'And again at Christmas,' thrusting the Child's face into the filth of the stable.
>
> (pp. 256, 257)

The 'heart of the matter', it seems, is pity.

The ending has multiple ironies. Louise, it is revealed, has been well aware of her husband's adultery, in spite of all his endeavours to conceal it. Scobie's attempt to conceal the fact of suicide fails, too. A final irony, however, occurs when Father Rank, the Catholic priest, talks to Scobie's widow. Scobie believed that in committing suicide he was damning himself. Rather like the priest who, in *Brighton Rock*, consoled Rose after Pinkie's death, Father Rank says:

> 'For goodness sake, Mrs. Scobie, don't imagine you – or I – know a thing about God's mercy . . . . . The Church knows all the rules. But it doesn't know what goes on in a single human heart.'
>
> (p. 297)

Thus, once again, the text suggests that, after all, the sinner may be saved: God may take Scobie's love (of God, or of fellow-humans) as a redemptive quality. As so often, Greene offers the prospect of a redeemed (if not sanctified) sinner; of the salvation of a man who, by orthodox standards, has been corrupt and destructive.

This final paradox of *The Heart of the Matter* can clearly be related to Greene's own endeavours to reconcile his faith with his adultery, and particularly with his notion that even adulterous love may, in some degree, be an aspect of divine love. It was one of the features which made the novel so controversial. Evelyn Waugh, a fellow-Catholic, said in a review:

> [T]housands of heathen will read it with innocent excitement, quite unaware that they are intruding among the innermost mysteries of faith . . . . . [T]he idea of willing one's own

damnation for the love of God is either a very loose poetical expression or a mad blasphemy . . . . .

(*CCE*, pp. 96, 101)

Waugh, Edward Sackville-West and Raymond Mortimer considered the possibility that Scobie was a saint; but Greene denied any such intention. Other Catholics condemned the work strongly. Ronald Brownrigg said that some readers might 'be muddled by *The Heart of the Matter* into thinking that what Christ said was "If you love me, break my commandments" '. The Reverend John Murphy declared that Scobie was a man of weak will, more afraid of women than God, who 'despaired when he should have repented'. The sceptical George Orwell questioned radically the plausibility of the novel:

If [Scobie] were capable of getting into the kind of mess that is described, he would have got into it years earlier. If he really felt that adultery is mortal sin, he would stop committing it . . . . . If he believed in Hell, he would not risk going there merely to spare the feelings of a couple of neurotic women. And . . . . . if he were the kind of man we are told he is . . . . . he would not be an officer in a colonial police force.

(*CCE*, p. 108)

The last point is shrewd. If he were that kind of man, he would hardly be an officer in the colonial police; but he could be a novelist such as Greene, who often felt that adultery (particularly with Catherine Walston) seemed to strengthen his faith; a novelist who sometimes had difficulty in distinguishing between sacred and profane love. In 'Congo Journal', Greene claimed that Orwell was wrong, for Greene had 'worked fairly closely with an old Commissioner in Freetown' who was humane and sensitive. But if Scobie were so humane, he would not have acquiesced in the murder of his servant. The demands of the plot seem to have twisted the characterisation into self-contradiction. Later, Greene said: 'I don't like the book much . . . . . Freetown is well described, but the dilemma of Scobie seems to me an exaggerated one' (*GGFR*, p. 555).

The Heart of the Matter was controversial, much publicised, banned in Eire, and chosen by the Book of the Month Club. It became an international best-seller. In Britain *The Ministry of Fear*, his previous novel, had sold 18,000 copies; within three years, *The Heart of the Matter* sold nearly 300,000 (*MW*, p. 356). Publishers promptly reissued his earlier novels, so that Greene's royalty-earnings soared.

Three years later, *The End of the Affair* made God an even more conspicuous presence in a novel of adultery. In this work, the protagonist, Bendrix, loves Sarah, who is married. Suddenly, after a bomb-explosion during an air-raid, she discontinues their relationship. Bendrix suspects that she has taken another lover. At last, after her death, he discovers that her other lover is actually God. What had happened was that when Bendrix seemed to have been killed in the explosion, Sarah had made a wager with God: 'I'll give him up for ever, only let him be alive'. Furthermore, it appears that Sarah had thereafter become a tutelary saint, performing miracles, in life and after death. Her kiss heals a strawberry-mark on a rationalist's cheek (thus also completing her cure of his rationalist scepticism). A boy with a grave stomach complaint dreams that she touches his stomach, and he is promptly healed. Bendrix prays to her to save him from taking another woman as a mistress; and he is promptly prevented from doing so by the importunity of her mother, who reveals that Sarah was baptized a Catholic. Henry, Sarah's widower, is led towards the Catholic faith, gaining consolation from her priest, Father Crompton. The more Bendrix defies God, the greater the reality that God has for him; finally his tone is that of a weary believer: 'O God, You've done enough'. Bendrix, a fiction-writer, has become a character in God's plot.

This novel exhibits a familiar tension in Greene's work. The setting is convincing, and so is the rendering of the stresses, guilts and jealousies of lovers; the complications of the plot are far less so. The evocation of wartime London, particularly the time of the V1 raids, is persuasively detailed. The central sexual relationship draws some details from Greene's wartime affair with Dorothy Glover and much material from the post-war affair with Catherine Walston. When Bendrix and Sarah copulate under her husband's roof, it reflects Greene's own experiences with Catherine at Thriplow. Henry Miles, the husband, has obvious kinship with Henry Walston: both are important public figures, involved in wartime administration; Miles, too, has the prospect of a knighthood. 'Crompton', the priest's surname, was Catherine's maiden name. Bendrix is an established novelist, gaining success, who once used the stream-of-consciousness method but has abandoned it (one recalls *The Bear Fell Free*, the rendering of Conrad Drover's character in *It's a Battlefield* or the introspections of *England Made Me*). The British edition was dedicated 'To C.'; the US edition 'To Catherine with Love'. Harry Walston declined to sue the author.

The novel's suggestion that adultery may lead, via a bargain

Greene with Catherine Walston on Capri

with God, to sainthood for an erring wife, is a characteristic Greenian paradox. But never before had Greene written a novel in which God intervened so directly and manifestly in the

61

arrangement of events. Even a believer might flinch at the extent to which the outcome appears to depend on supernatural intervention. Bendrix's life saved by Sarah's wager with God, Smythe's strawberry-mark cured by her kiss, Bendrix rescued by the dead Sarah from fornication with Sylvia Black, Parkis's boy healed by Sarah's ministry: it's a long list, and the supernatural aura is strengthened by a number of dreams by which Sarah appears to be communicating consolingly from heaven to earth. If the evidence had been more ambiguous, it might have been more plausible. Greene himself later recognised this. In his introduction to the 1974 Collected Edition text, he says:

> I realised too late how I had been cheating – cheating myself, cheating the reader . . . . . The incident of the strawberry mark should have had no place in the book; every so-called miracle, like the curing of Parkis's boy, ought to have had a completely natural explanation.

Accordingly, he revised the novel, so that in the later version the strawberry-mark (a congenital disfigurement normally permanent unless treated by surgery) becomes urticaria or nettle-rash, a malady of the skin which is characterised by itchy red or whitish raised patches and which is usually caused by an allergy. So, whereas the 1951 text refers to the 'purple crumpled strawberry mark' on Smythe's cheek and gives Bendrix the comment, 'I've read somewhere these marks are hysterical in origin' (pp. 94, 234), the 1974 text refers to 'gross livid spots' and lets Bendrix comment, 'I've read somewhere that urticaria is hysterical in origin' (pp. 84, 208). Consequently, the cure appears markedly less miraculous, though it is still part of a large sequence of evidence that Sarah, the adulterous sinner, has become a saint awaiting formal canonisation.

For *The End of the Affair*, which, he told Catherine Walston, was '*your* novel', in 1952 Greene was awarded in New York the Catholic Authors' award for fiction. An article in *Time* magazine bore the caption 'Adultery can lead to sainthood' and suggested that Greene might be a new Dostoyevsky. In 1955, the predictable film followed; an indifferent version, with Van Johnson as Bendrix and Deborah Kerr as Sarah. Greene, on the set, noted that Johnson chewed gum during his love-scenes; but he thought Kerr's performance 'extremely good'.

The other important novel of this period, *The Quiet American*, draws on Greene's experiences in Vietnam. His reports of the visit to the front-line at Phat Diem and of his flight in the bomber which destroyed a sampan are transferred with few alterations to the novel. During his tour of Vietnam, Greene frequently took opium, enjoying the resultant 'white nights' of tranquillity. In the novel, the protagonist, Fowler, similarly smokes opium: a vice perhaps appropriate to a reporter who seeks detachment. (Like Greene, he is separated from a Catholic wife who declines to grant him a divorce.) Fowler is eventually drawn into political commitment: he instigates the murder of Pyle, an American working for the CIA. Fowler's motives are mixed: by removing Pyle, he is removing a rival for the love of Phuong, his own mistress. But he also believes he is removing a dangerous 'innocent': a well-meaning but ignorant American whose schemes to establish a 'Third Force' in Vietnam have entailed the killing of citizens by plastic bombs which he has provided.

Greene's anti-Americanism is a strong feature of the novel. He evidently believed the novel's political thesis: that some of the terrorist explosions in Saigon, particularly one in the rue Catinat, were the work not of the Vietminh insurgents but of the CIA in conjunction with a maverick Vietnamese Colonel. The historical evidence, according to Norman Sherry's investigations (*Life* II, pp. 426–34), refutes Greene's thesis. The fact that US citizens were not killed by the particular explosion that Greene recalled was a matter of chance, not calculation. In any case, it is difficult to see how US interests could be advanced by actions which would suggest to the world the inadequacy of defences against communist and nationalist insurgents. When Fowler 'takes sides', he does so with a communist agent.

Greene later said that he was not anti-American but critical only of certain US policies. Nevertheless, as we have seen, even in *The Lawless Roads* a general distaste for the materialistic affluence of the USA is manifest; and frequently Greene conveys hostility to US culture. He once told Malcolm Muggeridge, about the Church, 'Russians only destroy its body, whereas the Americans destroy its soul'. His sympathy with the underdog led him easily into opposition to the upperdog of the modern world. He also resented the fact that, having been briefly a member of the Communist Party, he fell foul of the McCarran Act of the 1950s, with the result that he experienced repeated difficulties in gaining a visa to enter the USA: frequently he had to make do with a short-term visa instead of the longer one he sought.

The Quiet American was widely praised by reviewers in Britain; but, not surprisingly, there were some hostile reviews in the USA, notably from *Newsweek*, which said that Greene had now played into the Russians' hands: *Pravda*'s enthusiasm, it remarked, showed that Greene's characters were close to Marxist stereotypes. In an American interview, against the background of the Cold War and the political witch-hunt led in the USÁ by Senator Joseph McCarthy (a Catholic), the author quoted Franklin D. Roosevelt and Tom Paine: 'The only thing to fear is fear itself'; 'We should guard even our enemies against injustice'.

1955–65

Greene continued to compound his adultery with attractive women, some of them twenty or more years younger than himself. In 1955 he began a relationship with Anita Björk, a very attractive Swedish actress who had recently been widowed. He frequently visited her at a house that he bought for her near Stockholm, and they vacationed at his villa in Anacapri. This relationship lasted for several years; but Greene gallantly assured Catherine Walston that it was less important than his with her.

Then in 1959, at Douala in the Cameroons, he met and made friends with Jacques Cloetta, his wife Yvonne and their daughter Martine. They had a house at Juan-les-Pins; and, when Greene settled in Antibes in 1965, they were near-neighbours. Yvonne, yet another attractive woman who found the blue-eyed author appealing, became Greene's companion for the remainder of his life: he called her his 'happy, healthy kitten', or simply 'HHK'. The late volume *Travels with My Aunt* is dedicated to her. She would spend afternoons and evenings with Greene, returning to her husband at night; an arrangement which seems to have suited Greene admirably. 'Fame', says Querry in *A Burnt-Out Case*, 'is a potent aphrodisiac. Married women are the easiest.....' Eventually, in *J'Accuse*, Greene would take up cudgels on behalf of Yvonne's daughter Martine, who was involved in litigation with her former husband and his influential associates.

'In 1957 I travelled more than 44,000 miles', he claimed. Greene's travels in this decade were as extensive as ever: the countries he visited included Poland, the USSR, China (where his endeavours as a secret agent were apparently fruitless), Goa, Tahiti, Haiti, the Congo, and Cuba (in the days of the Batista regime and later when Fidel Castro became dictator). His janiform nature is illustrated by his ability to enjoy the decadent pleasures of the Batista era while assisting Castro's rebels. In *Ways of Escape* (p. 241) he recalls, for instance, one sojourn with a female friend in Havana:

> [We] had been to the Shanghai, we had watched without much interest Superman's performance with a mulatto girl (as uninspiring as a dutiful husband's), we had lost a little at roulette, we had fed at the Floridita, smoked marijuana, and

seen a lesbian performance at the Blue Moon. So now we asked our driver if he could provide us with a little cocaine.

(The driver promptly sold Greene a quantity of boracic powder.) On the same visit to Havana, the author agreed to smuggle warm clothing to Castro's partisans, who were based in the mountains. When Greene, in Vietnam, had interviewed Ho Chi Minh, the resultant account was warmly sympathetic to the communist leader: 'I am on my guard against hero-worship, but he appealed directly to that buried relic of the schoolboy.' There is more than a touch of hero-worship in Greene's essay on his meeting with Fidel Castro, who is depicted as charismatically lively, shrewd, pragmatically idealistic, close to the people, generous, and akin to St Paul, being 'Pauline in his labours and in his escapes'. The author 'argued for the possibility . . . . . of cooperation between Catholicism and Communism'. At least Greene's essay concludes by noting astutely that whereas passenger aeroplanes arriving in Havana are 'almost empty', those departing have 'every seat filled'.

Pre-revolutionary Cuba, with its night-clubs, strip-shows and lotteries, formed the setting of *Our Man in Havana* (1958). This novel is distinctly 'an entertainment', with strong elements of broadly satiric comedy. Greene mocks his employers in the British SIS by depicting them as naïve, absurd and incompetent. (The asinine Hawthorne is based on 'C', Sir Stuart Menzies, head of MI6: see *Life* II, pp. 171–2.) Wormold, the hero, is recruited as an agent, and responds by employing imaginary informants so that he can collect their pay; he sends to London plans for a Cuban secret weapon which are in fact drawings based on a type of vacuum cleaner that he sells. His fantasies become lethal as rival agents attempt to assassinate his supposed informants. Escaping assassination himself, he shoots and kills the treacherous Carter: thus Greene again takes vicarious revenge on the Carter who was his juvenile tormentor. Eventually, when Wormold is recalled to London, the full extent of his deception is tardily recognised, but the deception is hushed up; MI6 actually rewards him with an OBE – Kim Philby's reward – and with the position of lecturer in espionage to new agents. (Here Greene recycles some plot-material of the tale 'Nobody to Blame'.) In future, Wormold can live happily with his partner Beatrice.

The whole novel works proficiently as a comedy-thriller. The narrator's view of the world is broadly benign, the satire almost genial. (The actual incompetence and lenience of the British security services provided good warrant for their depiction in the novel.)

Even the sinister Cuban police-chief, Segura, reputedly a torturer, is depicted as a character capable – at least in his private life – of benevolence. The most serious note is probably that sounded by Wormold when he makes a speech at a banquet: in it (p. 220), he compares rival nations to rival firms making vacuum cleaners:

> 'There's not much difference between the two machines any more than there is between two human beings, one Russian – or German – and one British. There would be no competition and no war if it wasn't for the ambition of a few men in both firms; just a few men dictate competition and invent needs . . . . .'

Though it mocks the rhetoric of the Cold War, *Our Man in Havana* does not purport to be making any probing analysis of international relations; it does well what it sets out to do – to entertain. A reviewer in the *Daily Telegraph* termed it 'as comical, satirical, atmospheric an "entertainment" as he has given us'. Greene's rueful postscript was:

> Alas, the book did me little good with the new rulers in Havana. In poking fun at the British Secret Service, I had minimised the terror of Batista's rule.
>
> (*WE*, p. 249)

A far more taxing work is *A Burnt-Out Case* (1961). In this, Querry, a famous ecclesiastical architect, travels into the Congo to a leper colony organised by Catholic priests. He is befriended by a doctor there and permitted to do practical work on behalf of the lepers. 'A burnt-out case', is, we are told, the name given to a leper in whom the disease has run its course; he or she is extensively mutilated and lacks feeling in those areas. Querry is a moral and psychological burnt-out case: depressed and rootless, he has lost his Catholic faith, his ambition, his sexual desire, his interest in everyday humanity. Gradually, however, he becomes involved in the work of the colony. Observing the community of priests, studying the conscientious work of Dr Colin, and planning the construction of new hospital buildings, he begins to awaken: he even experiences contentment.

> Querry said to Colin, 'You know I am happy here.' He closed his mouth on the phrase too late; it had escaped him on the sweet evening air like an admission.

This, however, is the calm before the storm: Querry's innocently helpful involvement with a young married woman is misconstrued by her husband, Rycker, who jealously shoots and kills him.

The novel is thoroughly researched. The African setting is as convincing as any in Greene's fiction, and the work of the leper colony is described in specific, knowledgeable detail. The European organisers, the priests and the doctor, are well differentiated; the African lepers, too, are depicted with fine discrimination, from Deo Gratias, Querry's helper, to the pot-bellied child of three with a finger in the corner of his mouth. The accounts of the modes of leprosy, its treatment and its social consequences, are unsentimental, unsparing and compassionate. It is the characterisation of Querry which is problematic. What makes him hard to credit is that repeatedly he seems to be a vehicle for thinly disguised autobiography. Greene the author seems to be infiltrating the characterisation of Querry, creating an oddly ambivalent and even embarrassing effect. The autobiographical connections are many and varied, extending even to the fact that the faces of both men adorned the cover of *Time* magazine. Querry, in an allegoric confession to Mrs Rycker, tells her that he was once successful, famous, wealthy, with many lovers, yet also devout: he believed that in his artefacts he was serving God ('the King' in the allegory).

> 'Sometimes people were a little perplexed that such a good man should have enjoyed quite so many women – it was, on the surface anyway, disloyal to the King who had made quite other rules. But they learnt in time to explain it; they said he had a great capacity for love and love had always been regarded by them as the highest of virtues . . . . . Even the man himself began to believe that he loved a great deal better than all the so-called good people . . . . .'
>
> (p. 198)

As artistic success grew, he tired of major works and produced relatively trivial ones; yet the critical industry burgeoned, and many interpreters of his work continued to stress its theological aspects. But a change came. His belief in God had been not emotional but based on a variety of grounds ('historical, philosophical, logical and etymological'); and the belief has died. He now feels that his work, and even his love-making with women, had been a matter of egotism and pride. One faint glimmering of hope is that his present state of vacancy 'might be his punishment': 'he wondered if his unbelief were not after all a final and conclusive proof of the King's existence'.

Querry is not Greene; but just as Querry's story to Marie Rycker is transparently confessional (his allegory of the jeweller refers to 'a building', rather than a jewel, that the man has completed), it also has features which seem to stem from Greene rather than from an architect. For instance, Querry says that his commentators write books in which 'There was nearly always a chapter called The Toad in the Hole: the Art of Fallen Man, or else there was one called From Easter Egg to Letters of Marque, the Jeweller of Original Sin'. These references bring to mind numerous critical essays on the theological aspects of Greene's fiction; it is hard to imagine that the work of a jeweller (or an architect) would be subject to such specifically theological interpretation. As for Querry's loss of religious conviction, this too was happening to Greene; in his later life, his views were modulating towards the agnostic. It is clear that once again, in a major characterisation, Greene is drawing on personal experience in a way which introduces tensions and, arguably, inconsistencies. Evelyn Waugh's diary-entries on *A Burnt-Out Case* are apt:

> [It] emphasizes a theme which it would be affected not to regard as personal . . . . . His early books are full of self pity at poverty and obscurity, now self pity at his success . . . . .
> His new novel makes it plain that he is exasperated by his reputation as a 'Catholic' writer.
>
> (*The Diaries of Evelyn Waugh*, 1976, p. 779)

Later in 1961, Greene published *In Search of a Character: Two African Journals*. The second item in this volume, 'Convoy to West Africa' (which had previously appeared in *The Mint*, an anthology, in 1946), is a journal of the perilous voyage to Freetown in 1941 which yielded material for *The Heart of the Matter*. The first item, 'Congo Journal', with its title reminiscent of Conrad's 'Congo Diary', is a fascinating study of the research for *A Burnt-Out Case*. Greene was aware of Conradian precedent: 'Heart of Darkness' is cited several times in the journal. Repeatedly one finds that convincing details in the novel derive from Greene's careful notation of events in the Congo. Greene was evidently unflinchingly courageous in taking such close interest in the lives and sufferings of the lepers and the modes of treatment: 'the man without fingers or toes nursing a small child: the man with elephantiasis, testicles the size of a football'. He had long been fascinated by the example of Father Damien (1840–89), the priest who worked in a leper colony on Molokai until he died of leprosy; and Albert Schweitzer (1875–1965) was a theologian world-famous for his labours at the hospital of

Lambaréné. 'Congo Journal' shows how the conception of Querry emerged by imaginative trial and error, helped along by a variety of personal encounters. The autobiographical element in the character is accentuated by Greene's footnote to the following journal entry (p. 26):

> Pursued by the schoolmaster who now tries to exercise a kind of spiritual blackmail. I am replying that I am not competent in matters of faith: he should apply to a priest.

('I'm not competent to discuss it', says Querry, in the novel, when Rycker seeks religious guidance from him.) The note is:

> I would claim not to be a writer of Catholic novels, but a writer who in four or five books took characters with Catholic ideas for his material. Nonetheless for years – particularly after *The Heart of the Matter* – I found myself hunted by people who wanted help with spiritual problems that I was incapable of giving. Not a few of these were priests themselves . . . . . I was already beginning to live in the skin of Querry, a man who had turned at bay.

In *Ways of Escape*, Greene similarly emphasises the nausea he had experienced as, following the international success of *The Heart of the Matter*, so many people turned to him for spiritual help. Without becoming an atheist, he felt that atheism was preferable to 'the piety of the educated, the established, who seem to own their Roman Catholic image of God'. During an exchange of letters with Evelyn Waugh, Greene used a quotation from a favourite Browning poem ('Bishop Blougram's Apology' again) to convey his own position:

> What have we gained then by our unbelief
> But a life of doubt diversified by faith,
> For one of faith diversified by doubt?
> We called the chessboard white, – we call it black.

His volume of tales entitled *A Sense of Reality* appeared in 1963. Of its four tales, 'A Visit to Morin' (which had first been published in the *London Magazine* in 1957 and had already been printed on its own as a booklet in 1960), clearly anticipates the depiction of Querry in *A Burnt-Out Case*. Its central character, Morin, is an ageing writer who once was acclaimed as a Catholic novelist but who has lapsed. He says that he has lost his *belief* in God, though he retains his *faith*. Having ceased to go to confession (because he enjoyed extra-marital sexual relationships too much to have a sincere 'purpose of amendment'), he has been appropriately punished.

> 'I can tell myself now that my lack of belief is a final proof that the Church is right and the faith is true. I had cut myself off for twenty years from grace and my belief withered as the priests said it would. I don't believe in God and His Son and His angels and His saints, but I know the reason why I don't believe and the reason is – the Church is true and what she taught me is true.'
>
> (p. 95)

Greene's love of paradox was never more keen than when he offered loss of belief as proof of the presence of the object of belief. The logic is akin to that of a person who feels that his loss of belief that the earth is flat is a punishment for his failure to attend meetings of the Flat Earth Society, and therefore is proof that the earth is indeed flat.

'A Visit to Morin' is rather drily didactic. 'Under the Garden', however, which Greene thought one of his best tales, is more vivid: the dying narrator records a childhood dream of a descent to a tunnel beneath a little island in a pond. Javitt, the bluff, tough ruler of this subterranean realm, offers Greenian wisdom to the juvenile quester:

> 'Be disloyal. It's your duty to the human race. The human race needs to survive and it's the loyal man who dies first from anxiety or a bullet or overwork. If you have to earn a living, boy, and the price they make you pay is loyalty, be a double agent . . . . . The same applies to women and God. They both respect a man they don't own, and they'll go on raising the price they are willing to offer.'
>
> (pp. 55–6)

Probably the most interesting story in this collection is the last, 'A Discovery in the Woods', which belongs to the tradition of post-nuclear-holocaust works: a genre which burgeoned in the 1950s as Cold War fears grew and international nuclear testing repeatedly polluted the atmosphere. Works in this genre include Marghanita Laski's *The Offshore Island*, David Campton's *Mutatis Mutandis* and *Little Brother, Little Sister*, Nevil Shute's *On the Beach*, and, supremely, William Golding's *Lord of the Flies*. Greene's 'A Discovery in the Woods', an interesting venture into science fiction, tells of children from a strangely primitive community who, on an exploration of a far hillside, discover a mysterious ruined building (actually a wrecked ship, the *France*) containing a skeleton: 'He's six feet tall and he has beautiful straight legs', says one of the stunted, deformed children. The vessel from the civilised world has served, we realise, as the Noah's ark for this new, blighted, primitive era that succeeds a nuclear holocaust. In this tale which has brief passing resemblances to Wells's *The Time Machine* as well as *Lord of the Flies*, Greene well exploits the techniques of delayed decoding and covert plotting. Delayed decoding occurs when an author describes an effect but delays or withholds an account of its cause; covert plotting occurs when a plot-sequence is presented so obliquely that only in retrospect, or at a second reading, will it be perceived as a coherent sequence.

In this decade, Greene also pursued energetically his career as a dramatist, employing an unpredictable diversity of theatrical modes. *The Potting Shed* opened in London in 1958, *The Complaisant Lover* in 1959, and *Carving a Statue* in 1964. Each had fine actors and directors. *The Potting Shed* occasionally recalls Eliot's *The Family Reunion*, in that the central character gradually learns of a crucial incident in his past and is liberated into new life. The crux of the plot is that in the past, as a boy, James Callifer had hanged himself on being deprived of religious belief by rationalistic argument; his uncle, a priest, had prayed: 'Take away my faith, but let him live.' The prayer was promptly answered: the apparently dead boy revived, but the priest lost his faith (though he continues to practise, an alcoholic pastor). At the same time, James's father, an atheistic rationalist whose friends include Bertrand Russell, lost his own 'faith', since his atheistic rationalism had been subverted by this seeming miracle. Near the end of the play, James has learnt of all this; he rediscovers religion, love and significance; he is restored to his estranged wife. The priest, meanwhile, feels that he is regaining his vocation. The drama offers an easy defeat for sceptical rationalism, and challenges the psychoanalytic viewpoint (which is prominently represented). As we have seen, the paradox that loss of belief in God may be evidence of the presence of God occurs also in *A Burnt-Out Case* and 'A Visit to Morin'. A crucial 'wager with God' (resulting in divine intervention) had provided the fulcrum of *The End of the Affair* and, arguably, of *The Heart of the Matter* (Book Two, Chap. 1). The dialectical basis of the play – the debate between atheistic rationalism, psychoanalysis and Catholicism – had featured in numerous works from *Stamboul Train* onwards. Even bizarre details are familiar: in lodgings at Nottingham (shared with a journalist), James feeds his dog with tinned salmon, and it is frequently sick: memories of Greene's time as a Nottingham journalist.

The first London production, in February 1958, had a fine cast: John Gielgud as James Callifer, Irene Worth as his wife, Gwen Ffrangçon-Davies as his mother. *The Times* (6 February 1958, p. 12) said: 'In several scenes of suspense Mr. Graham Greene leads up with deft strokes of characterization to a revelation with a strong emotional and spiritual impact.' *Punch* declared it well acted but 'not altogether persuasive'; a harsher view was that of Brian Inglis in the *Spectator* (14 February 1958, p. 203), who said that the play was 'trite' intellectually:

> The psychiatrist appears to have picked up his craft by assiduous reading of *The Seventh Veil*; the rationalist is a figure preserved by some feat of taxidermy from around 1900; and the reasons for the priest's moral collapse are desperately unconvincing.

Furthermore, he said, the acting is inadequate: 'a parish amateur dramatic society . . . . . would do better than this distinguished but bewildered cast'.

The Potting Shed ran for just three months. *The Complaisant Lover* proved much more successful: a comedy of marital infidelity in which the husband finally asserts control over his wife's lover, condoning a *ménage à trois* in such a way as to chasten his rival. Hence the ironic title: here it is the lover, not the husband, who is expected to become 'complaisant'. Once again, a superb cast was employed: Paul Scofield was the lover, Phyllis Calvert the adulterous wife. The central role, that of Victor Rhodes, the cuckolded dentist, was an ideal part for Sir Ralph Richardson; indeed, it may well have been composed with that actor in mind, for Richardson excelled in roles like this, in which he could display endearing eccentricity and crafty innocence. He gained many plaudits, though Alan Brien (in the *Spectator*) complained that it was a 'much over-praised performance' by a self-indulgent veteran. *The Times*, however, applauded the play for being thoroughly entertaining and for offering a smooth transition from the farcical comedy of the first half to the serious comedy of the second; Ralph Richardson was 'masterly'. The play was so popular that its run at the Globe Theatre lasted a year, from June 1959 to June 1960.

During the 1950s a double revolution took place in the British theatre. John Osborne's *Look Back in Anger* (staged in 1956) inaugurated a range of works (by himself, Arnold Wesker, David Mercer and others) offering a more realistic, 'angry' and socially critical kind of drama. Samuel Beckett's *Waiting for Godot* (staged in London in 1955) was followed by kindred plays by Harold Pinter and Tom Stoppard, which showed that radical, 'absurdist' drama could be successful at the box-office. Greene's response was to move away from the middle-class 'drawing-room naturalism' of his previous works to the stark and bleak stylisation of *Carving a Statue*. This employs just one set: the studio of a fanatical artist in which stands a vast, incomplete sculpture intended to represent God: a statue so vast that only shins and feet can be seen on stage. Whether God is created in the sculptor's (or man's) image or the sculptor is created in God's image is one of the questions set by the play. The father largely ignores his son or treats him callously; his obsession is the work of art, which, it is clear, he is unlikely ever to complete. The boy has two girl-friends: one is sexually assaulted by the father; the other (who is deaf and dumb) dies in a motor-accident after being raped by a lascivious doctor. The harshness of the play's allegoric suggestions is represented well in the following exchange of dialogue (p. 56):

> *Father:* God doesn't love. He communicates, that's all. He's an artist. He doesn't love.
> *Son:* Did He hate his son?
> *Father:* He didn't love or hate him. He used him as a subject.

One of the main sources of the play, Greene explained, was the life of Benjamin Haydon, the early-nineteenth-century painter who had grandiose ambitions but limited talents. (He committed suicide by both shooting himself and slashing his throat with a razor.) The notion of God as an aesthete, quoted above, might have been suggested by Conrad's remarks in *A Personal Record*: 'I have come to suspect that the aim of creation cannot be ethical at all. I would fondly believe that its object is purely spectacular.' There is more than a hint of Beckett in the play: the single set, the bleak action, the suggestion that the central task will never be completed, the ruminations on a possibly hostile deity. Sometimes *Waiting for Godot* comes to mind, sometimes *Endgame*; but *Carving a Statue*, less formally experimental, remains characteristically Greenian in its pre-occupations. Greene denied that it was symbolic, saying that it displayed merely 'an association of ideas'; but the term 'symbolic' seems a reasonable critical short-hand for the play's mode. Either way, *Carving a Statue* failed (it was withdrawn after just six weeks at the Haymarket Theatre), even though some praise was won by Sir Ralph Richardson as the father and Dennis Waterman as his son. 'Pretentious and steadily untheatrical', said

73

Eric Keown in the *Illustrated London News*; 'threadbare', said *The Times*. Greene himself called it 'an abortion', criticised Richardson's interpretation, and declared:

> Never before have I known a play so tormenting to write or so fatiguing in production as *Carving a Statue*. I was glad to see the end of it, and to that extent I was grateful to the reviewers who may have hastened the end.
>
> (*WE*, p. 236)

Stylised, bleak, expressionistic, bold, negative, contrived and nasty: *Carving a Statue* at least showed that Greene, at the age of sixty, was still a restless and venturous creator.

The later years

1965–75

Although Greene was now in his sixties, he still travelled widely, and exotic and dangerous regions continued to beckon him. In 1967, for example, in Israel during the aftermath of the Six-Day War, he was taken close to the Egyptian front-line just at the time when the Egyptians began to shell Israeli-held territory; shells and bullets flew overhead as Greene and his guide crouched behind a sand-dune. During this visit one of his hosts was the renowned military strategist, General Moshe Dayan (who, to Greene's satisfaction, entertained him at an *Arab* restaurant). On other journeys he travelled as far as Argentina and Paraguay in search of material. One of his novels, *Our Man in Havana*, travelled rather further, having been the reading material of a Russian cosmonaut during his voyage through space.

The range of literary productions in this decade looks quite impressive, though it is noticeable that an increasing number of the books are gatherings of earlier material. These books include *Collected Essays* (1969), *Collected Stories* (1972) and *The Pleasure-Dome* (1972, a selection of his film reviews). *A Sort of Life* (1971), the first volume of his autobiography, incorporated material which had previously appeared in the form of essays and prefaces. At last there emerged the biography of John Wilmot, *Lord Rochester's Monkey* (1974), which he had written over forty years previously during the early years of his marriage. He revised it while residing at Antibes, in circumstances detailed in the tale 'May We Borrow Your Husband?', near the ramparts overlooking the sea. Rochester, the libertine poet, the debauchee and adulterer, the carouser, the Hobbesian sceptic who yet underwent a deathbed repentance and renewal of faith: an ideal subject for Greene. Indeed, Greene's own life may have been influenced by that of Rochester, of whom he says: 'The spirit was always at war with the flesh; his unbelief was quite as religious as the Dean of St Paul's faith.' The colourful biography is an apt labour of fascination if not of love.

Greene's retrospective preoccupation during this period is strongly evident in *Travels with My Aunt: A Novel* (1969). The subject, Greene said, was old age and death; but he found it enjoyable to write, and what emerges is a comic picaresque in which Aunt Augusta is the *pícara* and her son a middle-aged Pooterish apprentice in various forms of lawbreaking. Greene remarked:

> If *A Burnt-Out Case* in 1961 represented the depressive side of a manic-depressive writer, *Travels with My Aunt* eight years later surely represented the manic at its height – or depth.
>
> (*WE*, p. 286)

(Greene associated this manic mood with his decision to leave England and settle permanently in France.) A striking feature of this comic novel is that it is a saturnalia of self-referentiality: it abounds in literary in-jokes for Greene's loyal readers. There's a scene in Brighton, a journey on the Orient Express, a lover called Visconti (who is termed 'a viper') in honour of Bowen's *Viper of Milan*, and a friend called Mario after Greene's flamboyant friend Mario Soldati. The aunt's relationship with a younger black lover echoes the situation of the ageing hôtelière and Marcel in *The Comedians*; and the name of that lover, Wordsworth, was borrowed from the Liberian quartermaster described in *Journey without Maps*. Greene said the novel simply unfolded without planning: 'I felt like a rider who had dropped the reins'; and that is largely how the book reads: loose, galloping, entertaining enough; though death finally enters even this Arcadian race-course. Another reason for the episodic nature of the work is that Greene decided to incorporate in it a number of tales that he had not developed for inclusion in *May We Borrow Your Husband?*. Although the work has its serious and black-comic elements, it is predominantly comic and nostalgic, inflected by whimsy and fantasy. The older Greene became, the more he was prepared to relax and to contemplate life with a smile rather than a sneer or scowl.

The two other novels of this decade are *The Comedians* (1966) and *The Honorary Consul* (1973). *The Comedians* (which initially sold 60,000 copies) is a political comedy-thriller set in Haiti during the era of the ghoulish dictator, Doctor Duvalier: an era of tyranny, corruption, voodoo, poverty, decay. Greene knew it at first hand, having visited the island thrice, most recently in 1963. One of the main characters in the novel is a familiar Greenian type: Jones is yet another likeable English middle-class confidence-tricker. After various shady and farcical escapades, he emerges as a courageous hero in reality, dying while defending a group of rebels against the harsh regime. A Marxist idealist, Dr Magiot, opposes the dictatorship and proposes a Greenian thesis, an alliance of Catholics and communists against tyranny; he also sounds a distinctively Greenian note of hostility to the USA when he remarks: 'I'm not sure I wouldn't fight for Papa Doc if the [US] Marines came.' Magiot is killed by Duvalier's Tontons Macoutes to reassure the USA that Haiti is a bastion against communism. This anti-American theme is to some extent counterbalanced by the sympathetic portrayal of Mr Smith, a liberal former presidential candidate, and his intrepid wife. (She saves the narrator, Brown, from a brutal death at the hands of the Tontons.) The novel finally hints that Brown might be led from disillusioned detachment to left-wing political commitment.

Understandably, *The Comedians* infuriated Duvalier. Soon Haitian embassies distributed a pamphlet entitled *Graham Greene démasqué* which denounced Greene as 'a liar, a *crétin*, a stool-pigeon . . . . . a spy . . . . . a drug-addict . . . . . a torturer'. From this, Greene concluded that 'a writer is not so powerless as he usually feels, and a pen, as well as a silver bullet, can draw blood' (*WE*, p. 270). Another consequence was the customary film. The impressive cast included Richard Burton, Elizabeth Taylor, Alec Guinness, James Earl Jones, Peter Ustinov and Lillian Gish; but it proved to be an expensive failure: 'negligible', said the *New Statesman*, criticising the script; 'Elizabeth Taylor was a disaster', remarked Greene.

The Honorary Consul is more consistent in tone than the previous novel. Its main political target is US foreign policy, particularly the policy of supporting right-wing South American dictatorships – in this case, the dictatorship of General Stroessner in Paraguay. Set on the Argentinian side of the border with Paraguay, the novel tells how guerrillas attempt to kidnap a US ambassador in the hope that some Paraguayan political prisoners will be released in exchange. Incompetently, they capture not the ambassador but Charley Fortnum, an alcoholic British Honorary Consul. The guerrillas include a Marxist and a former Catholic priest; they are aided by Dr Plarr, a sympathiser who has been enjoying an adulterous relationship with

Fortnum's young wife. Eventually Plarr and the kidnappers are surrounded and are ruthlessly shot; Fortnum is rescued and returns to his wife. He knows of her infidelity but forgives her. A central contrast in characterisation is that between the cynical Dr Plarr and the innocently trusting and loving Fortnum.

The novel would have been improved by editorial pruning. The ratio of ethical debate to action, particularly in the last third of the novel, is too high; suspense wilts as discussion extends. Father León, the guerrilla who reluctantly resumes his priestly duties during the siege, seems to have stepped from the hinterland of Greene's old preoccupations: a figure deployed for the sake of debate rather than a credible character in his own right. He does at least offer the interestingly heretical idea (which can be traced back to Thomas Hardy's *The Dynasts*) that God has a malevolent as well as a benevolent aspect, and may be helped to evolve into full benevolence by the interaction of human beings with their Creator: ' "[T]he evolution of God depends on our evolution. Every evil act of ours strengthens His night-side, and every good one helps His day-side." ' (p. 286).

Greene deemed the *The Honorary Consul* 'perhaps the novel I prefer to all the others'; but he knew that while General Stroessner remained in power, he would never be able to return to Paraguay, 'that sad and lovely land'.

Meanwhile, he continued his progress as a playwright with *The Return of A. J. Raffles* (1975), subtitled 'An Edwardian Comedy in Three Acts based somewhat loosely on E. W. Hornung's characters in *The Amateur Cracksman*'. Raffles, the gentlemanly safebreaker, becomes involved with the Oscar Wilde set (specifically Lord Alfred Douglas) and burgles Wilde's foe, the Marquess of Queensberry. All ends genially; the Prince of Wales is depicted as a thoroughly decent, likeable and tolerant man of the world; the Marquess is defeated; and the work as a whole is a whimsically nostalgic tribute to Hornung and some putative cultural qualities of turn-of-the-century England, notably the elegance and gentlemanly cameraderie of the upper middle class. One of the settings is Albany, the luxurious block of flats (or of 'suites of chambers') in Piccadilly in which Greene had resided in the 1950s. The play reflects the atmosphere of the new 'permissive era', too: it includes a scene of nudity, and homosexuality is prominent. (When Lord Alfred asks a friend whether Raffles was bisexual, the reply is: 'Of course not. He never looked twice at a woman.') *The Return of A. J. Raffles*, with its gags and ludicrous confusions, was one of Greene's increasingly frequent holidays from Greeneland to a more benign region. This farcical comedy was produced by the Royal

Shakespeare Company in London for a six-week run at the Aldwych, with Denholm Elliott as Raffles and Paul Rogers as the Prince. Some reviewers were disappointed; but Richard Mayne, in the *Times Literary Supplement* (12 December 1975, p. 1486), commented: 'Nobody loses, except the police and some of the newspaper critics, who seemed not to have had the good time the rest of us enjoyed.'

1975–85

Greene's main base was now his flat in Antibes, where Yvonne Cloetta continued to make regular visits as his lover. Her daughter, Martine, had separated from her husband, Daniel Guy, but was then involved in bitter disputes with him over the custody of the children. Greene thereupon wrote the pamphlet *J'Accuse* (1982, the title rather presumptuously borrowed from Émile Zola), in which he suggested that the husband was an unbalanced criminal protected by corrupt officials in Nice. This led to lawsuits: Daniel Guy was awarded damages against Greene and his publishers.

During this period Greene was intricately involved in Central American politics. In a relationship initiated in 1976 by General Omar Torrijos Herrera, dictator of Panama, he visited Panama several times as the dictator's guest, becoming his friend and enthusiastic admirer: an admiration recorded in *Getting to Know the General* (1984), which describes the leader as 'a patriot and an idealist who had no formal ideology, except a general preference for Left over Right'. When the Panama treaty of 1977 was ratified at Washington by Torrijos and President Carter, in the presence of such notorious generals as Stroessner of Paraguay, Videla of Argentina and Pinochet of Chile, Greene was proud to be a member of the Panamanian delegation. The treaty granted various concessions to Panama, including conditional sovereignty over the Canal from the year 2000.

Greene also visited Belize and Costa Rica, and had a further friendly meeting with Fidel Castro of Cuba. Indefatigably, he travelled in Nicaragua after the victory of the Sandinistas, for he had been warmly sympathetic to the cause of the Sandinista guerrillas there and had given them financial aid. (After implementing admirable social reforms, the Sandinista government was beset by economic crises and soon suffered electoral defeat.) The author twice acted as an intermediary during negotiations following political kidnappings in El Salvador. In 1981, General Torrijos was killed in an air-crash: *Getting to Know the General* voices the suspicion that CIA agents had planted a bomb on the plane. Greene held amicable meetings with Colonel (later General) Noriega, who subsequently became dictator of Panama but was deposed and arrested by US armed forces in 1989. Both Torrijos and Noriega had presided over regimes of corruption and brutality. On reading how the author was so flatteringly fêted and lavishly entertained in Panama, one suspects that he was being manipulated and exploited by politicians; and Greene himself remarked: 'I have never hesitated to be "used" in a cause I believed in, even if my choice might be only for a lesser evil.'

In 1963, Kim Philby, Greene's former boss at the British Secret Intelligence Service, defected to the Soviet Union. From the 1940s onwards, the British security services had given generous hospitality to numerous traitors: among them, Philby, Blake, Burgess, Maclean and Blunt. Paid by the British taxpayer to secure British interests, these people had increased their incomes by passing secrets to the USSR. Guy Burgess and Donald Maclean had defected in 1951 (and John Cairncross had resigned soon afterwards); George Blake was jailed in 1961, but later escaped to Moscow; and Anthony Blunt's treachery (which cost him his knighthood) was discovered in 1964 but not publicly revealed until much later. Philby was responsible for sending numerous agents to their deaths; yet Greene remained on friendly terms with him until the end of his life, visiting him several times in Moscow. Of course, Greene passed parts of his correspondence with Philby back to the SIS. The author was thus an intermediary between MI6 and the KGB. Greene wrote the introduction to Philby's book, *My Silent War* (1978), in which he sought to defend the traitor by offering such claims as these: Philby genuinely believed in the superiority of the Soviet system; he was very courageous; and he resembled the Catholic conspirators against Queen Elizabeth I. 'Perhaps my childhood experience of divided loyalties has helped me to sympathize with people like Kim Philby. . . . .'

In 1960 Evelyn Waugh told a correspondent: 'I think [Greene] is [a] secret agent on our side and all his buttering up of the Russians is "cover".' The truth is more complicated: Greene retained a long and deep-seated hostility to several aspects of the USA, and repeatedly and influentially expressed sympathy with several aspects of Marxism; but he also enjoyed the gratifications (and material advantages) of work as an informer for the security services. The SIS, he said, was 'the best travel agency in the world'. He noted the literary precedent: Daniel Defoe had worked both as a government agent and as a novelist, and some of his political writings had been regarded as propaganda for the forces he was purportedly opposing.

The Philby defection forms part of the background to *The Human Factor* (1978). This is one of the best of Greene's post-war novels. In *Our Man in Havana*, he had depicted the SIS as bungling and incompetent. In *The Human Factor* it is depicted as Machiavellian, ruthless, and collaborative with the Apartheid regime in South Africa. The hero, Castle, employed by MI6, has a black wife and adopted son. Out of gratitude to communists, who helped the woman and her son to escape from South Africa, he has been passing British secrets to the Russians. His office comes under suspicion; his colleague Davis, wrongly thought to be the traitor, is murdered by his own employers. Castle then escapes to Moscow. In a bitter ending, he learns that his information was regarded as of minor importance; it was being passed back to London by a Russian agent in order to fool London into thinking that the Russian was really on the British side. So Castle has merely been helping to establish the credentials of a triple agent. Furthermore, although he had been promised that his wife and son would soon be allowed to follow him, the promise is not kept. Castle, it seems, will have a lonely existence in bleak Moscow for a long time to come. (In his flat there, he reads Defoe's *Robinson Crusoe*; a castaway consoled by a castaway.) The world of spying is thus shown by the novel to be a world of bluff and double bluff, of multiple treachery and profound cynicism. When we are told that 'a manic depressive has that touch of schizoid about him essential for a double agent', we may, recalling Greene's diagnosis of himself as a manic-depressive, further understand his divided allegiances.

As for Apartheid, the novel attacks it in three ways. One is by the suggestion that the South African regime might, in collaboration with Germans and the CIA, be prepared to use nuclear weapons against a Black African invasion-force. The second way is by illustrating the ruthless treatment of its victims by BOSS, the South African security service. The third is by the sympathetic depiction of Castle's wife and her son.

The Human Factor, while lacking the imaginative intensity of the best of the early novels, offers an effectively coordinated and richly ironic narrative. There are some implausibilities, but in the main it is lean, deft and proficient as an intelligent espionage thriller; compared with the thrillers of John le Carré, it is somewhat more substantial and subtle in characterisation, and morally more ambiguous. *The Human Factor* proved to be yet another Greenian best-seller, enhancing even further his international reputation.

The subsequent novel, *Doctor Fischer of Geneva* (1980), was, deservedly, far less successful; for it is short (little more than a protracted short story), slight and trivial. As a satire on the greed of the rich or as an allegory of materialistic corruption, it remains unconvincing, being so unlikely in its plot and characterisation. Paradoxically, whereas *The Human Factor* yielded a disappointing film, *Doctor Fischer of Geneva* became, thanks largely to the sardonic acting of James Mason, an effective film for television.

Far more enjoyable as a novel was *Monsignor Quixote* (1982), a genial comic novel set in Spain, in which the modern-day counterpart to Don Quixote is a benevolently innocent old priest. A Marxist ex-mayor is his Sancho Panza, a battered Seat car his Rosinante. Greene offers ingenious present-day equivalents, variously whimsical, farcical and satiric, to scenes in Cervantes's novel, concluding with a death-scene rather more sentimentally pietistic than the original. The beguiling televised version made apt use of Alec Guinness as Quixote and Leo McKern as his Marxist friend.

The Tenth Man was published in 1985 but had been written many years previously: begun in 1937, completed in 1945 as a story for a film that was never made, and then left in the archives of MGM until exhumed by a researcher. It is hard to imagine that this overly ingenious novella of double imposture could have become an effective film. Other minor works of this period are the playlet *Yes and No* and the comedy *For Whom the Bell Chimes*, both first performed at the Haymarket Studio, Leicester, in March 1980, and both published in a limited edition in 1983. *Yes and No* makes gentle mockery of Harold Pinter, Sir John Gielgud and Sir Ralph Richardson. *For Whom the Bell Chimes* is a farcical black comedy with some debt to Joe Orton: the corpse of a murdered woman makes embarrassing appearances on a swivelling bed; a killer escapes; a rogue has a love-scene with a transsexual police officer. It brings to mind but fails to match Orton's linguistic intensity, his zestful language of bizarrely skewed cliché and cynical epigram. Greene remarked:

> The fate of the play is not important – the fun of testing the spoken word, of cutting and altering and transforming, of working with a group, of escaping solitude[,] is everything.
>
> (*WE*, p. 238)

Finale

1985–91

The last of Greene's novels to be published in his lifetime was *The Captain and the Enemy* (1988), an uneasy mixture of familiar ingredients. Once again, Berkhamsted is a setting; once again, as in his first novel, *The Man Within*, the young hero is rescued from school by an older male; again, the older male is the raffish gentleman-trickster type (like Jones in *The Comedians*); and, as in *The Comedians*, the trickster is vindicated by a heroic death. In this case, he dies during an attempt (betrayed by the CIA) to bomb President Somoza of Nicaragua. As in *The Man Within*, the young protégé is an informer against his mentor. The setting of the later part of the novel is Panama: Greene draws on his recent experiences with General Torrijos and his henchman, José Martínez, known as Chuchu. The structure is loose, and the work as a whole seems rather weakly derivative from previous materials; it gives a sense that a social narrative of a considerably earlier period (concerning the Captain, Liza, and Jim as a boy) is being grafted on to a tale of current politics.

The retrospective aspect of Greene's late period was maintained by further gatherings of past material. *Yours, Etc.* (1989) is a selection of his letters to the press. *The Last Word and Other Stories* (1990) includes one tale not previously published ('A Branch of the Service'), but all the others had appeared in magazines: there was even an item, 'The New House', from the *Oxford Outlook* of 1923. Numerous pieces of journalism and some introductions to books were gathered in *Reflections* (1990). Posthumous collections included *A World of My Own: A Dream Diary* (1992) and *The Graham Greene Film Reader* (1993). The general effect of these volumes is to emphasise both his astute literary husbandry (nothing wasted, much recycled) and his astonishingly productive, diverse and adventurous longevity as a writer.

Greene's eminence was acknowledged by the awards that he had garnered over the years. He had been appointed a Companion of Honour in 1966 and enrolled to the Order of Merit in 1986. Balliol, his old college, had made him an Honorary Fellow in 1963. Honorary doctorates were conferred by Cambridge University (1962), Edinburgh (1967), Oxford (1979) and Moscow (1988). Prizes awarded to him included the Shakespeare Prize (Hamburg, 1969), the John Dos Passos Prize (1980), and the Jerusalem Prize (1980). In France, he was made a Chevalier de la Légion d'Honneur (1967) and a Commandeur des Arts et Lettres (1984). He was made an Honorary Citizen of

Anacapri in 1978 and was awarded the Medal of the City of Madrid in 1980, the Grand Cross of Panama's Order of Vasco Núñez de Balboa in 1983, and Nicaragua's Order of Rubén Darío in 1987.

Even in his last years, he continued his travels: between 1986 and 1988, for example, there were several visits to Moscow, where he had conversations with Philby; he met Mikhail Gorbachev, and visited Siberia; and in 1989 he flew to Ireland to be the presiding judge in a GPA Book Award competition. In Spain, in the company of his devoted follower Father Leopoldo Durán (a model for Monsignor Quixote), he had made bibulous tours and meditative retreats to a monastery, though he told journalists that he was now an agnostic. In Panama in 1987 he presented the unsavoury Manuel Noriega with a gift from Nicaragua's President Ortega.

In view of his lifestyle, particularly his hard drinking (his devotion to whisky – 'the medicine against despair' – could almost be termed the most enduring of his love affairs), he had enjoyed remarkably good health. With undiminished energy, he had survived illnesses in some of the most unhealthy regions of the world. In 1979 he had recovered well from an operation for intestinal cancer. Ten years later, however, he collapsed and needed thereafter to undergo frequent blood transfusions to compensate for a form of anaemia. In 1990 he moved from Antibes to Corseaux, a village near Vevey in Switzerland. There he was nursed by Yvonne Cloetta, assisted by her daughter, Martine, and by his daughter, Lucy Caroline. Eventually, pale and weakening, he was taken to the Hôpital de la Providence. Father Durán attended his bedside and administered last rites. Graham Greene, eighty-six years old, died on 3 April 1991.

During the burial service at Corseaux's cemetery, Durán declared: 'My faith tells me that he is now with God, or on the way there.' The mourners included both Yvonne Cloetta, Greene's partner, and Vivien Greene, his wife of so many years. Subsequently, in England, a Requiem Mass was held at Westminster Cathedral, the citadel of Roman Catholicism in the land. The Cardinal Archbishop of Westminster was present, and among those paying tribute were Louise Dennys (his niece), Muriel Spark (the novelist whom he had helped in her early days as a writer) and Sir Alec Guinness (the leading actor in the film of *Our Man in Havana*).

Among numerous reported tributes from fellow-writers were William Boyd's praise of Greene's 'democratic and humane qualities': 'Applied to Greene, the old saw about being "a citizen of the world" is very true'. Anthony Burgess said:

He always showed, when it was necessary, a becoming humility and was always aware of himself as a sinner and as a popular writer. He admitted to the exploitation of the Catholic faith for sometimes sensational ends. But he was convinced, justly, that the wrongs of the world could only be judged *sub specie aeternitatis* [under the aspect of eternity].

And Sir William Golding declared:

Graham Greene was in a class by himself . . . . . He will be read and remembered as the ultimate chronicler of twentieth-century man's consciousness and anxiety.

2 Contexts and issues

Religious matters

The following extracts are all comments by Greene.

From an undated letter to Vivien, probably of early December 1925 (*Life* I, p. 259):

> I've suddenly realised that I *do* believe the Catholic faith. Rationally I've believed for some time, but only this evening imaginatively.

From a letter to Vivien, 7 December 1925 (*Life* I, p. 260):

> One can believe in every point of the Catholic faith, and yet at times like this hate the initiator of it all, of life I mean.

From 'Henry James: The Religious Aspect', 1933 (*CE*, p. 49):

> The Anglican Church had almost relinquished Hell . . . . . but no day passed in a Catholic Church without prayers for deliverance from evil spirits 'wandering through the world for the ruin of souls'.

From 'The Lost Childhood', 1947 (*CE*, p. 17):

> Goodness has only once found a perfect incarnation in a human body and never will again, but evil can always find a home there.

From *A Sort of Life*, 1971 (*SL*, p. 165):

> I dislike the word [God] with all its anthropomorphic associations . . . . .
> With the approach of death I care less and less about religious truth. One hasn't long to wait for revelation or darkness.

From an interview in the *Observer*, 12 March 1978, p. 35:

> I'm a Catholic agnostic.

From *The Other Man*, 1983 (pp. 154, 157, 158, 161, 172–3):

> (When I was baptised, I made it clear that I had chosen the name of Thomas to identify myself not with St Thomas Aquinas but with St Thomas Didymus, the doubter.) I eventually came to accept the existence of God not as an absolute truth but as a provisional one.
>
> Personally, though I have never believed in hell, the evil which surrounded me [at school] prepared me for the paradoxes of Christianity.
>
> I don't like the term 'sin': it's redolent of a child's catechism. The term has always stuck in my throat, because of the Catholic distinction between 'mortal' and 'venial' sin. The latter is often so trivial as not even to deserve the name of sin. As for mortal sin, I find the idea difficult to accept because it must by definition be committed in defiance of God. I doubt whether a man making love to a woman ever does so with the intention of defying God . . . . . The word 'mortal' presupposes a fear of hell, which I find meaningless. That being the case, I fear that I'm a Protestant in the bosom of the Church.
>
> I don't believe in hell: if God exists – I'm not convinced He does – He is omniscient; if He is omniscient, I can't bring myself to imagine that a creature conceived by Him can be so evil as to merit eternal punishment.
>
> With age . . . . . doubt seems to gain the upper hand. It's my own fault. I've never been much of a religious person . . . . . If I went to Communion, I would have to confess and make promises. I prefer to excommunicate myself.

Survey

Greene had a conventional Anglican upbringing. At Oxford, however, he was atheistic. In the early tale, 'The Trial of Pan' (1923), Pan is brought before God; his music proves so seductive that God's followers defect to the pagan nature-deity. In 'The Improbable Tale of the Archbishop of Canterbridge' (1924), God is revealed to be a Satanic aesthete, who, when shot by the Archbishop, confesses and dies. (He had caused wars in order to 'make the poppies of a brighter scarlet, because they were dipped in blood'.)

After Greene's conversion to Catholicism, his concern with

religious matters became appropriately intense; his creative imagination became preoccupied with the debate between Catholicism, scepticism and communism; sometimes psycho-analysis was another participant. He explored a range of heretical and even blasphemous attitudes: Manichæism exerted its appeal; so, later, did forms of evolutionary theology. In his old age, his Catholicism was increasingly eroded by doubt and an inclination to agnosticism. At any one time of his adult life, his ideas were layered, complex, variable and paradoxical. He combined a desire for certainty with a distrust of authority; superstitious yearnings were offset by a salty scepticism; he relished the heterodox, supported the underdog, and was an eloquent Devil's Advocate.

As we have seen, Greene had at least two grounds for his conversion to Roman Catholicism in 1927. He was keen to win Vivien for marriage; and the course of instruction with Father Trollope had, he said, provided him with rational grounds for belief. Significantly, though, his second baptismal name was 'Thomas': 'I explained to the priest that I was taking the name of Saint Thomas the Doubter . . . . .' (*R*, p. 305).

Such conversions were not highly unusual. Vivien herself was a Catholic convert; so, later, was Catherine Walston, the most influential of Greene's lovers. G. K. Chesterton, the associate of the Catholic Hilaire Belloc, had converted to Catholicism in 1922; Eric Gill, the artist and writer, in 1913; and Evelyn Waugh would follow in 1930. Of the writers most admired by Greene, Conrad (though predominantly a sceptic) was an exile from Catholic Poland, and his 'Heart of Darkness' conveys a strong sense of supernatural evil. Henry James, Greene felt, was an honorary Catholic, in that his works, at their best, expressed the realities of Hell and Purgatory. (T. S. Eliot, entering the Anglican Church in 1927, chose its Anglo-Catholic extreme.) Ford Madox Ford was a Catholic, and Greene so admired his novels that he arranged for a series of them to be republished. Querry would have been aware that Sir Giles Gilbert Scott was a renowned Catholic architect.

In the two decades after the Great War, of course, many intellectuals felt (erring) that that war was an indictment of the liberal tradition and its rationalistic, democratic ideals; they therefore reacted against that tradition. Some (Auden, Spender, Isherwood, MacDiarmid, Caudwell, Day Lewis) veered towards Marxism; others (Pound, Yeats, Lawrence, Eliot, Percy Wyndham Lewis, Roy Campbell) towards right-wing politics; some – including a number of these named authors – towards religion or mysticism: Campbell, for instance, became a Catholic in 1935.

Having advocated communism in various poems of the 1930s, Auden (turning to Anglo-Catholicism) suppressed some and revised others so that they expressed Christian views. Greene's novels recurrently reflect that polarisation of debate which was so marked a feature of the 1930s and which, influenced by the depression, mass unemployment and the emergence of rival totalitarian states, was dramatically intensified by the Spanish Civil War.

Greene's conversion coincided with a general revival of the Catholic Church in England. There were some 1,710,000 English Catholics in 1912, but 2,360,000 in 1939. The number of priests rose from 3,800 in 1914 to 5,600 in 1939. Conversions were 9,000 in 1917, over 12,000 in 1929 and over 8,000 in 1943. (See Edward Norman's *Roman Catholicism in England*, 1985.) Notable events included the restoration of the shrine of Our Lady of Walsingham in 1934, the canonisation in 1935 of two English martyrs, Sir Thomas More and Cardinal John Fisher, and the construction of Liverpool Cathedral, begun in the 1930s though not completed until 1967. It was a faith maintained by members of the nobility (often descendants of recusant families), of the middle classes and the intelligentsia, and of the urban working class (particularly in the north-west of the country); indeed, its communicants were largely urban and predominantly from the working class. Cardinal Bourne, Archbishop of Westminster from 1903 to 1935, condemned uncontrolled capitalism but denounced the General Strike of 1926 as sinful.

Greene frequently proclaimed the virtue of disloyalty, the value of challenging orthodoxy. (As we shall see, he would criticise Shakespeare for having conformed to the Elizabethan Protestant establishment.) In a country in which the established Church was Anglican, Greene by becoming a Catholic was siding with a minority faith. Yet it retained the appeal of a long-established tradition, of a faith with a rich history, an elaborate ritual, a clear categorisation of moral vice and virtue, the drama of the Mass, a personal Confessional, and a vividly strong eschatology. It proclaimed the objective reality of Heaven, Purgatory and Hell; while, in Greene's view (in the 1930s and 1940s), Anglicanism was moving towards compromise with agnosticism. Furthermore, in large areas of the world, notably in Central and South America, it was the faith of the poor and downtrodden: a faith in the Jesus who had cast the money-changers from the temple and assigned Dives, the rich man, to Hell; so there were obvious ways in which Catholicism could blend with Greene's left-wing political sympathies as they developed. He criticised the Vatican for its opposition to the worker-priests, those radical clerics who, whether in Mexico or France, espoused left-wing political action. Greene is such a persuasive advocate, so often associating his priests with the poor and needy (peasants in Central America, lepers in the Congo), that one may temporarily forget the Inquisition and the long historical association of the Roman Catholic Church with reactionary and repressive regimes. In nineteenth-century Paraguay, for instance, Catholic priests participated in the torturing and killing of the many victims of the Paraguayan tyrant, Francisco Solano López. During the Spanish Civil War, the Vatican supported General Franco. In the Second World War, the Vatican was neutral. (Franco, Hitler and Mussolini had all experienced a Catholic upbringing.) After the War, Pope Pius XII was much criticised for not having spoken out against Nazi persecution of the Jews. Catholic prayers referred to 'the perfidious Jews'.

One obvious paradox of Greene's outlook was his hope for a marriage of the Roman Catholic Church and communism. In Moscow in 1987, he told Mikhail Gorbachev:

> We are fighting – Roman Catholics are fighting – together with the Communists, and working together with the Communists. We are fighting together against the Death Squads in El Salvador. We are fighting together against the Contras in Nicaragua. We are fighting together against General Pinochet in Chile.
>
> (*R*, pp. 316–17)

He remarked that Marx condemned Henry VIII for closing the monasteries; but this was a rather disingenuous way of masking the obvious contrast between Catholicism and Marxism. Karl Marx was militantly atheistic; he stated that religion was the opium of the people; he argued that religious teachings were but the means by which the many were kept in their place, and they stemmed not from divine revelation but from economic necessities. The *Communist Manifesto* declares: 'Law, morality, religion, are to him [i.e. the proletarian] so many bourgeois prejudices, behind which lurk in ambush just as many bourgeois interests.' Marx and Engels specifically scorned 'Christian Socialism':

> Nothing is easier than to give Christian asceticism a Socialist tinge. Has not Christianity declaimed against private property, against marriage, against the State? Has it not preached in the place of these, charity and poverty, celibacy . . . . . ? Christian

> Socialism is but the holy water with which the priest consecrates the heart-burnings of the aristocrat.

Greene said that although he supported Marxist *economics*, Marxist philosophy was 'as dry as Bentham and as outdated as Ingersoll' (*R*, p. 219).

Of course, down the centuries there have been priests who sided with the people against exploiters; but there have been more who sided with authority. If the Church produced a Las Casas to champion the South American Indians, it also produced a Torquemada and the ruthless priests of the Inquisition. Greene even tried to justify Torquemada, on the grounds that he had helped to bring about the better order which prevailed centuries later; which is rather like praising Hitler because the Third Reich gave way to a democratic Federal Germany. The Catholic Church (which, financially, is a huge business enterprise with vast investments) negotiated a concordat with Hitler in 1933. In 1949 Pope Pius XII urged Catholics to oppose communism, and even excommunicated Italian Catholics who joined the Communist Party. Some Marxist regimes have been relatively tolerant of Catholicism; others have been oppressive, and keen to persecute the Church. In Poland in the 1980s, during the early days of the Solidarity movement, many priests cooperated with Solidarity in resisting the Marxist dictatorship.

In practice, Greene assailed numerous aspects of Catholicism. He frequently criticised the 'hearty materialism' of the Catholic Church of the USA, whose hierarchy, he said in 1963, helped to maintain the Cold War (*R*, pp. 199, 219). He regretted the supersession of the Mass in Latin (an international common language) by the Mass in national vernaculars; he regarded with distaste the Vatican's affluence, and was scornful of the Vatican's attempts at censorship and its prohibition of artificial contraception. He upbraided the Archbishop of Paris for withholding a full Catholic funeral from the novelist Colette (who had been twice divorced); and he clearly disliked those parishes in which, in his view, a comfortable priest ministered to a complacent middle-class congregation.

> [We] can always turn away from Rome to some dry mountainside where a stigmataed priest spends hour upon hour in the confessional attending with kindness and insight to the worries of the poor.
>
> (*R*, p. 199)

He was thinking of Padre Pio. In 1949 he visited the Franciscan monastery where Padre Pio mysteriously bore the stigmata, wounds like Christ's on hands, feet and side. 'I can recall the stigmata, the dried blood sticking out. It would dry and then it would bleed again and then dry again.' Greene was impressed by Pio, but '[the] Vatican disapproved of him' (*Life* I, p. xx). Pio, in his humble setting, was certainly more important to Greene's imagination that were the splendours of the Vatican: 'how much more difficult sanctity must be under the Michelangelo frescoes . . . . . than in the stony fields of Apulia where Pio is confined' (*CE*, p. 396). Eventually, in 1991, shortly before his death, Greene contrasted President Gorbachev favourably to Pope John Paul II:

> Gorbachev began to see that doubt was a virtue . . . . . But this pope has gone in the opposite direction. He has become ever more dogmatic. The curia under Wojtyla is getting more like the old Soviet politburo.
>
> (*Sunday Times Magazine*, 17 September 1995, p. 20)

Commenting on the atheistic Communist regime in East Germany in 1963, he said: 'Official atheism I am able, perhaps mistakenly, to regard as a passing phase (I prefer in any case atheism to agnosticism under the guise of official Christianity) . . . . .' (*R*, p. 208). Repeatedly his novels depict Anglicanism satirically, as a faith so vague and flaccid as to be virtually agnosticism. One thinks of the funeral service of Hale in *Brighton Rock* or of Sarah in *The End of the Affair*. (In the latter, the service 'was so inhuman. Like a conveyor belt'; the clergyman 'talked about the Great All . . . . . I thought he was saying the Great Auk'.) Greene regularly regarded cremation with distaste, as though it were a vulgar mimicry of Hell's fires, a vandalism of God's image, or an intrusion of modern technology on the mysteries of death. 'Resurrect that body if you can', says the atheistic Bendrix to God after Sarah's cremation. Farrant's funeral, in *England Made Me*, is bleak and mechanical; Minty experiences 'a horror of the death by fire'. In *Travels with My Aunt*, Augusta accidentally touches a button and thus incinerates the corpse before the funeral. 'A Position in Life' (*R*, pp. 323–4) mocks a crematorium's public relations officer. Again, *Brighton Rock*'s satire is so good that it needs to be quoted:

> 'Our belief in heaven,' the clergyman went on, 'is not qualified by our disbelief in the old medieval hell. We believe . . . . . that this our brother is already at one with the One.' He stamped his words like little pats of butter with his personal

mark. 'He has attained unity. We do not know what that One is with whom (or with which) he is now at one. We do not retain the old medieval beliefs in glassy seas and golden crowns. Truth is beauty and there is more beauty for us, a truth-loving generation, in the certainty that this our brother is at this moment reabsorbed in the universal spirit.' He touched a little buzzer, the New Art doors opened, the flames flapped and the coffin slid smoothly down into the fiery sea. The doors closed, ... the clergyman smiled gently from behind the slipway, like a conjurer who has produced his nine hundred and fortieth rabbit without a hitch.

(pp. 45–6)

The phrasing – 'at one with the One', 'like little pats of butter', 'with whom (or with which)' – is so sharp that the passage represents Greene at his satiric best.

Greene seems, however, to have made little allowance for the diversity of modes of Anglican worship – let alone Protestant worship. High Church Anglicanism preserved liturgical formalism; he could, if he had wished, have found Anglican clergymen with robust conceptions of Heaven and Hell, or with strong left-wing leanings: he knew of the 'Red Dean of Canterbury', Dr Hewlett Johnson. He disliked Buchmanism and the Oxford Group of the 1930s, the movement which promoted the 'Moral Rearmament' campaign (founded in 1938). Spiritualism, too, is treated satirically in his works for offering a debased, vulgarised notion of the afterlife ('Everything is very beautiful on the upper plane. There are flowers everywhere'); but he concedes it a modicum. In *Brighton Rock*, for example, the planchette board tells the truth, albeit in cryptic form. (Greene said he wrote *The Confidential Agent* with 'the automatism of a planchette'.) The fortune-teller in *The Heart of the Matter* is a truth-teller. The priest in *The End of the Affair* says: 'I'm not against a bit of superstition. It gives people the idea that this world's not everything . . . . . It could be the beginning of wisdom' (p. 216). And there was certainly 'a bit of superstition' in Greene's own attitudes: his preoccupation, for example, with omens to be found in dreams, in coincidences and in apparently random occurrences.

For readers of biographies of Graham Greene, one obvious paradox is that while espousing Catholicism he led a life of sexual infidelity and promiscuity. Christ's seventh commandment is: 'Thou shalt not commit adultery'; Greene repeatedly broke the commandment. He even claimed, when committing adultery with Catherine Walston in the 1940s and 1950s, that he felt closer to God when sinning with her. He tried to square the circle by suggesting sometimes that awareness of sin strengthens one's faith in God; sometimes that adultery, to the extent that it is an expression of love, might help to bring a person closer to God's love. (He appears to confuse Eros and Agape, profane and sacred love, illicit sexuality and the Creator's love of humankind.) To Catherine he wrote in 1950 that God might well bless their adulterous relationship; and, later, he added:

> I have certainly been to the sacraments far more often in our five years than in the previous eight. So with me – as far as you are concerned – there's no real conflict, and sometimes I hate the conflict I cause in you.
>
> (*Life* II, p. 502)

He was often capable of revising the Church's teachings in ways which matched his own desires; on the other hand, *The End of the Affair* strongly suggests that there were more conflicts within Greene than he acknowledged in those letters to Catherine.

In 'The Lost Childhood', he had said that Bowen's *The Viper of Milan* made sense of his early sufferings: 'she had given me my pattern . . . . . perfect evil walking the world where perfect good can never walk again' (*CE*, p. 18). In *Essais Catholiques* (pp. 9–10), he declared that in the era of Belsen, it seemed that Satan ('notre éternel ennemi') had let his mask fall, 'parce qu'il croit, dans son orgueil satanique, que le dernier combat approche' ('because he believes, in his satanic pride, that the final struggle is imminent'). Yet that dark vision, which, in its emphasis on dynamic evil, sometimes resembled Manichæism, lightened as he aged. He probably had himself in mind when he remarked that an old Catholic convert is one who has passed from enthusiasm to acceptance and doubt (*R*, p. 212). In 1988, three years before his death, he said:

> I say my prayers. I go to mass. I never believed in hell. There's a big question mark over heaven. I'm not an atheist, which is a form of dogma and I'm against dogma. I'm agnostic.
>
> (*Sunday Telegraph Magazine*, 28 August 1988, p. 18)

Ten years earlier, in a *New York Times Magazine* interview with V. S. Pritchett, he had reportedly called himself a 'Catholic atheist'. In another interview of 1988 he even remarked: 'I'm not sure I believe in God.' Thus, although he was following some of the procedures of a Catholic believer, he was denying and doubting the most central tenets of the faith. He denied Hell, doubted Heaven, doubted even God, and saw Purgatory as merely part of 'this life'. Father Leopoldo Durán, his enthusiastic hagiographer, felt that Greene maintained a core of faith and 'disbelieved his disbelief'; but there is ample evidence that, in Greene's old age, his Catholicism had been almost completely subverted by scepticism and doubt. That qualification 'almost' is important. One of Greene's many paradoxes was the claim that faith might be compatible with disbelief. He could be sceptical about scepticism itself. In any case, he had remarked that 'no human being is capable of judging another' (*Life* II, p. 471).

Some aspects of religion in Greene's literary works

> After the death of Henry James a disaster overtook the English novel . . . . . For with the death of James the religious sense was lost to the English novel, and with the religious sense went the sense of the importance of the human act. It was as if the world of fiction had lost a dimension: the characters of such distinguished novelists as Mrs Virginia Woolf and Mr E. M. Forster wandered like cardboard symbols through a world that was paper-thin.
>
> ('François Mauriac', *CE*, p. 115)

Greene famously declared that he was not a Catholic novelist but a novelist who happened to be a Catholic. In his literary works there is immense diversity in the rendering of religion. Sometimes God seems to figure as an essential character (in *The Power and the Glory*, *The Heart of the Matter* and *The End of the Affair*, for instance), as though an additional dimension has been restored. Readers are then lured into speculations on a major character's afterlife. Sometimes the religious views of the texts seem relatively orthodox; sometimes they seem relatively heretical. Indulgence-collecting is burlesqued in the tale 'Special Duties'. Pharisaical Catholic bigotry is fiercely assailed in *A Burnt-Out Case* and *The Living Room*. In some works, loss of belief is sympathetically presented, while other texts have a thoroughly secular atmosphere.

MYSTICISM, LAZARUS AND THE WAGER WITH GOD. A number of Greene's fictional works strongly invoke supernatural agency. In *Rumour at Nightfall*, to take an early example, the Protestant hero marries the heroine in a Catholic ceremony, during which he experiences a mystical vision: the church seems to be filled with an uncanny light; he becomes a convert. Again, a 'Lazarus' motif recurs in various texts. The tale 'The Second Death' (1929) depicts a dying man who, in the past, was raised from the dead; and the narrator says that he himself was once given sight by a stranger: 'I felt a cold touch like spittle on my lids'. The story thus offers a version of the miracles of the raising of Lazarus (John 11: 1–45) and the healing of the blind man by means of clay mixed with spittle (John 9: 1–12). A macabre contrast is offered by the horror-tale, 'Proof Positive'. In *The End of the Affair*, as we have noted, Sarah makes a wager with God that if He will save her lover's life, she will abandon the adulterous affair; the life is saved, and thereafter she becomes a miracle-worker. *The Potting Shed*, again, features a wager with God. This time, a Catholic priest says that if God saves the child's life, the priest is willing to lose his faith in return. The child is saved, and the priest indeed loses his faith. In these last two works, the strong endorsement of the active presence of God creates obvious critical problems for the reader. A Roman Catholic is likely to find their plots more credible than would the sceptic; yet even the Catholic may find them distasteful in their blurring together of religion and superstition, in their depiction of God as one who descends to the childish level of swaps and forfeits. If all life is a gift of an omnipotent God, the 'wager' is fraudulent, as if a gambler were to steal a bookmaker's money to bet against the bookmaker. *The End of the Affair* comes dangerously close to offering sin (rather than repentance for sin) as a medium of exchange for grace.

THE VIRTUE OF EVIL. In 1930, in the essay 'Baudelaire', T. S. Eliot said:

> In the middle nineteenth century, ... an age of bustle, programmes, platforms, scientific progress, humanitarianism and revolutions which improved nothing, an age of progressive degradation, Baudelaire perceived that what really matters is Sin and Redemption . . . . . To a mind observant of the post-Voltaire France . . . . . the recognition of the reality of Sin is a New Life; and the possibility of damnation is so immense a relief in a world of electoral reform, plebiscites, sex reform and dress reform, that damnation itself is an immediate form of salvation – of salvation from the ennui of modern life, because it at last gives some significance to living . . . . .
>
> It is true to say that the glory of man is his capacity for salvation; it is also true to say that his glory is his capacity for damnation. The worst that can be said of most of our malefactors, from statesmen to thieves, is that they are not

men enough to be damned. Baudelaire was man enough for damnation . . . . .

(*Selected Essays,* 1932, pp. 375, 377)

The argument has a provocative paradoxicality. Would God perhaps, after reading Eliot's essay, send to Heaven the man who is 'man enough for damnation'? Or, if that man has blasphemously put secular salvation ('significance') before heavenly salvation, would God send him to a region of Hell appropriately replete with 'the ennui of modern life'? Since sloth and gluttony are deadly sins, would a 'manly' devotion to either of them guarantee us the glory of man's capacity for damnation while redeeming us from the ennui of, say, a devotion to humanitarianism?

To an agnostic or atheist, Eliot's claims may seem as speciously entertaining as some Wildean *jeu d'esprit*; but they are an index to Eliot's most earnest preoccupations. They provide a commentary on much of *The Waste Land* and of Eliot's early mature poetry, those works pervaded by the feeling that with the secularisation of morals and with the consequent absence of a sense of sin and virtue, meaninglessness pervades human experience as surely as ennui haunts lust.

The comments on Baudelaire reveal an unholy union between the Christian and the Romantic traditions. Dante's God sent the morally nondescript (those who lived without praise or blame) to the most ignominious of dooms. Hell proper was too good for them – that was reserved for definite sinners – so they had to congregate dismally on the fringes of Hell, in the dreary Vestibule. '[T]he deep Hell receives them not, for the wicked would have some glory over them' (*Inferno* III, lines 41–2). From the Romantic tradition comes an over-valuation of sincere, intense, single-minded, passionate experience: better a bow of burning gold and arrows of desire than a prudential or humane reluctance to be the wielder of lethal weapons. Blake and Shelley deemed the rebellious Satan the true hero of *Paradise Lost*, and Blake declared: 'Sooner murder an infant in its cradle than nurse unacted desires.' Romantic literature abounds in charismatic hero-villains: characters like Ann Radcliffe's Montoni or Emily Brontë's Heathcliff, who, though wicked, seem more intensely vital than do relatively respectable, civilised beings. Conrad's Kurtz belongs to this tradition. As Bertrand Russell pointed out, some features of Romanticism lead to Hitler and Auschwitz.

Graham Greene was familiar with Eliot's essay on Baudelaire. As early as 1933 (in an essay on Henry James), Greene quoted from the very passage cited above. In his fiction, the most forceful depiction of Eliot's paradox is in *Brighton Rock*, which suggests that the guilty copulation of Rose and Pinkie, fraught with a sense of sin, is better (by 'virtue' of its sinfulness, which makes it more significant) than the secularly hedonistic copulation of Ida Arnold and Phil Corkery. Eliot said: '[T]he sexual act as evil is more dignified, less boring, than as the natural, "life-giving", cheery automatism of the modern world.' Pinkie retains at least a belief in Hell; he transcends the secular ethic. Harry Lime, in *The Third Man*, clearly belongs to the tradition of charismatic villains; like Pinkie, he is a Catholic who holds a stronger belief in Hell than in Heaven.

In 'The Lost Childhood' (*CE*, pp. 17–18), Greene wrote: 'Goodness has only once found a perfect incarnation in a human body and never will again, but evil can always find a home there. Human nature is not black and white but black and grey.' 'To be a Catholic . . . . . is to believe in the Devil', he said in a review of Eliot's *After Strange Gods*.

THE HOLY SINNER. The notion of the virtue of evil relates to the milder paradox of the holy sinner. Near the end of *Brighton Rock*, the priest refers to a remarkable Frenchman:

> 'This man decided that if any soul was going to be damned, he would be damned too. He never took the sacraments, he never married his wife in church. I don't know, my child, but some people think he was – well, a saint.'

The Frenchman was Charles Péguy (1875–1914), a poet who was killed in the Great War. He provides the epigraph of *The Heart of the Matter*:

> Le pécheur est au coeur même de chrétienté . . . Nul n'est aussi compétent que le pécheur en matière de Chrétienté. Nul, si ce n'est le saint. [The sinner is at the very heart of Christianity . . . Nobody is as competent as the sinner in the matter of Christianity. Nobody, unless it is the saint.]

Highly paradoxical, not to say dangerous. Who wants a Heaven that contains a Pinkie, or a Hitler? What of the sinner's victims? Of course, Péguy's paradox may briefly bring to mind various features of the New Testament. Jesus was rebuked by the Pharisees for consorting with publicans and sinners (Matthew 9: 11), and, addressing the chief priests of the temple, he said: 'the publicans and the harlots go into the kingdom of God before you' (Matthew 21: 31). He also said: 'Joy shall be in heaven over one sinner that repenteth, more than over ninety and nine persons, which need no repentance' (Luke 15: 7). But there is a big difference between the orthodox teaching that a *penitent* sinner may gain absolution and salvation, and this notion that a wilful and persevering sinner may, by that very perseverence in sin, be specially privileged in the eyes of God, and may be deemed saintly by human beings.

The 'saintly' element lies in that suggestion of altruism, of solidarity with the sufferers: 'if any soul was going to be damned, he would be damned too'; 'Péguy . . . . . risked damnation himself in order to save another soul' (*CE*, p. 132). To the extent that the action is altruistic, perhaps it deserves lenient treatment by the Almighty. Thus the innocent Rose in *Brighton Rock* so loves Pinkie that she is willing to be damned with him rather than lose him. 'It's mortal sin', he says, embracing her; 'I love you', she responds; 'Wherever you go, I'll go too.'

> What was the good of praying now? She'd finished with all that: she had chosen her side: if they damned him they'd got to damn her, too.
>
> (p. 275)

Again, in *The Heart of the Matter*, Scobie seeks to treat his 'mortal sin', his premeditated suicide, as altruistic; by his death, he reasons, he will be liberating his lover, his wife and God from his continuing sinful presence as an adulterer:

> I can die and remove myself from their blood stream. They are ill with me and I can cure them. And you too God – you are ill with me. I can't go on, month after month, insulting you . . . . . You'll be better off if you lose me once and for all . . . . .
> He stood with the gin bottle poised and thought: then Hell will begin, and they'll be safe from me, Helen, Louise, and You.
>
> (pp. 280–1, 285)

There are various ways of judging this attitude. Perhaps, we may suppose, God thinks: 'Scobie was altruistic; he laid down his life for those he loved. Even though, formally, he was committing a mortal sin, I'll be merciful. He deserves salvation. Let him go to Heaven.' Or perhaps God thinks: 'Well, Scobie was trying to be altruistic, so although he appears to be committing a mortal sin, I'll be lenient: I'll sentence him to Purgatory, not Hell.' Perhaps God thinks: 'What arrogance! A mortal presumes to be helping me, the Omnipotent, by destroying the life that I have given. What pride! To Hell with him!' An atheist might be inclined to say to Scobie: 'That's a fine mess you've got yourself into. If you really believed in the God of Catholicism, you wouldn't have involved yourself in adultery. Alternatively, if you wanted adultery, you should have ceased to be a Roman Catholic. As it is, the contradiction in your value-system is destroying you. It looks like the nervous breakdown of a man suffering from a form of religious mania.'

Greene once said that *The Heart of the Matter* was 'about a man who goes to Purgatory'; later, he disliked the self-pitying Scobie and the novel as a whole. George Orwell astutely observed:

> The cult of the sanctified sinner seems to me to be frivolous, and underneath it there probably lies a weakening of belief, for when people really believed in Hell, they were not so fond of striking graceful attitudes on its brink.
>
> (*CCE*, p. 107)

'BETWIXT THE STIRRUP AND THE GROUND': THE REDEMPTIVE PARADOX. In *Brighton Rock*, Pinkie quotes (imperfectly) William Camden's poem, 'Epitaph for a Man Killed by Falling from His Horse':

> My friend, judge not me;
> Thou seest I judge not thee.
> Betwixt the stirrup and the ground,
> Mercy I ask'd, mercy I found.

Pinkie envisages a final escape-route: 'One confession when he was safe to wipe out everything . . . . .'

Greene exploited one of the great paradoxes of Catholicism. On the one hand, it specifies mortal sins: those sins punishable by an eternity in Hell. On the other hand, it offers to such mortal sinners various means of eluding entry to Hell. The first route is confession accompanied by contrition, and a sincere resolve not to sin again ('a firm purpose of amendment'); these entail a readiness to undertake any penance meted. Then the priest may absolve the sin, however grave. If an individual is dying, the presence of a priest, though extremely desirable, is not essential. At death's door a mortal sinner might repent when no priest was present; and, if the repentance were sincere, God's grace might grant the sinner forgiveness. Pinkie reflects: 'You could be saved between the stirrup and the ground, but you couldn't be saved if you didn't repent.' God, of course, can see into one's inmost being; so a person who, in the eyes of other people, is clearly heading for Hell, might nevertheless (thanks to God's grace) gain admission to Heaven. No doubt, many sinners must atone by years of suffering in Purgatory; nevertheless, Purgatory is a preparation for Heaven. Archbishop M. Sheehan's *Apologetics and Catholic Doctrine*, a standard handbook for Catholics which Greene knew, offers the following definitions. Heaven is 'an abode of perfect and everlasting happiness'. Hell is 'an abode of eternal suffering' in which the wicked experience both 'the pain of loss' and 'the pain of sense', the latter being agonies caused by the fires mentioned by Jesus (Matthew 13: 49–50). Purgatory is 'an abode of purification' in which souls experience both the pain of loss and, according to Saints Bonaventure and Thomas, extreme pain of sense. (One crucial difference between Catholicism and Protestantism is, of course, that the latter denies the existence of Purgatory.)

The *Catholic Dictionary* (which bears the Imprimatur) says: 'It is very hard to decide in particular what is or is not mortal sin.' Venial sins are reparable.

> Mortal sin is, on the contrary, irreparable, and a man who is guilty of it has lost every principle of vitality, so that he is as unable to recover life as one who has suffered bodily death.

That sounds final; but the next sentence is: 'Renewal cannot come from within, but only from the Almighty power of God, who can make even the dead hear His voice and live.' Sheehan stresses that this power is shared with priests, and points out that in the second century the Montanists were expelled from the Church 'because they contested her right to forgive the sins of idolatry, adultery, and murder'. Certainly Jesus said that a sin against the Holy Ghost cannot be forgiven either in this world or the world to come (Matthew 12: 32); nevertheless, explains Sheehan charitably, 'His emphatic words do not denote absolute impossibility but extreme difficulty . . . . . "with God all things are possible".'

At the end of *Brighton Rock*, the wheezing priest suggests that even Pinkie might attain Heaven, thanks to 'the terrible strangeness' of God's mercy. In *The Heart of the Matter*, Scobie commits suicide: a terrible mortal sin, the sin of despair. His widow says: 'He must have known he was damning himself'; but her priest retorts: 'For goodness sake, Mrs. Scobie, don't imagine you – or I – know anything about God's mercy.'

In the play *The Living Room*, after Rose's suicide, Michael, her lover, says to Father Browne: 'Oh yes, your Church teaches she's alive all right. She teaches she's damned.' Father Browne replies: 'We aren't as stupid as you think. Nobody claims we can know what she thought at the end. Only God was with her at the end.'

A striking feature of several of Greene's most important works is the principle of eschatological suspense. The reader is led to consider what will happen to the protagonist in an afterlife: does Heaven, Hell or Purgatory await? To heighten the suspense, Greene drives a wedge between two aspects of Catholicism. On the one hand there is Catholicism's very specific codification of sins and their consequences. On the other hand, there is Catholicism's recognition that God's wisdom transcends that of any human being. Consequently, God's judgement of a soul may be far different from any that we may, on the available evidence, postulate or expect. Greene reflected this division when he said on one occasion that Pinkie 'goes to hell', and, on another, 'I don't think that Pinkie was guilty of mortal sin' (*GGFR*, p. 528; *OM*, pp. 158–9).

When the novelist Colette was denied a priest at her funeral, because she had been twice divorced, Greene promptly criticised Cardinal Feltin, the Archbishop of Paris. Perhaps she had been deemed an impenitent sinner, Greene acknowledged:

> But to repent means to rethink one's life, and no one can say what passes through a mind trained in habits of lucidity when it is confronted with the imminent fact of death . . . . . Your Eminence, through such a strict interpretation of the rule, seems to deny the hope of that final intervention of Grace upon which surely Your Eminence and each one of us will depend at the last hour.
>
> (*Life* II, p. 471)

This sounds gallant, fair-minded and devout. Nevertheless, by stressing the insuperable ignorance of mortals and the amplitude of divine grace, Greene appears to call in question the authority of the Church to which he belongs. Perhaps he recalled Laertes' words to the priest at Ophelia's burial: 'I tell thee, churlish priest, / A minist'ring angel shall my sister be / When thou liest howling.'

In his late years, Greene doubted that any souls lay 'howling' in Hell. As he said in *The Other Man* (p. 161):

> I don't believe in Hell: if God exists . . . . . I can't bring myself to imagine that a creature conceived by Him can be so evil as to merit eternal punishment. His grace must intervene at some point.

Greene's 'Catholic' novels often exploit a tension between the evocation of the Hell-fires postulated by orthodox Catholicism and a theology which, to the extent that it stresses either divine grace or divine transcendence of human comprehension, veers towards the liberal, the heterodox and the heretical.

THE MANICHÆAN HERESY. Manichæism is a system of religious doctrines taught by the prophet Mani or Manichæus (*c.* 216– *c.* 276 AD). It postulates a primordial conflict between goodness (or spirit or light) and evil (or matter or darkness); the world is almost entirely subject to the Prince of Darkness, though a few enlightened souls, the puritanical Elect, may find their way to salvation. Woman is the gift of demons, sent to lure men to fornication. Procreation serves the ends of darkness, because each birth entails an increase of matter and a further dispersal of the light; it is the production of another subject for the realm of darkness, and a prolonging of the captivity of light. Greene provides a simplification and a revealing slip: 'A Manichean believes that the world is wholly in the hands of God . . . I mean of the Devil' (*OM*, p. 115). In the essay 'The Young Dickens' (1950), Greene argues that in various works of Dickens, particularly *Oliver Twist*, the depiction of virtue is sentimental and unconvincing, but the depiction of evil is nightmarishly convincing.

> In this Manichæan world we can believe in evil-doing, but goodness wilts into philanthropy . . . . .
> [Is] it too fantastic to imagine that in this novel, as in many of his later books, creeps in, unrecognized by the author, the eternal and alluring taint of the Manichee, with its simple and terrible explanation of our plight, how the world was made by Satan and not by God, lulling us with the music of despair?
>
> (*CE*, pp. 108, 110)

Though a heresy, it is 'alluring'. Greene felt its allure often enough when writing his grimmer texts of the 1930s and 1940s. Indeed, his characteristic imaginative terrain, 'Greeneland', by its emphasis on the dark, seedy, sordid, disgusting aspects of the world, comes very close to suggesting, if not endorsing, a Manichæan interpretation of experience. From Brighton to Africa, from Trier to Mexico, corruption finds ample soil. The imagery of *The Name of Action* has a distinctly Manichæan quality: Kapper, the revolutionary, is associated with 'perpetual night', materialism and sexual promiscuity; he overthrows a puritanical (and sexually impotent) dictator and feels a bitter hostility to the Virgin Mary, 'the mother of his eternal enemy'.

Manichæism has some resemblances to Jansenism, which is based on the doctrines of the Roman Catholic Bishop, Cornelius Jansen (1585–1638). Jansenism (condemned in papal bulls) emphasises the corrupted state of the world; its followers therefore seek to retreat from the world's blandishments and to await the grace on which the salvation of the fortunate few depends. The doctrine was virtually one of predestination. Another echo of Manichæism was the Albigensian heresy of the twelfth and thirteenth centuries, which declared that matter was evil; Jesus's body was an appearance, not a material reality. St Augustine was a Manichæan before his conversion. The Bible declares that even since the Atonement, Satan has a terrible power over the world and its votaries, so that he is called 'the god of this world' (2 Corinthians 4: 4).

Of course, Greene's reading of Shakespeare, Jonson, Webster and Tourneur, not to mention such satirists as Rochester and Swift, would have given him ample precedent for the literary expression of disgust at a befouled world and at the human body's subjection to lust, disease and corruption. Pinkie, a debased descendant of the Jacobean malcontent or the satiric misanthrope, reflects:

> That was what happened to a man in the end: the stuffy room, the wakeful children, the Saturday night movements from the other bed. Was there no escape – anywhere – for anyone? It was worth murdering a world.
>
> (*Brighton Rock*, 1938, pp. 127–8)

Greene repeatedly cited a passage from Cardinal Newman's *Apologia pro Vita Sua* (1864); he quotes it as one of the epigraphs to *The Lawless Roads*. Newman there considers the many woes of the world, 'the defeat of good, the success of evil, physical pain, mental anguish, the prevalence and intensity of sin': 'a vision to dizzy and appal'. He asks why these woes exist.

> I can only answer, that either there is no Creator, or this living society of men is in a true sense discarded from His presence . . . . . *if* there be a God, since there is a God, the human race is implicated in some terrible aboriginal calamity.

The 'terrible aboriginal calamity' is the Fall. To orthodox Catholic theologians, the Fall of Man is *felix culpa*: the *fortunate* Fall, since it led ultimately to the coming of Christ to the world

103

and to the general redemption by the Atonement. Newman's almost Manichæan negativity here, his stress on an enduring calamity, his image of a human race 'discarded from [God's] presence', pulsed in Greene's pessimistic imagination; it helped Greene to make sense of the depressing and sometimes horrific vistas he encountered, whether they were in Mexico or Africa or Europe.

THE EVOLUTIONARY HERESY. To Catholics as to Protestants, God is perfect and unchanging. It would be a gross heresy to suggest that He is imperfect and in process of meliorative evolution. (In order to harmonise with the terms used by Greene and the Church of his day, I use the traditional masculine pronoun for the deity; God alone knows what the correct pronoun should be.)

Greene knew well the writings of Thomas Hardy. In *Jude the Obscure*, *The Dynasts* and such poems as 'The Sleep-Worker' and 'God's Education', Hardy offered the theory of 'evolutionary meliorism'. He entertained the idea that the Creator, the 'First Cause' or 'Creative Will', has been creating blindly and automatically; human beings possess the awareness that their Creator lacks. Eventually, however, the Creator may evolve into consciousness (as creatures on earth have evolved), see what a mess it has made so far, and atone by reforming the creation – 'Consciousness the Will informing, till it fashion all things fair!'

In Greene's *The Honorary Consul*, the idealistic priest, Father Rivas, offers a kindred idea:

> 'The God I believe in must be responsible for all the evil as well as for all the saints. He has to be a God made in our image with a night-side as well as a day-side . . . . . I believe the time will come when the night-side will wither away, like your communist state . . . . . It is a long struggle and a long suffering, evolution, and I believe God is suffering the same evolution that we are, but perhaps with more pain.'
>
> (p. 285)

He is speaking in character; as he is a priest who has lapsed temporarily in order to side with Marxist rebels against dictatorship, it is understandable that his imagination should effect a blending or confusion of Marxist evolutionism with religious aspirations. Rivas is not Greene; but Rivas is offering an imaginative solution to a problem that was inevitably perplexing Greene. As the author's belief in Hell waned and faded, the stronger would become the heretical sense that God may be the immediate author of evil. For Aeschylus in *The Oresteia*, for Shelley in *Prometheus Unbound*, for Marx in *The Communist*

Manifesto, for Hardy in *The Dynasts* and eventually for Father Rivas in *The Honorary Consul*, an evolutionary metaphysic is an imaginative way of reconciling the woes of known history with the better world that is desired.

The notion that God has 'a night-side as well as a day-side' is suggested in the harsh play *Carving a Statue*, in which the sculptor seeks photographs of child-killers to help him sculpt a statue of the God who sent His own son to die for man's sins. Eventually, the sculptor feels that he has been depicting Lucifer, not God. The play suggests also, however, that any human attempt to define or depict God may be thoroughly marred by human sins.

Near the end of *In Memoriam* (1850), Tennyson had imagined that, in course of evolution, humans would be so improved in nature that they would become a transcendent 'crowning race':

> the crowning race
>
> Of those that, eye to eye, shall look
>   On knowledge; under whose command
>   Is Earth and Earth's; and in their hand
> Is Nature like an open book;
>
> No longer half-akin to brute,
>   For all we thought and loved and did,
>   And hoped, and suffered, is but seed
> Of what in them is flower and fruit . . . . .

And they would then blend with the deity who is:

> One God, one law, one element,
> And one far-off divine event,
> To which the whole creation moves.

In 1959 appeared Pierre Teilhard de Chardin's *L'Avenir de l'homme* (translated as *The Future of Man*, 1964). Teilhard, a Catholic priest, argued that the purpose of evolution was to unite human beings to the divine. With the growth of rationality and love, humans approach 'a divine centre of convergence':

> That nothing may be prejudged, and in order to stress its synthesising and personalising function, let us call it the *point Omega*. Let us suppose that from this universal centre, this Omega point, there constantly emanate radiations hitherto only perceptible to those persons whom we call 'mystics' . . . . .

> Is it not conceivable that Mankind . . . . . will detach itself from this planet and join the one true, irreversible essence of things, the Omega point?
>
> (*The Future of Man*, 1964, pp. 122–3)

In the 1972 text of *A Sort of Life* (Penguin, p. 120), Greene said that instead of the term 'God', 'with all its anthropomorphic associations', he now preferred 'Chardin's Omega Point'. (In the 1971 text he had muddled Teilhard's jargon, referring to 'Noosphere' instead of 'Omega Point'.) The optimistic teleology of Teilhard blended with the more benign moods of Greene's old age; it had a certain appeal to a man who was now a grandfather. A curious consequence was that his view of the deity was then similar to the view he had once satirised: 'Omega Point', in its mystical vagueness, seems not far removed from 'the universal spirit', the One 'with whom (or with which)' Fred Hale might have attained unity.

LOSS OF BELIEF AS PROOF OF FAITH. As we have seen, one of the most ingenious religious paradoxes in Greene's work is voiced in 'A Visit to Morin' and *A Burnt-Out Case*. Both Morin and Querry reflect that the state of unbelief might be proof of God's existence. They suppose that for their sins or their neglect of Him, God has punished them by letting their belief die; but if they infer that this has happened, then, logically enough, their faith is maintained. Thus, 'faith' is tantamount to the hope that what is now not believed may yet have a basis; it is a strange trust that is actually nourished by scepticism.

There are strongly autobiographical features in these two works, and the paradox offered there may well have appealed to the older Greene. Certainly it helps to explain the co-existence of his sceptical pronouncements in interviews and his friendly relationship with Father Durán; it helps to explain the co-existence, in Greene's late period, of markedly secular and markedly Catholic works, of *The Human Factor* and *Monsignor Quixote*. Once again, we see that Greene was thoroughly Pyrrhonian: like a devoted follower of the great sceptic, Pyrrho of Elis, he was prepared to be sceptical about scepticism.

CHARITY.

> And now abideth faith, hope, charity, these three; but the greatest of these is charity.
>
> (1 Corinthians 13: 13)

I've written some bad books, but I've also failed in charity . . . . .
                                                           (*OM*, p. 164)

After Greene's death, the *Sunday Times* reported that though
some observers had estimated his wealth to be about ten million
pounds, 'the personal estate of the man whose novels sold more
than 20 million copies in 27 languages is about £200,000' (24
November 1991, p. 2). The explanation was that well before his
death, Greene had established Verdant S. A.: its name, with its
play on 'Green(e)', had come to him in a dream. This was a
Swiss corporation which collected his royalties and paid him a
salary, a familiar procedure for reducing income tax liabilities.
Had he stayed in England, he would have made a larger tax
contribution to public amenities. The corporation supplied funds
to his family and made donations to a number of causes or
groups approved by the author, ranging from the left-wing
guerrillas of Nicaragua to the Trappist monks of Galicia. Outside
the ægis of Verdant, Greene had helped various younger writers,
among them Muriel Spark and Vincent O'Donnell.

One feature of Greene's fiction is so frequently recurrent that
it may be taken for granted and underestimated. That feature is
the value of charitable action: the altruistic deed motivated
perhaps by pity or even love – even if an element of pride or
vanity is sometimes present. Such altruism flowers in both
obvious and unlikely places. On a large scale, it is present in the
léproserie depicted in *A Burnt-Out Case*, in the labours of the
priests and the doctor among the lepers; it is often implicit in
the actions of the fugitive hero of *The Power and the Glory*, and
he is charitably helped by many people, including even his
pursuer, the lieutenant. Scobie's decision (in *The Heart of the
Matter*) to help the Portuguese captain appears charitable,
though he feels corrupted: 'corrupted by sentiment'. In Scobie's
view there is also a form of charity in his own eventual suicide.
On a small scale the virtue may be briefly evident in characters
who are made more sympathetic thereby: in Carleton Myatt (of
Stamboul Train), when he lends his fur coat to Coral Musker, or
in Ida Arnold (of *Brighton Rock*), when she gives a pound to
Charlie Moyne. Then there is the more extensive generosity
patiently extended by Wormold, in *Our Man in Havana*, to his
daughter Milly. Charity may take the form of forgiveness, as
when Charley Fortnum forgives Clara (in *The Honorary Consul*).
In the political field, the virtue is represented by whose who risk
or give their lives in what, to the author, is a worthy cause: Jones
at the end of *The Comedians*, the Captain at the end of *The
Captain and the Enemy*. Charitable actions may sometimes be

quixotic, misguided or fruitless; but, in their representation of apparent altruism in a harsh world, they constitute one of the most important ethical features of Greene's works.

Political matters

The following extracts are all comments by Greene.

From a letter to Vivien, 6 May 1926, during the General Strike (*Life* I, p. 300):

> Great triumph! Last night we [at *The Times*] got off a properly printed four page paper, with one machine working. The only paper in London to do it. The strikers are getting nasty though. Last night about 9.30 they set us on fire . . . . .

From Greene's diary, 11 August 1933 (*Life* I, p. 461):

> Joined the I.L.P. My political progress has been rather curved.

From *A Sort of Life*, 1971 (pp. 37, 41):

> I was easily aroused to indignation by cruelties not my own . . . . .

> I was ready to be a mercenary in any cause so long as I was repaid with excitement and a little risk.

From *The Other Man*, 1983 (pp. 19–20, 60, 80, 81, 84–5, 87, 88, 93):

> I'm a committed person. I'm bound by certain ideas, though not by any clear political line. I've often felt a strong pull towards the Communist party (but never towards the extreme Right). I shouldn't be a good recruit, though, for my loyalty would change with circumstances . . . . .

> At the time of the [Cuban] revolution I felt very close to the Fidelistas' struggle. I brought them a large suitcase full of winter clothes . . . . .

> *The Comedians* is the only one of my books which I began with the intention of expressing a point of view and in order to fight – to fight the horror of Papa Doc's dictatorship . . . . . I don't want to use literature for political ends, nor for religious ends.

> I've been a modest help to the Sandinistas [Nicaraguan

Communists] in buying bullets which, I hoped, would eventually hit Somoza . . . . . But you see in such a case it isn't the writer who is involved – it's a character called Graham Greene who happens to be a writer.

I did what I could when Daniel and Sinyavsky were sent to prison. I asked the Russians to stop translating my books . . . . . I resigned from the American Institute of Arts and Letters to make a stand against the war in Vietnam . . . . . I certainly upset General Stroessner with an article on Paraguay and with passages from *Travels with my Aunt.*

I for my part very seldom commit myself a hundred per cent . . . . . but politics are in the air we breathe, like the presence or absence of a God.

I refuse to belong to this party or that.

The temptation to double allegiance tends to disappear before American capitalism and imperialism. I would go to almost any length to put my feeble twig in the spokes of American foreign policy.

From an interview in the *Sunday Times*, 1 April 1984, p. 33:

I would certainly have voted for her [i.e. Mrs Thatcher] in 1979 . . . . . I still believe in her honesty, but I don't like her policy . . . . . I consider myself a social democrat, not a Marxist. I don't like the extreme left slant in the Labour Party.

Survey

Greene's political allegiances changed in the course of time, and, during much of his life, were layered like the skins of an onion, with an elusive centre. The extent of his involvement with British and foreign secret service agencies is not yet fully known, and, by the nature of the case, may never be fully known. Greene combined the conservative and the subversive, the patriotic and the communistic, hostility to socialism and approval of it, a fascination by power and a distrust of the powerful, a sympathy with the underdog and a revelling in the world of expensive and decadent pleasure.

'A novelist . . . . . 'E's a spy', says Savory in *Stamboul Train.* Greene certainly worked for the British Secret Intelligence Service (SIS) between 1941 and 1944. His duties in Sierra Leone

and London are indicated, if not fully specified, in *Ways of Escape.*
His sister Elisabeth and her husband, Rodney Dennys, were both
involved in secret service work. Greene had displayed an interest
in becoming a confidential informant or secret agent (for Dublin
and for Germany) during his Oxford days. He may well have
been involved in espionage work before the Second World War,
notably in the Baltic states (*MW*, pp. 189, 316). After the war,
although he had officially left SIS, he continued to send back
reports during his travels until the early 1980s. In French
Indo-China, the French forces suspected him of being a British
agent, and he denied being one; but they were right (see *Life* II,
pp. 481–8). The link with SIS partly explains the frequency of his
journeys to politically sensitive and contested parts of the world.

In the article 'Malaya, the Forgotten War', he urged the West
to take effective action to defeat communist movements in Asia.
Nevertheless, he came to be regarded in the USA as a
'fellow-traveller' of communism, in view, for example, of his
sympathetic accounts of Ho Chi Minh of Vietnam and of
left-wing revolutionaries in Central and South America. Evelyn
Waugh, as we noted, speculated that Greene's pro-communist
views were a bluff, a cover for secret service work. Another view
might be that Greene was predominantly sincere in his support
for communism and was hoodwinking the security services into
subsidising his travel. The truth is probably a mixture. Graham
always liked to have his travel subsidised if possible; he liked help
in reaching locations that might be used in his fiction. In *The
Spy's Bedside Book* he quotes Balzac's maxim: 'The trade of the spy
is a very fine one, when the spy is working on his own account.'
Regarding a proposal from Greene to carry out some espionage
in Finland in 1952, an SIS officer reported to his superiors:

> Bear in mind that he would certainly wish to be remunerated
> for any out-of-pocket expenses. Despite the money he makes
> out of making the great British public worry about its soul, he
> is extremely mercenary.
>
> (*MW*, p. 37)

The SIS ('the best travel agency in the world') certainly
facilitated Greene's journeys and meetings with knowledgeable
informants abroad. We have seen that in the 1940s Greene
became a friend of Sir Alexander Korda; and Korda's company,
London Films, had long provided cover for British agents. Korda
himself had completed valuable work in filming the North
African coast as preparation for the allies' wartime invasion of
that region. Sherry and Shelden cite evidence that Greene

reported back to SIS when he was in Poland (1955), in Vietnam (1955), in the Soviet Union (late 1950s) and in China (1957), and argue that he was repeatedly sending information to the service during his travels (*Life* II, Chap. 34; *MW*, Chap. 2 *et passim*). Yet, we may recall, in *Our Man in Havana* and *The Human Factor* the SIS is depicted as variously incompetent and treacherously unreliable.

During Greene's long career, there is some patchy, intermittent evidence of right-wing sympathies and connections. There was his delight in strike-breaking while working for *The Times* in 1926, and his jubilation then on hearing of the arrest of Shapurji Saklatvala, a Communist MP. In 1936 his account (in the *Daily Mail*) of the funeral of King George V is romantically patriotic, declaring: 'Just as much as Charles I, the King has laid down his life "for the common people of England and their liberties".' Another factor is the anti-Semitism of various novels between 1930 and 1938; the depiction of Kapper, the revolutionary leader of *The Name of Action*, is a clear example. Among Greene's associates, Victor Cazalet, the main investor in *Night and Day* magazine, expressed the hope that 'General Franco will win a victory for civilisation over Bolshevism', and Douglas Jerrold, who employed Greene at the offices of Eyre & Spottiswoode, was also a Franco sympathiser (as indeed was Herbert Greene for a while). Between 1948 and the late 1970s the Information Research Department, a section of the Foreign Office, produced anti-communist propaganda; some of it was published by Bodley Head, the firm of which Greene was a director between 1958 and 1968. During interviews in the 1980s, he said he would have voted for Margaret Thatcher in 1979; she seemed more trustworthy than the Labour leaders: 'I don't like the extreme left slant in the Labour Party.' John Carey, the literary critic, has remarked that Greene sought 'to keep in with the Establishment, while posing as a rebel and a misfit'.

More than a pose, and more like an obsession, however, is his long-term hostility to many aspects of the United States. His sympathy with the underdog entailed considerable antipathy to that upperdog in international affairs. He criticised the USA for its vulgar materialism and its interference abroad, and was particularly critical of the Central Intelligence Agency. During the Cold War, American fears of communism led to covert and overt support for numerous right-wing regimes; the CIA was an important channel of such support. In South and Central America, Greene sided with Marxist regimes and with dictatorships which, in his view, were left-inclined. He gave favourable publicity (in essays and novels) to Castro in Cuba, to

Allende in Chile, to the Sandinistas in Nicaragua and, of course, to the unsavoury Torrijos in Panama. *The Honorary Consul* suggests that the CIA participated in the torturing of South American dissidents; in *The Human Factor,* the Agency is involved with the British and South African security forces in supporting the Apartheid system. Looking to the east, in both *The Quiet American* and *Ways of Escape* Greene gives the CIA a large share of the blame for a terrorist atrocity in Saigon.

Greene's communist friends included Claud Cockburn (from Oxford days) and later Kim Philby. The author's visit to East Germany in 1963 resulted in an essay which was remarkably sympathetic to the Marxist dictatorship there. Notoriously, he once claimed that if he had to choose between living in the USA or the USSR, he would choose the USSR. He was a critical friend of the Soviet system: he was not blind to the persecution of dissident writers there, and protested against their incarceration; but in the main he seemed to give rather more sympathy to the Soviet regime than it deserved. Similarly, with hindsight, one can see that his anti-US views were sometimes excessive. After all, the USA had come to the rescue of Britain during the Second World War, and the Marshall Plan had helped the recovery of the whole of Europe in the war's aftermath. There is no doubt, however, that the CIA has been deeply involved in the politics of South and Central America. The toppling in 1973 of Chile's Marxist President, Salvador Allende, was widely regarded as evidence of this. The Iran-Contra scandal of the late 1980s revealed that funds had covertly been used to support the Contras, the rebels seeking to overthrow the left-wing government of Nicaragua. US troops intervened directly in Panama in 1989. Certainly Greene had a case, but he pushed it too far; and sometimes he gave the impression of wilfully biting the hand that fed him. Obviously, he had been helped along the route to wealth and fame by US publishers, US film-makers, US readers and reviewers, and US interviewers.

In his novels and articles, he frequently expressed a hope for a union of Marxism and Catholicism. In *Stamboul Train* Czinner, the idealistic Marxist, experiences nostalgia for Catholicism; so does D., the Republican emissary in *The Confidential Agent.* At the ideological climax of *The Power and the Glory,* the Marxist lieutenant is drawn to friendship with the Catholic priest who is his captive; the lieutenant is in some respects a priest *manqué.* In *The Honorary Consul,* the Marxist (Aquino) fights alongside the priest (Rivas) in their vain resistance to the Paraguayan dictatorship. Certainly, Catholicism and Marxism have, in practice, certain structural similarities, being hierarchical, authoritarian and dogmatic; each claims ownership of a master-narrative which explains history; both purport to bring salvation to the masses. Locally, in some areas of the world, they have established common ground for political action. In the main, however, as was shown by the Spanish Civil War, they are so obviously opposed that Greene's hope for their union seems particularly Utopian – or Dystopian.

Anti-Semitism and the case of Stamboul Train

Anti-Semitism, whose history extends over many centuries, was internationally widespread between the two world wars. It could be found among all classes; depressingly, it could be found in the writings of some of the most brilliant cultural figures. Writers admired by Greene included some who expressed strongly anti-Semitic views: G. K. Chesterton (a Catholic), T. S. Eliot and Ezra Pound. In *The New Jerusalem* (1920), for example, Chesterton, while denying that he was anti-Semitic, argued that Jews were loyal to each other rather than to the nations in which they lived; accordingly, there should be a law 'that every Jew must be dressed like an Arab' (pp. 271–2). He added:

> Jews and Gipseys . . . . . are in different ways landless, and therefore in different ways lawless . . . . . It is normal for the nation to contain the family. With the Jews the family is generally divided among the nations . . . . . Even when the purpose is not any sort of treachery, the very position is a sort of treason . . . . . [If] the advantage of the ideal [of Zionism] to the Jews is to gain the promised land, the advantage to the Gentiles is to get rid of the Jewish problem . . . . . I would leave as few Jews as possible in other established nations, and to these I would give a special position best described as privilege; some sort of self-governing enclave with special laws and exemptions . . . . .
>
> (pp. 277–99)

In Eliot's 'Burbank with a Baedeker' (1920), we read:

> The rats are underneath the piles,
> The jew is underneath the lot.
> Money in furs.

(In later editions 'jew' became 'Jew'.) Eliot assured his Virginian audience, in the lectures of 1933 published as *After Strange Gods* (1934):

> I think that the chances for the re-establishment of a native culture are perhaps better here than in New York. You are farther away from New York; you have been less industrialised and less invaded by foreign races . . . . . The population should be homogeneous . . . . . What is still more important is unity of religious background; and reasons of race and religion combine to make any large number of free-thinking Jews undesirable . . . . . And a spirit of excessive tolerance is to be deprecated.
>
> (pp. 16–17, 20)

Ezra Pound's *Cantos* poured scatological abuse on the conspiracy of Jewish financiers who, in Pound's view, were responsible for the corruption and subversion of civilisation. During the Second World War, Pound would serve the Fascist cause in Italy, and in propaganda broadcasts for Rome Radio he reviled the 'Kikes' (Jews) who, he alleged, had caused the war.

> [T]he big Jew has rotted EVERY nation he has wormed into . . . . . The sixty Kikes who started this war might be sent to St Helena as a measure of world prophylaxis . . . . . The Jews have worked out a system, a very neat system, for the ruin of the rest of mankind . . . . .

In Greene's second novel to be published, *The Name of Action*, the English hero, Chant, supports Kapper, the revolutionary leader, a Jewish poet whose speciality is vulgar satire. In the course of time Chant becomes disillusioned in the revolutionary cause and finally sides with the toppled dictator of Trier. Early in the narrative, soon after Chant meets Kapper, we are told this (p. 38):

> Chant . . . . . caught his first glimpse of what was happening behind the black, shifting curtain of the Jew's eyes, dark halls and clammy mysteries and perpetual night. Must I, too, he wondered, become a part of that dream and let myself be shifted here and there by that imagination always in darkness?

(One is reminded of Max Bewer's anti-Semitic cartoons, in which the Jew is a sinister night-creature.) Kapper's home is squalid and grimy, and when he looks at the dictator's beautiful wife, he does so with 'those dark, desecrating eyes'. To him the Madonna is 'the mother of his eternal enemy':

> There was nothing higher than the world to which this Jew

could appeal, no supernatural tribunal to find his work of value. It was with envy that he looked through the window at the moonlit court in which the Madonna stood.

(p. 183)

In the thematic structure of this novel, Kapper is associated with revolution, murder, bawdily reductive satire, the sordid underworld, and with widespread vice and fornication; one of his henchmen bears 'a grey syphilitic scar'. The dictator has tried to inaugurate a puritanical regime; when Kapper is victorious, the prostitutes emerge from hiding and saturnalia can begin. Furthermore, with gross implausibility, the dictator's beautiful wife chooses not to follow her devoted husband but to stay with Kapper; there is a bond of dark attraction between them.

The anti-Semitic animus of *The Name of Action* is so marked that one may suspect that this is one of the reasons for Greene's decision to suppress the work; for the novel was never reprinted in the collected editions which appeared when Greene became internationally lauded. In any case, it is generally an unconvincing work. Greene did include it, however, in the list of publications in his post-war *Who's Who* entries. Furthermore, he chose not to suppress *Stamboul Train*, a work in which anti-Semitism appears more pervasively, subtly and tellingly. I give here an extensive account of this novel, because what makes the issue of its anti-Semitism difficult is that in some respects this is an admirable work, a deft, lively and shrewd political thriller.

As we have noted previously, with *Stamboul Train* Greene moved rapidly towards characteristic maturity as a writer. The cinematic qualities are still strikingly effective. Greene had long been an enthusiast for films; he was an astute film reviewer (as when he praised the emotional economy of Erich von Stroheim's *Greed*, which first appeared in 1923), and in *Stamboul Train* scene after scene is observed with sharpness, variety, mobility. The jump-cutting from character to character (sometimes from dialogue to dialogue) is handled with confident dexterity. The experience of train travel, away from the clammy darkness of the Channel coast deeper into the continent, further towards the cold and snow of Yugoslavia, is strongly evoked by a wealth of lively detail.

The characters of *Stamboul Train* are sharply etched and contrasted, often in a satirical pattern, as the novel accelerates towards its comprehensively cynical conclusion. Dr Czinner, the communist, is travelling to Yugoslavia to face a trial at which he hopes to denounce the tyrannical regime; but he is denied a public martyrdom: arrested at the border, he is shot there. On the journey, he feels a confessional yearning for the Catholic faith of his childhood; but the only priest available is a garrulous Anglican, Opie, who suggests that a psycho-analyst would be a more effective counsellor. A central character is Coral Musker, a showgirl, who is befriended by Carleton Myatt, a Jewish businessman. She loses her virginity to Myatt. He experiences tentative feelings of love for her, and, when she is arrested with Czinner at the border, he makes a vain attempt to rescuse her. Instead, he fortuitously rescues only Grünlich, a brutal killer (whose name, with an authorial wink, means 'Green(e)-like'). Coral is then rescued by a predatory lesbian, Mabel Warren, not for any altruistic reason but because Mabel is seeking a new sexual partner; though Coral, who has a coronary disease, then dies from a heart-attack in Mabel's car. As the summary indicates, the plot is certainly melodramatic, but it is grippingly well-paced, and repeatedly the characterisations have the vividness of sharp cameos; intimately shrewd detail invests them all.

In the final chapter, set in Istanbul, the cynicism reaches its merciless conclusion. Carleton Myatt decides to dismiss thoughts of Coral in order to woo and marry the more attractive Janet Pardoe; and the main reason for Myatt's decision is financial. Janet is the niece of Stein, another Jewish businessman involved in a tricky transaction with him. By marrying Janet, Myatt will become the 'family member' whom Stein hopes to see on the board of the amalgamated company; and such cooperation will enable Myatt to buy out Stein and establish a lucrative monopoly.

'There is a splinter of ice in the heart of a writer', said Greene (*SL*, p. 185); he repeatedly claimed that a novelist should strive for objectivity. As one looks back over *Stamboul Train*, a kind of iciness, a systematic ruthlessness, is evident; and one senses not objectivity so much as a determination to eliminate the reassuring patterns of moral justice and romantic fulfilment offered by conventional popular fiction. The text makes this opposition explicit, both by its satiric treatment of Quin Savory (the pipe-smoking popular novelist based on J. B. Priestley), who seeks to 'bring back cheerfulness and 'ealth to modern fiction', and by such remarks as this: 'Novelists like Ruby M. Ayres might say chastity was worth more than rubies, but the truth was it was priced at a fur coat or thereabouts.'

Accordingly, in Greene's novel, the left-wing idealist, Czinner, dies ignobly and apparently in vain (unless his truncated speech has influenced one of the soldiers who hears it); the tyrannical regime in Yugoslavia is unshaken, a coup against it having already failed; the weak, gentle and kind Coral perishes; the callous killer, Grünlich, survives; and Myatt's heart is hardened. By the standards of fiction-writing in 1932, the outcome is remarkably harsh, with cruel irony heaped upon irony. Its treatment of sexuality, whether heterosexual or lesbian, whether crucial or incidental, is also, by the general standards of the time, remarkably explicit, and may partly account for the commercial success of the book. 'I thought it was the dirtiest book I had ever read', recalled one purchaser (*Life* I, p. 442). In cynicism and frankness, and in certain technical devices like the rapid interweaving of different characters' dialogues, Greene may have learnt lessons from Aldous Huxley's *Crome Yellow* (which he admired); though the descriptive intensity is distinctively Greenian.

His previous novels had a psychologically blurred quality caused by the awkward mixture of personal preoccupations and narrative requirements. In *Stamboul Train* Greene seems fully in command of the fictional material, deploying it instead of slithering into it. The novel is adroit in its interweaving of several themes. These include: the claims of communism versus the claims of religion (a dialectic which would reach its culmination in *The Power and the Glory*); attitudes to religion; the injustice of class divisions in society; the difficulty of disentangling idealism and altruism from vanity and self-interest; the techniques of the successful writer (whether novelist or journalist) and the ways in which such a writer distorts the truth and manipulates the public (a discussion which would extend to *A Burnt-Out Case*); and, crucially, the justice or injustice of anti-Semitism. It is in its voicing of the last theme that *Stamboul Train* seems, in the post-Holocaust world, most controversial.

Of the central figures, the most important in the narrative is Carleton Myatt: 'most important' in the sense that the final emphasis falls on the outcome of his encounters and deliberations. During his journey, he experiences anti-Semitic prejudice in numerous forms, some mild, some extreme, from railway staff, fellow passengers, villagers and soldiers. He is clean and fastidious, but Mrs Peters calls him 'A dirty little Jew', and even an old woman who glimpses him briefly as he drives by in a taxi shouts 'Dirty Jew'. Intermittently the narrator seems to be opposing such prejudice: its vileness is often made evident, most notably when Myatt faces a brutal guard at Subotica who strikes at him with a rifle-butt, saying 'Go away, you Jew':

[In] the small hungry eyes shone hatred and a desire to kill; it was as if all the oppressions, the pogroms, the chains, and the envy and superstition which caused them, had been herded into a dark cup of the earth and now he stared down at them from the rim.

(p. 244)

117

Yet it is evident that one of the central questions posed by the plot-structure is this: will Myatt give way to the temptation to step out of a familiar stereotype and be altruistic, brave and loving, or will he, in his own life, choose to be governed by that stereotype of the mercenary, scheming, manipulative rich Jew? Eventually, it is the stereotype which prevails. And, as it prevails within Myatt, so it prevails within the narrative. After fighting a resourceful rearguard action, the narrative is, in this respect, defeated by the very anti-Semitic prejudice which it has sought to analyse and has intermittently criticised.

Myatt himself believes that Jews are more duplicitous in business matters than are English gentiles. We are told that Eckman, a Jew who has become a convert to Christianity, keeps 'a chained Bible by his lavatory seat', so that every visitor will know of his conversion. Coral, reflecting on the Jews she has met in the world of the theatre, thinks that they are 'mean with a commonplace habitual meanness, generous in fits and starts, never to be trusted'. Myatt treats her generously and even attempts a heroic rescue; but, by the end of the novel, it appears that he, too, was generous only 'in fits and starts'. Taking the hand of the Jewess, Janet, he 'wondered whether Mr. Stein had the contract in his pocket'.

Stamboul Train was written before Kristallnacht, before the pre-war pogroms in Nazi Germany, before the horrors of Belsen, Dachau and Auschwitz. Nevertheless, after the war, Greene made no substantial changes to the novel. In the Introduction which he wrote for the 1974 edition, he said: 'Hitler had not yet come to power when *Stamboul Train* was written. It was a different world and a different author – an author still in his twenties.' For some of the characterisations, he added, 'the old writer can salute his young predecessor with a certain distant respect'; and one of them is 'Mr Stein the fraudulent businessman'. In the post-war conflicts between Israel and the Arab world, Greene spoke out on behalf of Israel; but the complex and insidious anti-Semitism of *Stamboul Train* he allowed to stand.

A Gun for Sale, too, remained substantially unchanged. The most depressing feature of the plot is that it presents with caricatural clarity a stale anti-Semitic thesis: the thesis of the destructive international conspiracy. In this novel, the arch-villain is Sir Marcus, the head of a powerful steel company. He has a 'family resemblance', Greene remarked, to the real-life Sir Basil Zaharoff (*WE*, pp. 69–70). He is gradually identified as a Jew, a Mason, a ruthless conspirator and a war-lover: he is 'That old devil' with 'the old wicked face'. Aided by Davis, a financial racketeer, he has hired Raven to kill a continental socialist who was once a friend of his. Sir Marcus hopes that this treacherous assassination of the socialist, a Foreign Minister who opposes war, will be blamed on Serbs, and that the consequence will be the outbreak of the Second World War. Of course, the preparations for that war, as well as the conflict itself, will further enrich not only Sir Marcus (because steel will be needed for armaments) but also his circle of rich friends. They, too, appear to be Jewish.

> Armament shares continued to rise, and with them steel . . . . .
> Sir Marcus had many friends, in many countries; he wintered with them regularly off Cannes or in Soppelsa's yacht off Rhodes; he was the intimate friend or Mrs. Cranbeim. It was impossible now to export arms, but it was still possible to export nickel and many of the other metals which were necessary to the arming of nations. Even when war was declared, Mrs. Cranbeim was able to say quite definitely that evening when the yacht pitched a little and Rosen was so distressingly sick over Mrs. Ziffo's black satin, the British Government would not forbid the export of nickel to Switzerland or other neutral countries . . . . . So the future really was very rosy indeed, for you could trust Mrs. Cranbeim's word. She spoke directly from the horse's mouth, if you could so describe the elder statesman whose confidence she shared.
>
> (pp. 159–60)

It seems depressingly obvious that Greene is offering the old anti-Semitic myth of a world-conspiracy of wealthy Jews to profit by war and death. As the historian John Röhl has shown, Kaiser Wilhelm II, who had instigated the Great War, was one of the influential bigots who alleged that in the 1930s, as in 1914, Jews and Freemasons were instigators of conflict. In England, the *Right Review* in 1937 denounced the 'international Yiddish money tyranny', while the *Saturday Review* praised Hitler and Mussolini. In 1939, Hitler invaded Poland; and, in the ensuing years of devastation, six million Jews died in the Holocaust.

A Gun for Sale is widely pervaded by prejudice. Even the seedy revue in which the heroine, Anne, performs is controlled by a 'Mr. Cohen' as well as by Sir Marcus's henchman, Davis. The back-street abortionist is 'Dr. Yogel'. The malevolence of Sir Marcus is so stressed ('his most vivid emotion was venom') that the reader is invited to feel approval when Raven eventually assassinates him. (The assassination, after all, is supposed to have the effect of averting war.) In *Stamboul Train,* Greene had at least attempted to question anti-Semitic prejudice: sometimes its injustice and cruelty were displayed; but here that prejudice is all too easily endorsed. Oddly enough, when *A Gun for Sale* was adapted for broadcasting, Greene insisted that even Raven, who in the text does not appear to be a Jew, 'should speak in a Jewish manner' (*Life* I, p. 628).

In the case of *Brighton Rock*, Greene did later revise the text to reduce the anti-Semitic animus which is evident in the first British edition. (The first US edition differs: see p. vii above.) Pinkie, the Brightonian racketeer ('I'm real Brighton') is challenged on his local territory by a gang from London which serves the wealthy Colleoni. The 1938 text makes clear that Colleoni is Jewish: 'a small Jew . . . . . [whose] eyes gleamed like raisins' (p. 84); he is at home in the opulence of the Cosmopolitan Hotel, where Jewesses sit like 'bitches'. His henchman, Crab, is a Jew; and his razor-wielding gang-members are Jewish, too. One of the means by which the narrator seeks to win an element of pity for Pinkie is to contrast the Catholicism of Pinkie and Rose to the Semitic kinship of Colleoni and his gang, just as the sense that Pinkie is at least a Brighton lad is accentuated by the recognition that his territory is being invaded by lawbreakers from the metropolis. 'You can't stand against Colleoni', the local police inspector tells him.

The Uniform Edition of *Brighton Rock* (1947, often reprinted) retained all these details; but, for the Collected Edition of 1970, Greene reduced the number of references to Jews. Whereas the 1938 Heinemann text, referring to Colleoni's gang, has 'the group of Jews stood in a bunch waiting' and 'The Jews with one accord came round them' (p. 150), the 1970 text has 'the group of men stood in a bunch waiting' and 'The men with one accord came round them' (p. 129); their faces are no longer 'Semitic'. Again, the 1938 text (pp. 11–12) reads:

> Down the broad steps of the Cosmopolitan came a couple of Jewesses with bright brass hair and ermine coats and heads close together like parrots, exchanging metallic confidences.

For 'Jewesses' in this passage the 1970 text substitutes 'women'. The sentimental crooner at Sherry's dance-hall was 'the Jew' (p. 69); he becomes 'the singer' (p. 60). Instead of an 'old Semitic face' (p. 88), Colleoni has an 'old Italian face' (p. 77). When Pinkie waits to meet him at the Cosmopolitan, 'A little Jewess sniffed at him bitchily and then talked him over with another little Jewess on a settee' (1938, p. 83); this becomes 'A little bitch sniffed at him and then talked him over with another little bitch on a settee' (1970, p. 73). The revisions are incomplete, for both texts say of Crab, 'He had been a Jew once, but a hairdresser and a surgeon had altered that' (by dyeing his hair and straightening his nose: pp. 113, 98–9).

As we have seen, other works by Greene, including his film reviews for the *Spectator* and *Night and Day*, are tainted by anti-Semitic remarks: for example, 'too perceptive dramatic critics . . . . . are able to recognize genius even when it speaks Yiddish' (*PD*, p. 222). On the other hand, Forbes (formerly Furtstein) in *The Confidential Agent* is a wealthy Jew who proves to be generous, considerate and gallant; and, in *The Honorary Consul* (1973), Gruber is presented fairly sympathetically as a Jew whose parents were killed by the Nazis: 'They had made their withered little plus two sign to that mathematical formula – the Final Solution' (p. 90). In *Travels with My Aunt* (1969), however, when Visconti says 'In my situation cash alone has a tongue', Henry Pulling enquires: 'Has Mr Visconti any Jewish blood?' (p. 288).

Between 1934 and 1939, Graham Greene's brother Hugh had worked in Berlin as a journalist for the *Daily Telegraph*, and that newspaper regularly printed his indictments of the Nazi regime in Germany: he visited Dachau and was appalled by what he saw. Herbert Greene's *Secret Agent in Spain* (1938), Chap. 4, depicted sympathetically the sufferings of German Jews victimised by the Nazis. So the novelist should have been well informed about the realities of the persecution of the Jews. Unfortunately, Greene's 'Notes from a Journal of the Blitz, 1940–1941' (published in the *Month*, November 1952) say that the only cowardly person that he saw during one bombing raid was a 'whimpering' casualty with a crushed foot: 'a large fat foreign Jew'. In *Ways of Escape*, he has become 'a large fat foreigner'; and in *A Sort of Life* (p. 85), Greene pays tribute to 'our old Jewish post warden' at that time, 'one of the bravest men I have known and the most unaware of his own courage'. In interviews, Greene said that after the war, during the Arab–Israeli conflicts, his sympathies lay with the Israelis. Writing during the aftermath of the Six-Day War, he noted (while on a tour of the front with the Israelis) that the truce had been broken by Egyptian artillery. He was on friendly terms with General Moshe Dayan, the Minister of Defence. In 1981 he was awarded the Jerusalem Prize (which included a sum of $5,000), 'to recognise an author who has contributed to the world's understanding of the freedom of the individual in society' (*MW*, p. 153). Interviewed in 1984, Greene said: 'I have never felt any kinship with the Arab causes; I prefer the Israelis.' Later, however, he was critical of Menachem Begin's premiership, and said 'Today some of my sympathies are with the Palestinians, because I don't see what chance they have of real autonomy so long as Begin remains in power' (*OM*, p. 116).

The texts discussed in this section offer various lessons and warnings. A novel which contains moral or political implications that we deplore may still, from a literary point of view, be a very good text. Creative writers are distinguished by their qualities of articulate intelligence and imagination, and not necessarily by their possession of an impeccable moral or political outlook. Chaucer and Shakespeare were, by most standards, remarkably humane; but even they endorsed some racist stereotypes. The literary ancestry of Greene's Colleoni and Sir Marcus can be traced back via Dickens's Fagin and Sheridan's Moses to Shakespeare's Shylock and the murderous 'cursed Jewes' of Chaucer's 'Prioress's Tale'. Greene said that a writer should espouse the virtue of disloyalty; but he retained, in various early novels and non-fictional works, a loyalty to certain prejudices which is now painful to observe. One lesson is that present-day readers and critics should be circumspect in their judgement of him; for posterity may find in us prejudices of which we are currently unaware but which time and historical change may make painfully conspicuous.

Various influences

Throughout his life, Greene was a rapid, voracious and retentive reader: a remarkably catholic reader, in the sense that he could appreciate and employ the most heterogeneous texts, ranging from the children's books of Beatrix Potter (which contributed phrases to *Brighton Rock* and *The Power and the Glory*) to the magisterial novels of Henry James, from Metaphysical poetry and Shakespeare's plays to the Victorian adventure-tales of Rider Haggard and the experimentalism of Joyce's *Finnegans Wake*.

Good evidence for these claims is provided by his book *British Dramatists*, his biography of Rochester, and the literary pieces (many of them book reviews) in *Collected Essays*. In the main, Greene is a fine literary critic: lucid, sharp and original. He conveys his enthusiasms, he moves well between the particular and the general, he strikes at the familiar from an unfamiliar angle; he renews one's interest; he reminds one of the peculiar magic conjured by a good tale. Often his Catholicism provides the originality of the approach, as when he seeks and locates a sense of the infernal in the works of Dickens or James. Sometimes an important factor is his sense of chivalry to the underdog, aided by his warm nostalgia for the pleasures of adventure-stories. 'Conrad, Dostoevsky, James, yes, but we are too ready to forget such figures as A. E. W. Mason, Stanley Weyman, and Rider Haggard, ... who enchanted us when we were young' (*CE*, p. 209). This chivalry may have strengthened his championship of Conrad's erstwhile collaborator, Ford Madox Ford; indeed, Greene was prepared to argue that in narrative technique, Ford (in *The Good Soldier*) had surpassed his master. On other occasions, he was brilliantly mischievous, as when he made such a poker-faced pseudo-intellectual analysis of Beatrix Potter's tales that the authoress, taking it seriously, wrote to protest against his 'Freudian' interpretation. (The analysis proved to be astute, even while offering a fine parody of critical hermeneutics.)

The epigraphs to his novels provide some indication of his range of reading: they are taken from (among others) Sir Thomas Browne, Shakespeare, John Donne, T. S. Eliot, Thomas Traherne, George Santayana, Alexander Kinglake, W. H. Auden, Oliver Wendell Holmes, Thomas Hardy, A. H. Clough, Lord Byron, John Dryden, Dante, George Herbert, Edwin Muir, Cardinal Newman, Thomas Dekker, Charles Péguy, Auguste Flaubert and Sören Kierkegaard. A recurrent theme in these epigraphs is the fallen, sinful, divided and ignorant state of human beings. Literary quotations, literary allusions and sly literary jests proliferate in his novels and tales. Modern authors appear, variously disguised, variously criticised: most obviously, J. B. Priestley as both Savory in *Stamboul Train* and the pipe-smoking author at the Royal Albion Hotel in *Brighton Rock*. Greene said that in the novella 'The Third Man', the literary character of the 'great English writer Dexter . . . . . bore certain echoes of the gentle genius of Mr. E. M. Forster'. Greene himself, working on his biography of Rochester, appears in 'May We Borrow Your Husband?'. Some quotations recur: Marlowe's *Doctor Faustus* is one favourite source ('Why, this is hell, nor am I out of it'; 'My heart's so hardened I cannot repent'); George Russell's 'Germinal' is another; Browning's 'Bishop Blougram's Apology' yet another. The tale 'Mortmain' gives a love-poem by Browning a crucial role in the plot, quotes Edmund Spenser and cites George Eliot's letters. 'Cheap in August' quotes Henry James and cites Thomson's *The Seasons*, Longfellow's poems, Anthony Trollope, Dylan Thomas, Truman Capote and Tennessee Williams.

Thus, scores of authors have left a verifiable imprint on Greene's writings. Two of the most important of them, and one of the most curious, I discuss in the following sections.

Joseph Conrad

When we scan Greene's career, his voyages, travels abroad, his literary range and the way in which first-hand observation was transformed into fictional narratives, he looks remarkably like a younger brother of Joseph Conrad: less powerful but enviously and industriously emulous. There is no doubt that one reason for Greene's restless journeys to dangerous or formidable regions was a desire to rise to the challenge presented by Conrad. The evidence is tangible: when Greene travelled in a paddle-boat up a tributary of the Congo, he held Conrad's 'Heart of Darkness' in his hand.

In Liberia, when Greene met Colonel Davis, he was at once reminded of the soldier of fortune, Captain Blunt, in *The Arrow of Gold*. Conrad journeyed to the Caribbean, the Far East, central Africa; so did Greene. Conrad's *Nostromo* was, in part, a critical response to US imperialism in Colombia and Panama; Greene extended this criticism, with particular attention to Panama, in *Getting to Know the General*. (Both men criticised the role of the United States in the secession of Panama from Colombia in 1903.) Incidentally, Conrad's friend Cunninghame Graham, who had travelled widely in Paraguay and written about the Jesuit missions there, had provided material for *Nostromo*; and, when Greene explored Paraguay, he remembered Cunninghame Graham and his writings.

Greene acknowledged that his earliest novels, *The Man Within*, *The Name of Action* and *Rumour at Nightfall*, were written under the influence of some of Conrad's inferior work. As we have noted, *The Man Within* seems indebted to the Conrad–Hueffer novel of piracy and trial, *Romance*. Then *The Name of Action* and *Rumour at Nightfall*, though so different from each other, both show the influence of *The Arrow of Gold* (which Greene later deemed 'Conrad's worst novel'). In *The Name of Action*, as in *The Arrow of Gold*, the hero experiences disenchantment with a political conspiracy and fights a duel over a seductive woman; in *Rumour at Nightfall*, the heroine (Greene explained) is an imitation of Conrad's Doña Rita. After the failure of these two novels, Greene tried to break away from an influence he now saw as 'too great and too disastrous': 'Never again, I swore, would I read a novel of Conrad's – a vow I kept for more than a quarter of a century' (*IS*, p. 48; *SL*, p. 208).

Although Conrad's more romantic fiction exerted a deleterious influence, there were other aspects of Conrad which proved particularly productive. Greene's greatest Conradian debt is probably to *The Secret Agent*, for Greeneland, that seedy, corrupt territory, has clear affinities with the base, murky world of Conrad's novel of political crime and espionage, of double agents and sordid circumstances. The debt is clear in *It's a Battlefield*, for Greene's Assistant Commissioner of Police (corrected from 'Commissioner' after the first edition) is clearly a twin of Conrad's Assistant Commissioner. Both have served in the tropics before returning to London; both like to leave their desks to explore the streets of the city; both deal with a Parliamentary Private Secretary who is devoted to a busy Minister. In a characteristic disguised acknowledgement, the first name of the hero, Conrad Drover, derives, we are told, from 'a seaman, a merchant officer' who had once lodged in his parents' home. Caroline Bury, though partly based on Lady Ottoline Morrell (who met both authors), is a counterpart to the 'lady patroness' of *The Secret Agent*: each is liberal in outlook and willing to give help to a convict with revolutionary sympathies. In these two novels, Conrad and Greene offer pessimistic vistas of struggling selves lost in the urban crowd, of fallible authority, of hypocritical idealists and rather naïve patronesses; in both works, a vulnerable figure is killed while making a futile political gesture. Like Conrad, Greene makes fastidiously perceptive notations of urban squalor. The pessimistic irony that political action may prove counter-productive, self-destructive or absurdly unavailing is common to both writers.

When Greene travelled to central Africa, he was consciously emulating Conrad. In 1890 the latter had kept a 'Congo Diary'; Greene in 1959 kept a 'Congo Journal'. In the essay 'Analysis of a Journey' and in *Journey without Maps*, Greene actually quotes his predecessor's diary when showing that he, like Conrad, associated the darkness of the interior of Africa with the darkness of the unconscious mind of a European. 'Heart of Darkness', of course, repeatedly formed a reference-point for Greene: it is cited in *Journey without Maps*, the 'Congo Journal' and *A Burnt-Out Case*. Both writers espouse a form of primitivism, for both suggest that the Africans are best left to themselves and are corrupted by the incursion of European (or American) trade and exploitation. Another connection is that Querry in *A Burnt-Out Case* has intermittent resemblances to the Marlow of 'Heart of Darkness'. Marlow looks compassionately on the suffering Africans and finds that his role is misinterpreted by fellow-Europeans, who think that he belongs to Kurtz's 'gang of virtue'; Querry is similarly compassionate to the suffering lepers and is infuriated by the attempts by Rycker, Parkinson and some of the priests to stereotype him as an intrepid idealist.

'Heart of Darkness' seems to have left its mark on *The Third*

Man. Martins is a weak descendant of Marlow; Harry Lime is a powerful descendant of Kurtz, that charismatic figure of eloquent corruption; and Anna shares the mournful fidelity of the Intended. The 'river of darkness' is transmogrified as the vast sewer beneath the city. Once again, Greene incorporated sly homage: one of Lime's loyal henchmen is known as 'Mr. Kurtz'. (A suspect character named Kurtz – a flawed idealist – also appears in *The Name of Action.*) The Conradian theme that loyalty to one person or cause may entail treachery to another was extensively developed by Greene, as we may be reminded by the quotation from *Victory* which is the epigraph of *The Human Factor*: 'I only know that he who forms a tie is lost. The germ of corruption has entered into his soul.'

Greene's admiration for Conrad was changeable and discriminating. He praised the Cambridge critic F. R. Leavis, who had emphasised Conrad's moral intelligence, for rescuing him 'from legend' – i.e. the legend of the romantic yarn-spinning master mariner (*WE*, p. 262). On re-reading 'Heart of Darkness' in 1959, Greene first found that Conrad's 'heavy hypnotic style' made him aware of 'the poverty' of his own style, but later considered the language 'too inflated' and Kurtz unconvincing (*IS*, pp. 48, 51). 'And how often he compares something concrete to something abstract. Is this a trick that I have caught?' – to which the answer is yes, though Conrad was not the only source.

One of the finest brief appreciations of Conrad is Greene's 'Remembering Mr Jones', in which, predictably seeking to give Catholicism credit for some merits of a predominantly sceptical writer, he finds 'the rhetoric of an abandoned faith':

> Conrad was born a Catholic and ended – formally – in consecrated ground, but all he retained of Catholicism was the ironic sense of an omniscience and of the final unimportance of human life under the watching eyes. . . . . 'The mental degradation to which a man's intelligence is exposed on its way through life': 'the passions of men short-sighted in good and evil': in scattered phrases you get the memories of a creed working like poetry through the agnostic prose.
>
> (*CE*, p. 184)

That review was written in 1937. Curiously, the remark about 'the memories of a creed working like poetry through the agnostic prose' now seems to apply quite well to some of Greene's own later works, such as *A Burnt-Out Case* and *The Human Factor.*

T. S. Eliot

It is a widely acknowledged platitude that T. S. Eliot's earlier poetry, particularly *The Waste Land*, exerted a powerful influence on writers and intellectuals in the 1930s. Cyril Connolly described it as 'a veritable brain-washing'. In Greene's case, the influence is to be found not in his poetry – *Babbling April*, for example, offers rather callow romanticism – but in the early novels.

As we have seen, Eliot's anti-Semitism, in which Jews are associated with affluence, corruption and subversion, finds an echo in Greene's fiction. The Jews of Eliot's poems (Bleistein, the 'Chicago Semite Viennese', Sir Ferdinand Klein, Sir Alfred Mond, Rachel *née* Rabinovitch with her 'murderous paws') are relatives of the Jewish conspirators in *A Gun for Sale*. Greeneland borrows numerous features of Eliot's urban (and soiled rural) terrain: the drab streets and refuse-strewn river-bank, the sordid or joyless acts of copulation, and the pervasive sense that the secular outlook drains life of meaning whereas the religious outlook restores significance. As Michael Shelden says:

> The mind that created *Stamboul Train* and *Brighton Rock* was teeming with memories of Eliot's yellow fog, the gloomy pubs and cheap hotels, the half-deserted streets, the rats and oily canals, scraps of newspapers swirling in vacant lots, stale smells of food and drink, the lonely typist in her furnished room, the random bits of overheard conversation and popular tunes.
>
> (*MW*, p. 99)

One of the two epigraphs of *The Name of Action* is a passage from 'The Hollow Men' which stresses the gap between the idea and the reality, the notion and the act: appropriate to a narrative illustrating vague idealism and disillusionment. Another connection is that the legend of the Fisher King, one of the sources of *The Waste Land*, influences the treatment of the dictator, Demassener. Among the unsavoury characters in *The Waste Land* is Mr Eugenides, who offers the narrator 'a weekend at the Metropole' –

> Mr. Eugenides, the Smyrna merchant
> Unshaven, with a pocket full of currants
> C.i.f. London: documents at sight

– and he is clearly a relative of Carleton Myatt, the Jewish currant-trader in *Stamboul Train*, who carries samples of the currants in his pocket, studies the trade documents, and makes calculations which take account of 'C.i.f.' (cost, insurance and freight). He offers Coral Musker accommodation not at the Metropole in Brighton but at a flat in Constantinople. (The Metropole features in *Brighton Rock*.) The Tarot Pack of *The Waste Land*, including the card that represents 'The Hanged Man', reappears in *A Gun for Sale*. In *Journey without Maps*, a quotation of several lines from *The Waste Land* accompanies a discussion of 'the deep appeal of the seedy'. More generally, Greene's fiction strove to vindicate Eliot's thesis that the thriller and the serious novel could be combined and given poetic intensity.

It is not surprising that when Greene met Eliot in 1935, and occasionally thereafter, his attitude was that of the respectful disciple towards a master. Yet their careers had common features. Both (poets, playwrights, reviewers) had worked editorially on magazines and became executives of publishing firms; both served as fire-wardens during the Blitz; both knew the throes of depression and marital incompatibility; both admired James, Conrad, Joyce and Pound, and enjoyed popular entertainments (notably the music-hall); both combined radicalism and conservatism; both were converts who used religion as a criterion of the world's situation; and both exploited 'the literary possibilities of a modern world plagued by disillusion and despair' (*MW*, p. 100).

Dunne and dreams

John William Dunne (1875–1949) was an early aircraft designer. His book, *An Experiment with Time*, appeared in 1927, and, though now largely forgotten, it was then much discussed and very influential. It received 'unexpectedly continuous attention by the public press', the author noted; and four editions were published by 1936. (He extended his theories in *The Serial Universe*, 1934.)

Dunne offered anecdotal evidence that certain dreams are precognitive: they truly foretell the future. For example: in 1902 he dreamt of a volcanic eruption; later in the year, he read in a newspaper that Mont Pelée had catastrophically erupted. To explain such coincidences, he offered a theory of 'serial time':

> *Every Time-travelling field of presentation is contained within a field one dimension larger, travelling in another dimension of Time, the larger field covering events which are 'past' and 'future', as well as 'present', to the smaller field.*
>
> (*An Experiment with Time*, 1927, p. 151; his italics)

One time-dimension is thus within another, which in turn is within another, like the skins of an onion or, to use his analogy, like the boxes within a Chinese box. In a dream, our attention is no longer directed by normal waking-state concerns; so our mind is free to roam, and may wander from one time-dimension into another: hence the previsionary glimpses. Dunne presents intricate arguments to vindicate the idea that a person in one time-dimension might be able to scan events in a different time-dimension; and, led to mysticism, he even claims to have proved 'the unity of all flesh in the Super-body and of all minds in the Master-mind' (1936, p. 233): there is 'a superlative general observer' (1927, p. 207). Dunne invites his readers to note and assess their own dream-experiences, and reports the results of a group experiment in which Oxford undergraduates were invited to send him accounts of their apparently precognitive dreams.

His theories have deterministic implications. He says that we have some limited scope for intervention to alter the foreseen future, but generally 'we live too much in ruts'. Each person resembles 'the amateur user of a pianola' who may change 'one perforated roll for another', but 'again a deterministic sequence start[s] from the point of interference'. If you reflect that the pianola roll is printed with perforations not by the player but by the machine at the roll factory, and that those perforations were originated by a different, distant player, Dunne is clearly implying that free will is limited to choices between destinies which have already been inscribed by some higher power.

Dunne's book may now seem cranky and pseudo-scientific, but in the late 1920s and the 1930s its show of evidence, its elaborate theorising and its basis in the familiar (the *déjà-vu* feeling and apparently anticipatory dreams) made various readers regard it as, if not convincing, certainly thought-provoking. It influenced the ideas and sometimes the structures of various literary works. The Bible and classical literature had told of prophetic dreams; Dunne gave old notions a new theoretical framework. Incidentally, as his book appeared just nine years after the Armistice, its intimations of immortality may have provided consolation for some relatives of people who had died in the Great War.

Greene enjoyed works by such popular novelists as Rider Haggard, Conan Doyle and John Buchan. In 1932 appeared Buchan's novel *The Gap in the Curtain*, which, in its plot and themes, is based solidly on Dunne's *An Experiment with Time*. The instigator of the main events is Professor Moe, a gaunt, intense yet frail genius. (He is called Moe partly because, the text hints, he is a modern Moses.) His theories are reported thus in

Chapter 1:

> Time . . . . . involved many new dimensions. There seemed to
> be a number of worlds of presentation travelling in Time, and
> each was contained within a world one dimension larger. The
> self was composed of various observers, the normal one being
> confined to a small field of sensory phenomena, observed or
> remembered. But this field was included in a larger field, and,
> to the observer in the latter, future events were visible as well
> as past and present.
>
> In sleep, he went on, where the attention was not absorbed,
> as it was in waking life, with the smaller field of phenomena,
> the larger field might come inside the pale of consciousness.
> People had often been correctly forewarned in dreams.

This is virtually a paraphrase of Dunne's basic ideas, which thus
provide the premises of a plot which hinges on an experiment in
group precognition and its intriguing consequences. Five of the
people involved in Moe's experiment do indeed foresee the
future. To that extent, the plot endorses Dunne's ideas; but it
also assails Dunne by suggesting that it is dangerous and possibly
lethal to indulge in such experiments. For example, a character
who has a prevision of his own death-notice in *The Times*
consequently worries himself to death: he dies of a heart-attack
in time to validate that notice. Another character offers the
moral of the story:

> 'Our ignorance of the future has been wisely ordained of
> Heaven. For unless man were to be like God and know
> everything, it is better that he should know nothing. If he
> knows one fact only, instead of profiting by it he will assuredly
> land in the soup.'

In *British Dramatists* (1942, p. 46), Greene noted that J. B.
Priestley 'has tried to enlarge the contemporary subject matter
with the help of Dunne'. Theories of precognition influenced
such plays of Priestley as *Dangerous Corner* (1932), *I Have Been
Here Before* (1937), *Time and the Conways* (1937) and *An Inspector
Calls* (1947). He said that *I Have Been Here Before* was indebted
mainly to Peter Ouspensky's *A New Model of the Universe*; but *Time
and the Conways* is heavily influenced by Dunne. Its time-scheme
is mixed: in an interesting theatrical experiment, Priestley puts
the last act in the middle. More precisely: Act 2 portrays events
which take place nearly twenty years after the events to be
portrayed in Act 3, so that the *déjà-vu* feeling is both depicted

and evoked. The result of this shuffling of the time-sequence is that Act 3 is shrouded in melancholic ironies. For example, when the young people are discussing their ambitions, Carol, a young actress, says she wants many things: 'I'd get it all in somehow. The point is – to live. Never mind about money . . . . . I'm *going to live*.' But Act 2 has already told us that she died young, after a painful illness and an unsuccessful operation. Perhaps, indeed, her fervent desire to live is a response to some premonition of that early death. But there is a glimmering of hope in the play. One character, the prescient Alan, a disciple of Dunne, declares that after death 'perhaps we'll find ourselves in another time, which is only another kind of dream', and offers to lend Kay a book on the subject, presumably *An Experiment with Time.* Priestley, in his introduction to the play, urges his public to 'read Dunne's work with the close attention it needs – and deserves'.

After 1929, Dunne's *An Experiment with Time* (formerly published by Black) was published by Faber & Faber, when T. S. Eliot was one of the firm's directors; and some of Dunne's notions seem to have influenced Eliot's verse-drama *The Family Reunion* and his long meditative poem *Four Quartets.* In *The Family Reunion,* Emily refers to the 'loop in time', anticipating the situation in which Harry is found to be carrying the burden of guilt for his father's criminal desires; and the sense of past and present is repeatedly confused as the Erinyes of Aeschylean drama assail the modern drawing-room, and more generally as echoes of the ancient *Oresteia* reverberate within the present-day situations. We are told that 'the past is about to happen, and the future was long since settled'. Dunne's notion of 'serial time' probably contributes to the metaphysical speculations of *Four Quartets,* augmenting the Christian paradox that the whole expanse of time is immediately present to a timeless God. The poem's famous opening certainly brings to mind that concept of serial time:

> Time present and time past
> Are both perhaps present in time future,
> And time future contained in time past[;]

and, in a spiralling movement with spiralling allusions, the poem proceeds to consider and evoke the *déjà-vu* feeling. Indeed, by its subtly overlapping echoes and recurrent images, it virtually generates precognitions in the reader's mind.

The most Dunnian of Graham Greene's works is *The Bear Fell Free*, a tale published as a booklet. The central events are these: Anthony Farrell, a shady character but a pioneering aviator, sets out on a solo flight across the Atlantic, changes his mind, tries to

131

return, and crashes to his death in the Irish Sea. (In *An Experiment with Time*, one example of the catastrophes that Dunne – the aircraft designer – had foreseen in his dreams was a plane crash in which the pilot was killed.) The technique of the tale is ostentatiously experimental, for the narrative leaps between future, present and past, jumbling the normal order, like a jigsaw puzzle whose pieces have been vigorously muddled. Knowingly, the tale offers an explicit leitmotif of the jigsaw puzzle: for instance, one of the characters is 'sorting out the muddle, patiently, like a child with a jigsaw puzzle'. When pieced together, the tale is a characteristic narrative of Greeneland. We find that Farrell is a feckless boaster; his socialist friend, Baron, has big plans but dies unexpectedly in the bath; Farrell's mistress, Jane, is unfaithful to him with his friend Davis; and Davis later (burdened by guilt) commits suicide. The bear of the title is a mascot which survives the plane crash. (Greene himself took a teddy bear mascot on his travels.) Near the end, the narrative, shedding punctuation, modulates towards a Joycean stream of consciousness: 'O my God it's Davis glad you could come Mr. Baron kiss me Hardy fine young Conway best friend a man ever King will receive you dead in his bath members of the Book Society . . . . . '

What relates the experimentalism to Dunne's theory is the attempt to suggest the simultaneity or overlapping and intersection of different periods of time. The tale exploits the ironies resulting from prolepsis. Dunne said that a greater mind subsumes all the lesser ones; the tale hints that the mind may be God's. Christ, we are told, is 'eternally dying for a jigsaw piece, but gladly one would mislay this piece'. The mishmash of the narrative, in which images of present death and treachery are mixed with images of wartime death and suffering, tends to give a reductive impression of muddle without progress, of a hopeless impasse. There is strong emphasis on literally and metaphorically fallen people, sharing a communion of guilt. Near the end, we are offered this:

> Birth and death simultaneously tainted with each other. Guilt and suicide in the maternity ward, guilt and suicide in the trenches, in Jane's flat guilt and suicide . . . . . Prayers no good for something already happened, memory no good with no past, hope no good with no future . . . . .

The Bear Fell Free is a slight but arrestingly strange item. In its techniques, it is so oddly and exceptionally experimental among Greene's works that it may, in retrospect, be regarded merely as a purgation of experimental ambitions after which Greene could resume, stylistically, a relatively orthodox course, rather like *Carving a Statue* among his plays. Nevertheless, the tale is a conspicuous pointer to Greene's extensive concern with prevision, time-jumps and dream-effects.

Dunne had invited correspondents to report nocturnal previsionary experiences. Graham Greene was already an assiduous recorder of his dreams. Of course, he was well versed in Freudian and Jungian ideas, and, during his psychoanalytic treatment by Kenneth Richmond, he had been trained to report his dreams for analysis. Gradually, he became remarkably adept at recalling and exploiting his night-self. In this, there was a mixture of psychological self-analysis, some superstition, and a pragmatic recognition of fertile material for literary husbandry. So efficient was Greene's literary economy that a selection of his dreams was eventually published as a book in itself: *A World of My Own*, 1992, an oddly oblique form of autobiography. In the introduction to that volume, he refers explicitly to Dunne's concept of prophetic dreams, and, on the basis of his own observations, remarks: 'I am convinced that Dunne was right' (p. xxi). In *A Sort of Life*, Greene claims, for instance, that at the age of five he had dreamed of a shipwreck on the night that the *Titanic* sank in 1912. (In a later version, Greene corrected his age at the time to seven, to fit the date of the sinking.) He also claimed that in 1944 he dreamed of a V1 pilotless aircraft before the first V1 raids on England began.

Of his novels, *It's a Battlefield* and *The Honorary Consul* each sprang from a dream, he said; so did the tales 'Under the Garden' and 'Dream of a Strange Land'. Sometimes, he remarked, one may, while writing a fictional work, identify so strongly with a character as to experience the character's dream rather than one's own. Thus, during the writing of *A Burnt-Out Case*, he had a dream which in its nature was one of Querry's, and promptly incorporated it into the text (at the end of Chapter 3 in Part Two), 'where it bridged a gap in the narrative which for days I had been unable to cross'. (After the dream of a lost opportunity, Querry seizes the opportunity to help Dr Colin.) The unconscious mind was Greene's quiet collaborator: if a literary obstacle seemed insurmountable, he would read the day's work over before sleep, and in the morning would often find that the obstacle had been removed by 'the *nègre* in the cellar' (*WE*, pp. 274–5). Querry's experience is the same: 'Problems which seemed insoluble would often solve themselves in sleep' (p. 51).

In 1959, Greene remarked that 'dreams can dictate the mood of a whole day and bring a dying emotion back to life' (*IS*,

p. 33). Repeatedly, his novels and tales incorporate significant dreams; indeed, it is probable that no other writer of predominantly realistic fiction has employed them so frequently. His first novel, *The Man Within*, is interfused by literal and metaphorical dreams. Andrews, in Chapter 2, has a nightmare which conveys his fear and guilt; later, his betrayal of Carlyon is seen as the destruction of that leader's 'sentimental blind dream of adventure'; and characters impinge on Andrews's consciousness in a dreamlike way: 'Like a dream the man had entered and like a dream he had gone.' Later, in the much sharper novel *Stamboul Train*, Chapter 2 offers in rapid succession the dreams of Myatt (revealing a mixture of sexual desire and business worry), Coral Musker (in which she is a victimised dancer) and Mr Opie (which blends religious hope with his love of cricket). In the late novel *Monsignor Quixote*, Quixote himself approaches death as a somnambulist: in sleep he conducts his final Mass. It appears that Greene's reading of Dunne accentuated an interest in dreams and prevision which pervades his fiction and creates distinctive thematic and textural effects.

Within a predominantly realistic narrative, dreams may provide the imaginative contrast of surrealism or fantasy, as in the following example from *The Heart of the Matter*. Scobie has a vision of peace which is fused with an ominous hint of a sinking like that of the *Titanic*:

> [H]e dreamed of peace by day and night. Once in sleep it had appeared to him as the great glowing shoulder of the moon heaving across his window like an iceberg, Arctic and destructive in the moment before the world was struck.
>
> (p. 59)

Then there is Scobie's vision of 'perfect happiness and freedom':

> Birds went by far overhead, and once when he sat down the grass was parted by a small green snake which passed on to his hand and up his arm without fear, and before it slid down into the grass again touched his cheek with a cold, friendly, remote tongue.
>
> (p. 81)

Within the hot, sweaty, smelly, sordid Africa of *The Heart of the Matter*, such dreams offer a contrasting lyricism (and a touch of refreshing coldness) while yet maintaining some of the thematic concerns. There is another general function, of course: Greene knew that to describe their dreams is an obvious way of giving psychological depth to characters that might otherwise seem too schematic – and schematic characterisation is an evident risk in some of his novels.

Sometimes the dreams have a Freudian import: they reveal the sexual desires or fears of the character. Sometimes they are not Freudian but Dunnian: precognitive; though the Bible doubtless provided Greene with the earliest introduction to the topic of prophetic dreams. Examples abound in his fictional works. In *Brighton Rock*, Rose dreams of Pinkie's death; later, he himself has a nightmare of death in the sea: 'no death was so bad as drowning'; and that is how he dies. In *The Heart of the Matter*, Helen Rolt dreams that she is gripped by Bagster, as she will be in reality after Scobie's suicide. Sometimes dreams have a metaphysical import (as had Dunne's theory): they seem to be the vehicles of divine revelation. In this category, the most important example is probably towards the end of *The Power and the Glory*. On the eve of his execution, the whisky-priest imagines that he is participating in a Mass, the wine served by Coral: which hints at his salvation – and at hers.

Precognition need not be confined to dreams. Near the close of *The End of the Affair*, it is revealed that Sarah's turning to Catholicism was anticipated long ago, when she was an infant. Although she retained no recollection of the fact, she had been secretly baptized into the Catholic faith. Greene said that this was based on a similar linkage in the life of Roger Casement, and commented: 'We are not necessarily in the realm of "magic" here or coincidence – we may be in the region of Dunne's *Experiment with Time*' (*WE*, p. 137). Sarah's future seems to have influenced her past. Perhaps, Greene reflected, this was true of himself. In *Ways of Escape*, he notes that his novel *The Confidential Agent* had offered a satirical account of a holiday camp like those established by Billy Butlin that flourished after 1945, even though the novel appeared before those camps were founded. (He is wrong: the Butlin camp at Skegness opened in 1937.) He continues:

> Dunne has written in *An Experiment with Time* of dreams which draw their symbols from the future as well as the past. Is it possible that a novelist may do the same, since so much of his work comes from the same source as dreams? It is a disquieting idea . . . . . Why in 1936 did I write of D [in *The Confidential Agent*] listening to a radio talk on the Problem of Indo-China? . . . . . Six years were to pass before the French war in Vietnam began and eight more before the problems of Indo-China became vivid to me . . . . .
>
> (*WE*, p. 92)

A 'disquieting idea', indeed. The concept of reversed causality, the later causing the earlier, would be explored by other novelists, notably by D. M. Thomas in *The White Hotel* (1981) and Martin Amis in *Time's Arrow* (1991). In *Time's Arrow*, the naïve narrator, travelling backwards through time, talks as though the Nazis in the extermination camp are creators of life: they convert smoke and ash and bone into living victims whose agonies dwindle into discomfort and eventual happiness as they return, backwards, to home, family, friends, and early days. The reversed sequence is narratorially generated as a device for ironic 'defamiliarisation'; the reader, perceiving the cruel ironies, reconstitutes the horrific historical sequence. In *The White Hotel*, we are invited to consider that the heroine's eventual hideous death has generated the symptoms of pain which she had experienced many years previously. Here the local reversal occurs within a normal forward progression of historical events.

The idea that reversed causality may actually occur is strongly deterministic. It implies a mystification of history which may, from one viewpoint, be consolatory. The bereaved may think: 'That's the way it had to be: that was the inscribed destiny.' The same mystification of history may, from another viewpoint, be depressingly fatalistic. Whether the historical event be the Holocaust, as portrayed in *The White Hotel*, or the Vietnam War, as discussed in Greene's *Ways of Escape*, the linkage with precognition may convey the sense that these man-made catastrophes were inevitable: a matter of mysterious ordinance rather than of political choice. Perhaps Dunne's *An Experiment with Time* should have been entitled *Time's Experiment with Us*.

Being somewhat superstitious, Greene told various friends about his forebodings that he would suffer an early death, perhaps by water. In spite of all the risks that he took, his longevity refuted the foreboding, and he died in Switzerland, far from the sea. Graham Greene's life-span was, among other things, a great experiment with time: an experiment which apparently refuted J. W. Dunne's.

Part Two
The Art of Greene

3 Greene on his art

From *Why Do I Write?*, 1948 (pp. 47–8, 49):

> Loyalty confines us to accepted opinions: loyalty forbids us to comprehend sympathetically our dissident fellows; but disloyalty encourages us to roam experimentally through any human mind; it gives to the novelist the extra dimension of sympathy . . . . .
> Propaganda is only concerned to elicit sympathy for the innocent, or those whom the propagandist likes to regard as innocent, and this he does at the expense of the guilty: he too poisons the wells. But the novelist's task is to draw his own likeness to any human being, the guilty as much as the innocent. Isn't our attitude to all our characters more or less – There, and may God forgive me, goes myself? . . . . . [T]hat is a genuine duty we owe society, to be a piece of grit in the State machinery . . . . .[I]sn't disloyalty as much the writer's virtue as loyalty is the soldier's?

From 'The Virtue of Disloyalty', 1969 (*R*, pp. 268–9, 270):

> Isn't it the story-teller's task to act as the devil's advocate . . . . .? The writer is driven by his own vocation to be a Protestant in a Catholic society, a Catholic in a Protestant one, to see the virtues of the Capitalist in a Communist society, of the Communist in a Capitalist state . . . . . He stands for the victims, and the victims change.

> Perhaps the deepest tragedy Shakespeare lived was his own: the blind eye exchanged for the coat of arms, the prudent tongue for the friendships at Court and the great house at Stratford.

From *A Sort of Life*, 1971 (pp. 63, 115, 141):

> [P]erhaps it is only desperation which keeps me writing, like someone who clings to an unhappy marriage for fear of solitude . . . . .

[I]f I were to choose an epigraph for all the novels I have written, it would be from 'Bishop Blougram's Apology':

> Our interest's on the dangerous edge of things.
> The honest thief, the tender murderer,
> The superstitious atheist, demi-rep
> That loves and saves her soul in new French books –
> We watch while these in equilibrium keep
> The giddy line midway.

I suppose . . . . . that every novelist has something in common with a spy: he watches, he overhears, he seeks motives and analyses character, and in his attempt to serve literature he is unscrupulous.

From *The Other Man*, 1983 (pp. 18, 37, 125–6, 130–1, 136–7, 161, 186):

My subject is rootlessness – but then my subject matter is my life, so there's no paradox.

My marked inclination towards melodrama stems from . . . . . adolescent reading.

I pay attention to the 'point of view' . . . . . and I re-read aloud what I have written, making a good number of corrections for the sake of euphony . . . . . In all my novels I'm content to have blank spaces which I don't know in advance how to fill. The characters are thus able to follow their bent more freely . . . . .

My first books were very bad, full of metaphors which I chose for their extravagance, influenced as I was by my readings in the 'twenties, when I was very attached to the English Metaphysical poets of the seventeenth century, who devoted themselves to highly complex rhetorical exercises. Today my early novels horrify me, they're so absurd. There's nothing worse than poetic prose.

[U]ntil one reaches a certain point one has to work very hard and with complete lucidity. Then something happens which is rather like an aeroplane taking off . . . . . One may have to stay at the controls, but the worst is over.

[A] writer is even more like a double agent than he is like God: he condemns and sustains his characters by turns.

I'm a good enough writer. Better than many. I'm not proud but realistic. I'm not modest, either. But I can't place myself among the giants.

4 The nature and origins of Greeneland

A crooner in *A Gun for Sale* sang of Greenland, thus encouraging critics to talk of 'Greeneland'. Apparently the term was coined by A. C. Marshall, who, in *Horizon* (May 1940), said that Greeneland was characterised by seediness. Eventually, *A Supplement to the Oxford English Dictionary* I (1972) included the word, defining it thus: 'A term used to describe the world of depressed seediness reputedly typical of the setting and characters of the novels of Graham Greene.' Whether the fictional location were Brighton or Mexico, London or Liberia, Vietnam or Sierra Leone, Greene transformed it into Greeneland: a distinctively blighted, tainted, oppresssive landscape. He, however, resisted the term.

> Some critics have referred to a strange violent 'seedy' region of the mind (why did I ever popularize that last adjective?) which they call Greeneland, and I have sometimes wondered whether they go round the world blinkered. 'This is Indo-China,' I want to exclaim, 'this is Mexico, this is Sierra Leone carefully and accurately described. I have been a newspaper correspondent as well as a novelist. I assure you that the dead child lay in the ditch in just that attitude. In the canal of Phat Diem the bodies stuck out of the water . . .' But I know that argument is useless. They won't believe the world they haven't noticed is like that.
>
> (*WE*, p. 77)

One response is, of course, that Greene repeatedly sought what others would seek to avoid: warfare, oppression, crisis, vice, squalor. He had chosen to go to Phat Diem in Vietnam, and there he had seen, as his journal for 16 December 1951 records, the child dead in the ditch and the canal 'thick with bodies'; meanwhile bombs and mortar shells exploded nearby. Such matters he chose to observe and to note; and the notations were amplified in the fictional works (in the case of Vietnam, in *The Quiet American*). Another response is that Greene, as he conceded, had a strongly depressive side to his temperament; and he tended to relish depressing vistas, redolent of decay or corruption or sleaziness. In *Journey without Maps* he acknowledged 'the deep appeal of the seedy'.

Examples abound. The Brighton of *Brighton Rock* has vulgar opulence, tawdry amusements, dog-muck on pavements, rusting prams in front gardens, murder and corruption among the holiday-makers. When the moon shines in at Pinkie's window, it's the moon of Greeneland: it shines on 'the door where the jerry stood', seeking out the chamber-pot. This is how Pinkie's 'honeymoon' with Rose begins at his lodgings:

> A smell of cabbages and cooking and burnt cloth hung about the dark passage. He nodded – 'That was old Spicer's room. Do you believe in ghosts?'
> 'I don't know.'
> He pushed open his own door and switched on the naked dusty light. 'There,' he said, 'take it or leave it,' and drew aside to expose the big brass bed, the washstand and chipped ewer, the varnished wardrobe with its cheap glass front.
> 'It's better than a hotel,' she said, 'it's more like home.'
>
> (p. 261)

In *The Heart of the Matter*, Freetown (as we infer it to be) has a climate of humidity so oppressive that Scobie puts blotting-paper under his wrist to absorb the sweat; cockroaches and ants besiege the rooms. Scobie goes into his bathroom, 'disturbing a rat that had been couched on the cool rim of the bath, like a cat on a gravestone'; and there he contemplates 'the tin bucket under the lavatory seat emptied once a day: the fixed basin with another useless tap: the bare floorboards: drab green black-out curtains' (p. 35).

Again, the opening of *The Power and the Glory* is a famous instance:

> Mr. Tench went out to look for his ether cylinder: out into the blazing Mexican sun and the bleaching dust. A few buzzards looked down from the roof with shabby indifference: he wasn't carrion yet. A faint feeling of rebellion stirred in Mr. Tench's heart, and he wrenched up a piece of the road with splintering finger-nails and tossed it feebly up at them. One of them rose and flapped across the town: over the tiny plaza, over the bust of an ex-president, ex-general, ex-human being, over the two stalls which sold mineral water, towards the river and the sea. It wouldn't find anything there: the sharks looked after the carrion on that side. Mr. Tench went on across the plaza.
>
> (1940 text, p. 3)

It's a superbly atmospheric and cinematic opening. As the buzzard rises, we have a buzzard's-eye view, cinematically a panning crane-shot over the brilliantly lit scene. Greene said that with films in mind, 'in a description one uses a moving camera instead of a stationary one' (*GGFR*, pp. 547–8). The paragraph has a quality of grim humour: 'he wasn't carrion yet'; 'ex-president, ex-general, ex-human being'. The heat is oppressive; the dust bleaches; there are repeated reminders of death. Even the river and sea offer not a sense of refreshment but more reminders of destruction, death and decay: 'the sharks looked after the carrion'. And Mr Tench is looking for ether because he is a dentist, an expert on decay within the living. His gesture of revolt is self-lacerating and ineffectual. Syntactically and rhythmically, the passage is already well crafted, though for later editions Greene polished it further, substituting 'vultures' for 'buzzards', 'towards them' for 'up at them', and 'One rose' for 'One of them rose'. It offers a lyrically pessimistic vista, an intense contemplation of a blighted environment.

In so many of his novels and tales, particularly those of the late 1930s and the 1940s, Greene's descriptive emphasis on blighted landscapes as the setting for blighted lives gave a distinctive and even parody-inviting character to his works. The pye-dogs and vultures, the slums and their refuse, the harlots and weary priests: all become a predictably obedient entourage to the author on his imaginative travels. (In 1949 the *New Statesman* ran a competition in which readers were entitled to submit parodies of Greene's work; the author entered under the name of 'M. Wilkinson' and came second with a passage in which a lonely boy looks with apparent contempt at 'the large breasts and the fat legs' of his aunt.) The various details in the characteristic descriptions of Greeneland may all be found in reality; what matters is his recurrent emphasis on them and his elision of more positive and life-enhancing features. And, though distinctive, such passages can be related to various traditions.

Here, for example, is a famous source of that adjective 'seedy':

> How weary, stale, flat and unprofitable
> Seem to me all the uses of this world!
> Fie on't, ah fie, 'tis an unweeded garden
> That grows to seed; things rank and gross in nature
> Possess it merely.

Greene's more bitter narrators are descendants of Hamlet and the vengeful malcontents of the Elizabethan and Jacobean stage, who survey with saturnine relish the corruption around them and invoke the skull beneath the skin. Another contributor is the satiric tradition, emphasising lust, squalor and the decay of the flesh, which extends from Shakespeare's *Timon* and Ben Jonson's *Volpone* to Pope's *Dunciad*, Swift's *Gulliver's Travels* and Matthew Bramble in Smollett's *Humphry Clinker*. This blends with the tradition of social satire in the English novel: Greeneland was in some respects anticipated by the depressing urban landscapes, decaying environments of sordid crime, in works by Dickens and Conrad. Dickens's *Oliver Twist*, *Bleak House* and *Little Dorrit* come to mind: the infernal rotting slums of *Bleak House* have established an outpost in the Carlton Hill slums of *Brighton Rock*. Parts of Conrad's 'Karain', *The Nigger of the 'Narcissus'*, 'The Return' and *Chance* stress urban ugliness and oppressiveness; and we have noted that *It's a Battlefield* has explicitly-registered continuity with *The Secret Agent*. In 'Heart of Darkness' Conrad had shown how even the primæval jungles of Africa could be degraded and defiled by the incursions of avaricious Europeans. The travel books, histories, tales and essays of Conrad's friend Cunninghame Graham (a writer cited by Greene) had repeatedly associated 'progress' with a materialism which inflicts on exotic regions an alien detritus: sardine tins, gin bottles, mass-produced shoddy goods.

Greene's characteristic work can also be related to the poetic tradition of urban realism and decadence. He admired Baudelaire's poems as well as Eliot's, and the 'decadent' poets of the 1890s had often enough depicted the city as a location of both squalor and corruption. Arthur Symons, Richard le Gallienne, John Davidson, Eugene Lee-Hamilton and W. E. Henley were among those who sought to reconcile the lyrical and the sordid. Lee-Hamilton, in the sonnet 'Baudelaire' (1894), provides an extreme example of *nostalgie de la boue* (gutter-nostalgia):

> A Paris gutter of the good old times,
>   Black and putrescent in its stagnant bed,
>   Save where the shamble oozings fringe it red,
> Or scaffold trickles, or nocturnal crimes.
>
> It holds dropped gold; dead flowers from tropic climes;
>   Gems true or false, by midnight maskers shed;
>   Old pots of rouge; old broken phials that spread
> Vague fumes of musk, with fumes from slums and slimes.
>
> And everywhere, as glows the set of day,
>   There floats upon the winding fetid mire
> The gorgeous iridescence of decay . . . . .

In addition, Baudelaire and the decadents gave prostitution and sexual 'deviance' new prominence in literature; and a characteristic aspect of Greeneland is the frequency with which prostitutes, brothels, promiscuous women, deviant adults and even depraved children appear. Of course, Greene knew well the depressing urban and psychological landscapes of Eliot's 'Love Song of J. Alfred Prufrock', 'Rhapsody on a Windy Night' and the 'Preludes': 'restless nights in one-night cheap hotels', 'The yellow fog that rubs its back upon the window-panes', 'faint stale smells of beer', 'A broken spring in a factory yard', 'that woman / Who hesitates towards you in the light of the door', 'The thousand sordid images / Of which your soul was constituted', alleviated faintly by 'The notion of some infinitely gentle / Infinitely suffering thing'.

Greeneland sometimes implies a despairing form of romanticism, a regret for an Eden blighted. At its darkest, it evokes that Manichæan sense of a world almost entirely conquered by the evil or the negative. The human characters variously fit that landscape. So many of them are failures or inadequates; often it seems that to possess understanding is to fail. Those who try to do good seem repeatedly to be striving against hopeless odds. The lords of the world are the rich, the powerful, the successfully corrupt, the insensitive. Again, we may recall that Cunninghame Graham repeatedly offered the paradox of 'the failure of success', claiming that those who are exemplary in moral terms are likely to be failures in worldly terms. (See his *Success*, 1902.) He also offered a memorable autobiographical essay, 'A Jesuit', describing a tobacco-priest (his luggage is merely a newspaper filled with cigarettes) who disembarks at a Paraguayan wilderness. All the other priests have been killed by the Indians; ordered by Rome to return to the region, this Jesuit accepts his lonely duty. 'I am the mission, that is, all that now remains of it.' One of his descendants was perhaps the Mexican whisky-priest of *The Power and the Glory*, another solitary in a different alien wilderness.

Roman Catholic critics have sometimes objected that Greene underestimates the positive aspects of religion and of the world about us: he fails to acknowledge 'all things bright and beautiful' that the hymn ascribes to God; he says too little of redemption, regeneration and the pervasiveness of divine love. All writers are selective; Greene selected what he wanted to emphasise; and for much of the time his imaginative outlook was sombre, even jaundiced. Fastidious, he sought and portrayed what offended his fastidiousness; sensitive, he sought and portrayed what lacerated that sensitivity. Love–hate relationships burgeoned; he himself knew them all too well: the love–hate relationship with promiscuity, with sexual passion, with the decadent and the depraved.

At his most parody-inviting, however, Greene seems almost complacent in the contemplation of the fallen world. The love–hate relationship modulates into an almost patronising love of the degraded. In *The Heart of the Matter* (p. 30), Scobie considers life in his African colony:

> Why, he wondered, swerving the car to avoid a dead pye-dog, do I love this place so much? Is it because here human nature hasn't had time to disguise itself? Nobody here could ever talk about a heaven on earth. Heaven remained rigidly in its proper place on the other side of death, and on this side flourished the injustices, the cruelties, the meannesses that elsewhere people so cleverly hushed up. Here you could love human beings nearly as God loved them, knowing the worst: you didn't love a pose, a pretty dress, a sentiment artfully assumed.

This is Scobie, not Greene; but Greene offers similar views in his non-fictional work, notably in *Journey without Maps* and *The Lawless Roads*. A Marxist academic, Arnold Kettle (in *An Introduction to the English Novel* II, Part 3), has criticised the easy identification here of 'the truth' with the worst. He proceeds:

> The question arises as to whether the sentimentality involved in seeing life as better than it really is, is necessarily worse than an opposite kind of sentimentality which takes pleasure in seeing the world as worse than it happens to be.

'Perverted sentimentality' is at work in this novel, says Kettle. 'Scobie *likes* the stink'; he isn't committed to fighting it. Conrad's Marlow is indignant about human corruption; Scobie partly embraces it and partly is ambushed by it. The plot-mechanism, Kettle adds, is not convincing but 'slick' and 'glib' in its repeated ironies. When Wilson visits a brothel, the narrator remarks that 'he had reduced himself to human nature': a facile negative essentialism. Kettle sums up: 'It is the way in which human nature in this novel is indeed reduced that constitutes its ultimate failure.'

One response to Kettle might be to show that Scobie knows less than he thinks he does; his pitying outlook merges with pride, complacency and myopia; so the critical distance between the narrator and the central character is sometimes greater than

Kettle allows. Another response might be that *The Heart of the Matter* is one text among many, and the narrator's outlook varies. A narrator is never identical with the author. Greene was an acute literary critic, not least of his own writings. *A Burnt-Out Case* challenges the kind of indictment offered by Kettle. The account of the *léproserie* in that novel is no gratuitous horror but is a careful, discriminating, accurate rendition of an African leper colony and the diligent work done there by the patients, the priests and the doctor. We know from Greene's *In Search of a Character* how careful he was to get exactly right the details of leprosy and its treatment. Here is no shoulder-shrugging 'acceptance' of pain and disease but a sympathetic rendering of the struggle to treat, cure or at least contain an appallingly disfiguring and crippling ailment. When Querry arrives at the colony, Dr Colin is understandably distrustful. Colin says to the Superior:

> 'I was afraid for a moment that we might have a leprophil on our hands . . . . . Schweitzer seems to attract them . . . . . Sometimes I wonder whether Damien was a leprophil. There was no need for him to become a leper in order to serve them well . . . . .
>
> The second day [Querry] was here, I took him to the hospital. I wanted to test his reactions. They were quite normal ones – nausea not attraction. I had to give him a whiff of ether.'
>
> (pp. 19–20)

Querry, the architect, does *not* 'like the stink'; he applies his talents to help the work of healing. Greene, in his way, also helps that work.

A further irony is that Arnold Kettle, the Marxist, seems not to have allowed for, or foreseen, the extent to which Greene's novels would express sympathy for characters who become involved in left-wing revolutionary struggles: such characters as Fowler in *The Quiet American*, Jones in *The Comedians*, Father Rivas in *The Honorary Consul*, or Castle in *The Human Factor*. Sometimes they may fail or be misguided; but they try to oppose tyranny in *this* world, rather than, resignedly, rest their hopes on the *next*.

5 'Novels', 'Entertainments', and the redemption of Greeneland

In the preface to his tale *Incognita* (1691), William Congreve made a distinction between novels, which were relatively realistic, and prose romances, which were relatively far-fetched. When *A Gun for Sale* appeared in 1936, the list of works which appeared in the preliminary matter showed that Graham Greene was now dividing his longer narrative works into the categories of 'Novels' (*The Man Within, It's a Battlefield, England Made Me*) and 'Entertainments' (*Stamboul Train* and *A Gun for Sale* itself). The two works he disowned, *The Name of Action* and *Rumour at Nightfall*, were excluded from the list. Greene explained that the 'entertainments' are melodramatic and 'are distinct from the novels because as the name implies they do not carry a message (horrible world)' (*CCE*, p. 160); he also hoped that by draining and absorbing the 'poison' of melodrama they would let the novels become more realistic.

The distinction was rather arbitrary: though the 'entertainments' may have been conceived as thrillers which might eventually be filmed, there is no marked generic distinction between, say, *A Gun for Sale* and *It's a Battlefield*, for both have ingredients of the popular thriller mixed with topical political content. (In the event, texts from both categories of his work were seized eagerly by film-makers.) Furthermore, *Brighton Rock* would be subtitled both 'A Novel' (in its first British edition) and 'An Entertainment' (in its first American edition). Certainly, there is a clear contrast between *The Heart of the Matter*, with its sombre realism and theological subtleties, and *The Ministry of Fear*, a relatively superficial thriller. In the span extending from *The Power and the Glory* at one extreme to *The Ministry of Fear* at the other, there remains a large and commodious middle area containing works which overlap in their modes. Eventually, Greene rescinded that division between 'novels' and 'entertainments'. By the time of the Collected Edition of the 1970s, all his long prose narratives were subsumed under the heading 'Novels'.

From the 1950s onwards, his literary works became more diversified, and comedy played an increasing role. One is reminded of the gentleman who told Dr Johnson, 'I have tried too in my time to be a philosopher; but, I don't know how, cheerfulness was always breaking in'. There are happy endings for the heroes of *Loser Takes All, The Potting Shed* and *Our Man in Havana*. Some of the stage plays are replete with comedy, even farce at times: examples include *The Complaisant Lover, The Return of A. J. Raffles* and *For Whom the Bell Chimes*. In the predominantly serious political novels *The Comedians, The Honorary Consul* and *The Captain and the Enemy*, there are ludicrous or farcical events, and there is some lightening of the atmosphere compared with his early serious novels: the sense of grim Greeneland dwindles; the descriptive style becomes lighter and less intense; a more secular atmosphere prevails. Some of the later works are largely light-hearted: notably *Travels with My Aunt* and *Monsignor Quixote*, with their atmosphere of picaresque adventure. In both, central figures are elderly people with qualities of blithe innocence or innocuous irresponsibility.

Travels with My Aunt is characterised by benevolently trans-formative recollection. Old locations are revisited, but now they belong not to Greeneland but to a relatively benign territory of picaresque comedy: Brighton is now beguiling, and this Stamboul Train conveys passengers to no lethal ambush. The Pooterish innocent and his mischievous old mother travel with apparent invulnerability through a modern terrain in which they seem to be anachronisms; but they adapt. Augusta enjoys an autumnal love affair, while Henry Pulling, experiencing Paraguay as a lotos-land, can conclude his narrative by quoting (with only the mildest of irony) Browning's lines, 'God's in his heaven – / All's right with the world!' Again, in *Monsignor Quixote*, the conflict between communist and cleric, which, in *The Power and the Glory*, culminated in the priest's execution, has been transformed into an affectionate, good-humoured running debate between two old friends as they advance from escapade to escapade in a land of sunshine, wine and hospitality. The ageing Greene called himself a 'Catholic agnostic' and acknowledged his disbelief in Hell; and this may be one reason for the diminution of anguish and of dark brooding in the later works. Another reason (recalling Conrad's late career) may be the inevitable reduction, in Greene's prosperous old age, of the intensity of his inner divisions and drives; a relative peace of mind seems to have arrived. Death strikes even in Arcadia, of course: Monsignor Quixote dies, as does Wordsworth in *Travels with My Aunt*, as did the Captain in *The Captain and the Enemy*. In *The Honorary Consul*, Stroessner's Paraguay will be no lotos-land to Plarr and his comrades. The later Greene has nevertheless opened some benignly Arcadian vistas as compensation for the infernal or purgatorial landscapes of the earlier, more intense, novels of Greeneland.

'A reputation is like a death mask. I wanted to smash the mask', he said (*WE*, p. 216). Greene resisted the stereotypes ('Catholic novelist', 'Grim Grin') that commentators imposed on him; he enjoyed literary explorations which were a recasting of his public identity; and in his old age he took his readers and himself on numerous holidays of the imagination.

6 Recycling, recurrences, and games with names

Greene testified to the husbandry of the creative writer: he is like 'a careful housewife, who is unwilling to throw away anything that might perhaps serve its turn' (*IS*, p. 17). Greene's imaginative and commercial husbandry was remarkable. For instance, he re-used, in work after work, certain locations, character-types and plot-situations, so that repeatedly one has a sensation of *déjà vu* or of the familiar within the unfamiliar. A 'transtextuality' is a narrative feature which appears in two or more different texts; and Greene offers a labyrinth of transtextualities.

In *The Human Factor*, the hero, Castle, cycles through Berkhamsted, 'across the canal bridge, past the Tudor school, into the High Street, past the grey flint parish church which contained the helmet of a crusader . . . . .' There are also the remains of a castle which may have given him his surname: he speculates that one of his ancestors was an artisan there. The location is probably as familiar to Greene's regular readers as to Castle; for this is the author's homeland, the area of his upbringing described in *Journey without Maps*, *A Sort of Life* and *Reflections*; it is the 'Denton' of the tale 'The Other Side of the Border', the 'Bishop's Hendron' of 'The Innocent', the 'Bankstead' of 'Doctor Crombie', and the schooltime location of Farrant in *England Made Me* and Jim in *The Captain and the Enemy*. As we have noted, the associated detail of the despairing man who sought suicide at the almshouses by the humpbacked bridge appears in several works, including *A Sort of Life*, *Journey without Maps*, *The Lawless Roads*, 'The Innocent', *The Captain and the Enemy* and *Reflections*. Thus, various umbilical cords connect Greene's real-life experience and his fictional world.

Further instances abound. Harston House in Cambridgeshire, the home of Greene's rich uncle Sir William Graham Greene, had gardens which contained a potting shed and a big pond with a small island. These featured in the play *The Potting Shed* and in various tales, including 'Under the Garden'. Oxford University and, particularly, Greene's Balliol (or 'Belial') College, appear in 'When Greek Meets Greek' and *The Great Jowett*. The Liberia of *Journey without Maps* provides the oppressive jungle of 'A Chance for Mr Lever'. The Freetown of 'The Other Side of the Border' reappears in *The Heart of the Matter* and *Ways of Escape*, as well as *Journey without Maps*. Mexico, and particularly its port of Frontera, with its vultures (or 'buzzards'), sharks and bust of Obregón, feature in *The Lawless Roads*, *The Power and the Glory* and 'The Lottery Ticket'. Nottingham, where Greene worked as a journalist and owned a dog which vomited after eating salmon, appears (sometimes as Nottwich) in *Stamboul Train*, *Journey without Maps*, *A Gun for Sale* and *The Confidential Agent*; the location and even the vomiting dog are used in *The Potting Shed*. Some of the Nottingham details are uncannily sharp: in a stationer's window, a printed card bears a Sassoon poem, 'Aftermath', with the refrain 'Have you forgotten yet?'; that card in the window is quoted in *Journey without Maps*, *A Gun for Sale* and *A Sort of Life*. The Gower Street area of London, where Greene worked in the Ministry of Information and was a warden during the Blitz (as *Ways of Escape* tells), is depicted in *A Gun for Sale*, *The End of the Affair* and 'Men at Work'. And this is only a brief selection of the recurrent locations. The repeated use of the same locations in both the fiction and the non-fiction is another of the methodological similarities between Greene and Conrad.

One of the most important associative clusters concerns childhood betrayal and bullying. Greene's 'The Lost Childhood' adapts its title from George Russell's poem 'Germinal', which says: 'In the lost boyhood of Judas / Christ was betrayed'. These lines echo in 'The Basement Room' and elsewhere; Greene quoted them in interviews. In 'Prologue to Pilgrimage', *Brighton Rock*, *The Lawless Roads* and *Reflections*, Greene associates bullying with 'a pair of dividers' used as a weapon. The childhood foe, Carter, is vicariously defeated in the form of fictional namesakes: for instance, Carter is the name of the embarrassed husband in the tale 'The Blue Film', of the harassed lover in 'Mortmain' and of the callous agent shot by Wormold in *Our Man in Havana*.

Another associative cluster began when, as a boy, Greene visited the dentist – 'I have never suffered greater pain than I did then' – whose house had 'the stained glass window representing the Laughing Cavalier which hid the chair of torture' (*SL*, pp. 35–6). For Greene, dental decay was a *memento mori*: 'death was in his carious mouth already' (*PG*, p. 12). Dentists as intimidating pain-inflictors feature in 'The Lottery Ticket', *The Power and the Glory* and *The Complaisant Lover*, and that same stained-glass window with the Laughing Cavalier has numerous re-appearances; like the shell-case used as an umbrella-stand, it is a travelling property of Greeneland. A poignant transtextual feature is the death of a child: Francis dies in 'The End of the Party'; in *Brighton Rock* Annie Collins, pregnant at fifteen, commits suicide, and so does Molly Carthew; hero-worshipping Else is murdered in *The Confidential Agent*; Scobie's daughter is dead in *The Heart of the Matter*; and, in *The Power and the Glory*, Tench has lost a son, a Mexican woman seeks a funeral service for her five-year-old Anita, the Indian woman loses her three-year-old boy, and Mr and Mrs Fellows lose their daughter.

When a reader identifies such recurrences in the fiction, there are various effects. In the case of the repeated location, one effect may be a gain in authenticity: repetition helps to induce suspension of disbelief. Another may be resonance and enrichment, as the recollected associations augment the immediate situation. Another may be a sense of ironic disparity, as when the benign Brighton of *Travels with My Aunt* contrasts with the malign Brighton of *Brighton Rock*. And another may be a sense of psychological intimacy with the author, as one moves with increasing familiarity through the initially private associative clusters of another person.

Of course, the recurrent use of the same real location in two or more fictional texts is not unusual, nor is the establishment of a close relationship between the author's career and the fictional events: Wells and Golding, in addition to Conrad, come to mind. Conrad and Golding, moreover, explored the use of transtextual narratives. For example, the story of Conrad's Tom Lingard unfolds in three texts, the story of Hamilton in two, the story of Marlow in four, and that of Golding's Edmund Talbot in three. Greene used this technique briefly when depicting Kite, the gangster. In *A Gun for Sale*, we are told of the circumstances of his murder by rival gangsters at a London station: he is surrounded, his throat is cut, he is carried through the barrier and dumped. In *Brighton Rock*, that murder of Kite proves to be the premise of the plot: we gradually learn that Pinkie is concerned to avenge his death: hence the ensuing action.

Another category of connections is that of 'close anticipations': one incident or character is not the same as, but closely anticipates, one in a later text. 'A Drive in the Country' features a cynical young thief who invites an innocent, vulnerable young woman to join him in a suicide pact. In the car, he gives her a revolver and instructs her in the method. She, however, runs away, leaving him to die. This is clearly an anticipation of the suicide pact initiated by Pinkie with Rose in *Brighton Rock*. Again, Ada, the plump, promiscuous middle-aged woman of the tale 'Jubilee', is a close relative of Ida Arnold in *Brighton Rock*; in both cases, this hearty, resilient woman takes the sexual initiative with a man who finds that he has encountered more than he bargained for. The tale 'The Lottery Ticket' presents, in brief, a range of material to be developed in *The Power and the Glory*: the little Mexican port where sinister birds hover, where a bust or statue overlooks the plaza; an official whose bad tooth is being painfully drilled by a dentist, and a good man executed. A curiously specific anticipation of incidents occurs in 'The Innocent' (1937). The hero recalls that when he was a young lad, he left in a hiding-place in a wall a love-message for an eight-year-old girl. Now, long afterwards, he revisits the hiding-place and retrieves the paper, and finds that it bears an obscene sketch of a man and a woman. 'I had believed I was drawing something with a meaning unique and beautiful; it was only now after thirty years of life that the picture seemed obscene.' In *The Human Factor* (published forty-one years later), Castle recalls that when he was ten he left a hidden message for a seven-year-old girl whom he loved: 'when he came back . . . . . he found the note was still there but disfigured by a vulgar drawing'; but this time, it is the girl, not the boy, who is the cartoonist. The similarities and the peculiar specificity imply an autobiographical source.

Of the recurrent character-types, one of the most easily identifiable, as we have seen, is the type based on Graham's brother Herbert: that of the con-man who repeatedly gets into financial scrapes through dubious schemes. Examples include Anthony Farrell (*The Bear Fell Free*), Anthony Farrant (*England Made Me*), Jones in *The Comedians* and the Captain in *The Captain and the Enemy*. Another, partly autobiographical, character is the writer who, after seeking to achieve detachment, moves towards commitment to a cause: Fowler in *The Quiet American*, Querry in *A Burnt-Out Case*. Another is the decent man cuckolded, a man who remains on civilised, sometimes even amicable, terms with his cuckolder: Demassener in *The Name of Action*, Henry in *The End of the Affair*, Victor Rhodes in *The Complaisant Lover* and Charley Fortnum in *The Honorary Consul*. In sexual triangles, Greene (guided, no doubt, by personal experience) sometimes depicts the woman as one who seeks to reconcile conflicting claims: usually the claim of loyalty to her husband with the claim of sexual adventure. Certainly Mary Rhodes in *The Complaisant Lover*, Sarah in *The End of the Affair*, Martha in *The Comedians* and Clara in *The Honorary Consul* belong to this category. The betrayal of a man by his supposed friend is a plot-device which extends from *The Man Within* to numerous novels and tales: 'The Third Man' is a famous example. Some of Greene's heroines are 'waifs' whose relationship to the male partner resembles at times that of pupil to mentor: Rose in *Brighton Rock*, Helen in *The Heart of the Matter*, Marie in *A Burnt-Out Case*.

Greene likes to play games with names; in his texts, significant patterns or pairings of names emerge. Most obviously (echoing Jonson's Corvino and Corbaccio in *Volpone*), there are the names associated with birds, usually unpleasant ones: Kite, Crowe (twice in *Brighton Rock*: Old Crowe and Violet Crowe), Crowe again ('The Blessing'), Krogh (twice), Crane, Henne-Falcon, Raven, Conder; in a variant of 'Cock Robin', Kite is killed by Raven. (A pleasant exception is Phuong, meaning Phoenix, in *The Quiet American*.) The name 'Sparrow' in *Travels with My Aunt* derives, says Greene, from John Sparrow, Warden of All Souls' at Oxford. There are aquatic names: Crab, Crabbe, Tench, Piker. Colour names: Pinkie Brown, Rose (French for pink) and Molly Pink (*Brighton Rock*), Rose again (*It's a Battlefield*, *The Living Room* and *Travels with My Aunt*), Blacker ('The Hint of an Explanation'), Browne (three in *The Living Room*) and Grünlich. Jewish names are sometimes borne by sinister characters: Kapper, Yogel, Goldstein. Some surnames are ostentatiously ordinary – Jones, Brown, Smith – and may (in the case of Jones and Brown in *The Comedians*) be taken for rogues' pseudonyms: Greene recalled the duplicitous 'Mr Jones' of Conrad's *Victory* and 'Gentleman Brown' in Conrad's *Lord Jim*. In *The Captain and the Enemy*, the shady Captain is known both as Brown and as Smith. Anna Schmidt in 'The Third Man' is using a false name to elude the Russians. Greene seems to have liked the name Sarah: he gave it to the sanctifiable heroine (based largely on Catherine Walston) in *The End of the Affair*, to the idealistic black heroine of *The Human Factor*, and (slightly modified as Sara) to the forbearing wife in *The Potting Shed*. Another name with strongly favourable associations for him was 'Coral' (which he associated with 'jewellery . . . . . suitable for young girls after their first communion'): hence the Coral Musker in *Stamboul Train* and Coral Fellows in *The Power and the Glory*; and the latter character is, of course, a communicant during the sentenced priest's final dream. In contrast, 'Mabel Warren' is the name that he gave not only to the predatory lesbian in *Stamboul Train* but also to the intimidating thirteen-year-old in 'The End of the Party' who, with her friend Joyce, fills Francis with justified apprehension: 'Their long pigtails swung superciliously to a masculine stride. Their sex humiliated him, as they watched him fumble with his egg, from under lowered scornful lids.'

Some of the linkages, whether deriving from recollection of real people or from private semantic associations, have a quality of disguised autobiography. The careful deliberation that Greene gave to such matters is evident from his remarks on the conversion of the name 'Rollo' to 'Holly' for the film *The Third*

Man. Joseph Cotten, who was to play the character, objected to the name Rollo, which (he thought) had homosexual connotations.

> I wanted the name none the less to be an absurd one, and the name Holly occurred to me when I remembered that figure of fun, the nineteenth-century American poet Thomas Holley Chivers.
>
> (*WE*, p. 124)

Holly is also the name of the main character in Haggard's *She*. Lime's surname, Greene explained, was suggested by the lime (quicklime) thrown on the corpses of hanged murderers: an echo of Wilde's 'Ballad of Reading Gaol'. Other literary associations, as we have seen, generate the names Kurtz (in *The Name of Action* and 'The Third Man') and Visconti (*Travels with My Aunt*). Occasionally there are sly references to personal sexual intrigues. A 'woman called Glover' is mentioned in *The Confidential Agent*; a loving Dorothy who seeks her gloves appears in *Travels with My Aunt*. The situation of Harry in *The End of the Affair* resembles that of Harry Walston. Catherine Walston might have winced on finding that in *The Honorary Consul* the best brothel is run by 'Mère Catherine', but she might have been cheered to learn that *The End of the Affair* was prompted partly by Greene's researches on St Catherine of Genoa. The hero of *The Confidential Agent* is called simply 'D.'. Greene said that the advantage of using only an initial was that it saved the character from having a specified nationality; but there was a disadvantage: 'Unfortunately, as I learnt before, if one uses an initial for one's principal character, people begin to talk about Kafka' (*IS*, p. 33).

Sometimes a name may have religious associative significance: Calver, the criminal in *The Power and the Glory*, has a name which seems designed to evoke 'Calvary' and thus heighten the analogy between the whisky-priest and Christ. Sometimes the very absence of a name may have religious significance. The whisky-priest has no name other than the common name he borrows for a while (that of a killed hostage); the anonymity is appropriate to his representative role as sustainer of the continuity of religion. Deo Gratias ('Thanks to God') was the actual name of an African at the *léproserie* visited by Greene, and in *A Burnt-Out Case* it has double significance: partly ironic, since the man is a leper; partly non-ironic, since caring for Deo Gratias helps to restore Querry. In turn, 'Querry' brings to mind the Latin verb 'quaere': question, search for, or seek in vain.

In idiomatic speech, the names 'Jesus', 'Christ' and 'God' are commonly used merely as everyday oaths, as expressions of surprise or annoyance perhaps. One of the ironies of *Brighton Rock* is that when Pinkie uses them so, the strongly religious thematic context restores some of their force as invocations of divinity; a bridge is thus built between the sordidly mundane and the transcendent.

7 'Leopards' and other stylistic matters

Greene's earliest novels (*The Man Within, The Name of Action, Rumour at Nightfall*) were technically flawed in numerous ways: the descriptive passages, for example, were often romantically turgid. Then, in *Stamboul Train*, he achieved an effective balance of functional descriptive richness and well-paced narrative, of external and internal analyses. By the time of *Brighton Rock* and *The Power and the Glory*, he had attained what most writers would desire: a style memorably distinctive and even idiosyncratic, harmonising in imagery with the themes of a suspenseful and engrossing plot-sequence.

One ingredient of that 'memorably distinctive and even idiosyncratic' style is the presence of what he and Vivien termed 'leopards': images that leap out at you; similes that have a striking, even grotesque quality. 'There was one, I remember, comparing something or someone in the quiet landscape of Sussex to a leopard crouching in a tree, which gave a name to the whole species' (*SL*, p. 190). Here, from *Brighton Rock*, are six examples of these characteristic similes:

> The sea stretched like a piece of gay common washing in a tenement square across the end of the street. (p. 111)

> The sun slid off the sea and like a cuttle fish shot into the sky the stain of agonies and endurances. (p. 187)

> [H]is virginity straightened in him like sex . . . . . (p. 124)

> The small pricked-out plants irritated him like ignorance. (p. 154)

> The sympathy didn't belong; it could be peeled off his eyes like an auction ticket from an ancient flint instrument. (p. 166)

> His words wilted out like a line of seaweed, along the edge of the Boy's silence, indifference and purpose. (p. 170)

Such 'leopards' can be found in Greene's writing at earlier and later periods; but their use seems to be most frequent in the period 1936 to 1948. Thereafter the frequency lessens, as Greene's style became more facile, more fluent and 'transparent', and less rich. In 1971, he said: '[It] took a great many years for me to get the beasts under control, and they growl at me yet' (*SL*, p. 190). Sometimes they bring to mind the surrealistic similes of Eliot's verse ('the evening . . . . . like a patient etherised'), but Greene suggested that they sprang from Metaphysical poetry.

Greene knew well the 'conceits' of Metaphysical poetry and the grotesque, bizarre similes of Jacobean drama. Helen Gardner defines a Metaphysical conceit as 'a comparison whose ingenuity is more striking than its justness, or, at least, is more immediately striking' (*The Metaphysical Poets*, Penguin 1957, p. 19). The most famous instance is John Donne's comparison, in 'A Valediction: Forbidding Mourning', of a pair of faithful lovers (who for a while must part) to the legs of a pair of compasses. Both are separate yet united; so the oddity of the comparison is justified by its logic, or rather by its mock-logic which yields the sense of wit. There is a related quality of the compressed riddle in John Webster's similes: 'I do love her just as a man pulls a wolf by the ears'; 'like the black and melancholic yew-tree, / Dost think to root thyself in dead men's graves, / And yet to prosper?' In *British Dramatists*, Greene praised Webster and Tourneur for expressing 'a kind of dark horror, a violent moral anarchy' by such imagery as this: 'We are merely the stars' tennis-balls'; 'What's the flesh? A little crudded milk, fantastical puff-paste.'

Nevertheless, Greene's 'leopards', which help to establish the atmosphere and preoccupations of Greeneland, remain distinctive. Take the first example in the list quoted above. In the Brighton vista, the sea can be seen at the end of the street, but here it is 'like a piece of gay common washing in a tenement square'; though 'gay', it is 'common' and associated with the poverty of a tenement. The blue expanse of nature is being demeaned by association, linked to the sleaziness of Greeneland.

The second example is dramatic, even melodramatic, and visually spectacular. The setting sun, staining the night sky red, is like a cuttle-fish which ejects its black ink when assailed (a bizarre linkage of the gradual with the sudden, tenuously justified by the marine associations of sun over sea); yet the red stain is 'the stain of agonies and endurances'. The text has recently referred to the bloody death of Kite, but now religious associations are evoked; one thinks of the tortures of martyrs and particularly of the crucified Christ. Sacred suffering oversees profane suffering. Again, the simile's rapid linkage of concrete to abstract gives it a quality of oxymoron, or compressed paradox. (Some later editions of *Brighton Rock* made nonsense of the imagery by rendering the sentence as: 'The sun slid off the sea and like a cuttlefish shot into the sky with the stains of agonies and endurances.' The added 'with' hurls the sinking sun aloft.)

The third example is paradoxical by its linkage of abstract to (relatively) concrete and by its analogy between customarily opposed items: virginity and a penis becoming erect. The justification is that the repressed and virginal Pinkie feels revulsion before the sexual: perversely, his frigidity can be aroused to a passionate disgust.

The fourth example again makes the abstract–concrete conjunction (though reversing the customary order) and resembles a Jacobean riddling simile: why should plants irritate a person 'like ignorance'? The answer is that Pinkie, who minutes ago was physically attacked, has gained knowledge of pain and fear. Hiding in a potting shed, he sees the objects around as representatives of the comfortable, harmless life of its owner: Pinkie feels the resentment of a person on the dangerous margin against someone safely ensconced in domestic normality.

Example five again links the abstract, 'sympathy', to the very concrete particular of the auction ticket. Both are removable: Prewitt's sympathy is superficial, a temporary veneer; beneath it, the simile suggests, lies a hard, egoistic temperament.

The final example, appropriately enough for this novel of Brighton, once more employs marine imagery. Spicer, who has been betrayed by Pinkie and will be murdered by him, has been speaking apologetically and haltingly to Pinkie. In the simile, the failing words resemble wilting seaweed left to die; Pinkie resembles the barren and impassive shore-line.

So, looking back over this sequence, we see that the similes sometimes further characterisation, and serve to integrate characters with the marine location and with themes of morality and religion. They have a provocative, paradoxical quality; and they impart a quality of drama, even of metaphysical melodrama, to the details of the text. One adapts to such stylistic flourishes during the reading of Greene; in isolation, some of the similes may seem strained. Nevertheless, the 'leopards' of *Brighton Rock* and *The Power and the Glory* are usually more effective in establishing atmosphere and implication than are the similes and metaphors found in the earlier novels. In *England Made Me*, for instance, there are some ludicrous analogies: 'Autumn . . . . . peeled like smoke from the naked thighs of a statue'; 'malevolence . . . . . lay like scurf over his overcoat'. Greene was his own best critic in this respect. Speaking of the style of *The Name of Action*, he said:

Here are examples of . . . . . my terrible misuse of simile and metaphor. Even the good can corrupt and perhaps I had been corrupted by much reading of the metaphysical poets. 'A revolver drooped like a parched flower to the pavement.' (I like to reverse this simile – 'A parched flower drooped like a revolver to the pavement.') 'The sound of far voices sprinkled over him like the seeds of a poppy bringing rest.' And here's a piece of pomposity which I had learned from Conrad at his worst: 'A clock relinquished its load of hours.'

(*WE*, p. 18)

Yet, only eight pages after this self-criticism, Greene recalls a Norwegian visitor who brought him a measure of hope, 'carrying it like a glass of akvavit down the muddy lane'.

The following two passages from *The Power and the Glory* further illustrate the pressure of paradox within Graham Greene's descriptions. Here is Coral Fellows at work:

When she had given her orders she went to the warehouse to inspect the alligator skins tacked out on a wall, then to the stables to see that the mules were in good shape. She carried her responsibilities carefully like crockery across the hot yard: there was no question she wasn't prepared to answer: the vultures rose languidly at her approach.

(p. 63)

Here, the first sentence is simple and factual; clear simple diction and syntax. The second sentence moves to analysis of her character; a characteristic 'leopard' leaps out: 'responsibilities' carried 'like crockery', suggesting deliberate care. Her forthright sense of responsibility and her honesty are noted, yet juxtaposed with the observation of the languidly rising vultures, so that again, even though there is no simile, the reader experiences that rapid juxtaposition of abstract and concrete, of internal with external. The narrator has moved with confident agility between the renderings of action, of character and of location. The style combines direct 'unliterary' reportage with an idiosyncratic idiom in which there is deliberation, a quest for the striking notation and the *mot juste* – as in that adverb 'languidly'. The vultures are ominous familiar denizens of Greeneland: Coral's life will be short.

The next passage is part of the description of the priest's tedious night in a crowded prison-cell:

[H]e sat silent and rigid against the damp wall, with his feet dead like leprosy under his haunches. The mosquitoes droned on: it was no good defending yourself by striking at the air: they pervaded the whole place like an element. Somebody as well as the old man had somewhere fallen asleep and was snoring, a curious note of satisfaction, as though he had eaten and drunk well at a good dinner and was now taking a snooze.

(p. 161)

Greeneland again: the prison-cell, mosquitoes omnipresent. Clear uncluttered diction and syntax, but repeated similes. Some strain is imposed to achieve a striking abstract simile: 'dead like leprosy' is a contortion of 'as dead as if they were the feet of a leper'. There is a tinge of paradox in the observation that even in this purgatorial cell, someone may not only sleep but may also, when snoring, seem to be expressing contentment. Generally, a graphically effective passage. By such close and vivid notation, Greene anchors in credible actuality the moral and theological debates and the insistent patterning of his plot-structures. Indeed, one might reflect that just as his similes often link the concrete to the abstract (usually, though not always, sharpening one's apprehension of both), so, on a much larger scale, his narratives attempt equivalent linkages. The nervously sensuous rendering of location and action precipitates moral and theological questions.

In detail and in large conception, some of Greene's works employ theological shock-tactics which generate a near-blasphemous dramatic effect. There was a distant but ample precedent for such shock-tactics in John Donne's 'Holy Sonnets', as when the poet implores Christ to identify the true Church:

> Betray kind husband thy spouse to our sights,
> And let myne amorous soule court thy mild Dove,
> Who is most trew, and pleasing to thee, then
> When she'is embrac'd and open to most men.

Or as here, when the poet beseeches God:

> Take mee to you, imprison mee, for I
> Except you'enthrall mee, never shall be free,
> Nor ever chast, except you ravish mee.

In contrast to the degree of poise and control that the sonnet form lends to Donne's boldness is the melodramatic prose of Scobie's dialogues with God:

'You have only to say the word,' he addressed God, 'and

163

legions of angels...' and he struck with his ringed hand
under the eye.....
O God, he prayed, his hands dripping over the wheel, kill me
now, now..... Vermin don't have to exterminate themselves.
Kill me. Now. Now. Now. Before I hurt *you* again.

(pp. 257, 273)

Greene acknowledged the influence of Metaphysical poetry
and of Conrad; but he was also strongly influenced, not always
for the better, by American traditions. Hemingway's style can
sometimes be detected in Greene's laconic passages of dialogue
and description. The following passage from *The Lawless Roads*
(pp. 94–5) is virtually a pastiche of Hemingway, with its
American slang ('got a little lit'), its simple syntax and its
childish repetitions of 'and': 'Then we went to the St. Regis and
had Bacardi cocktails and got a little lit and talked of the
American debt and the Immaculate Conception.....' Here's an
example from *The Quiet American* (p. 23):

> [The] gold and the young green and the bright dresses of the
> south, and in the north the deep browns and the black clothes and
> the circle of enemy mountains and the drone of planes.....

Certainly the Hollywood movie influenced his scenic
montages, some dialogues (terse, understating) of his lovers, and
the 'tough guy' diction and cynical jesting of gangsters in his
thrillers. American crime fiction also may have contributed to
the effective staccato style of his action scenes, illustrated in these
two passages from *Brighton Rock* (pp. 151–2, 332):

> Then somebody from the stand shouted 'Bogies' and they all
> moved together, coming quickly at him in a bunch. Somebody
> kicked him on the thigh, he clutched a razor in his hand and
> was cut to the bone.

> The lights petered out along the road to Peacehaven: the
> chalk of a new cutting flapped like white sheets in the
> headlight: cars came down on them blinding them. He said:
> 'The battery's low.'

Sometimes the prose combines the tough style with a more
'literary' (perhaps latinate) diction, as when Fowler, in *The Quiet
American*, is shown Pyle's corpse (p. 16). Here the laconism of
'like a tray of ice-cubes' offsets the elegance of 'frozen into
placidity':

They pulled him out like a tray of ice-cubes, and I looked at him. The wounds were frozen into placidity. I said, 'You see, they don't re-open in my presence.'

An Americanism which can be found in Greene's writing across the decades is (in the UK at least) a solecism: the idiomatic but ungrammatical use of 'like' in positions where 'as' should be used. In *Brighton Rock*, for example: Cubitt moves drunkenly, 'like a statue might move'; 'he'd got her like you got God in the Eucharist'; 'She was stamped with him, like his voice was stamped on the vulcanite'; 'The woman hooked on another smile, like you hook on a wreath'. (In later editions, Greene sometimes restored 'as'.)

Many of these illustrations show that the vivid distinctiveness of Greene's style derives largely from its high proportion of surprising similes: they add glints of drama, even melodrama. Thus, in *The Honorary Consul*, 'When he bent to kiss her cheek he could smell the hot chocolate in her cup like a sweet breath from a tomb.' A related feature, often but not necessarily exploiting similes, is the use of aphorisms which tend to the hyperbolic; sometimes they blend the narrator with a character. Examples:

Each love affair was like a vaccine. It helped you to get through the next attack more easily.

The whole globe was blanketed with his own sin.

They were companions cut off from all the world: there was no meaning anywhere outside their own hearts.

[Peacehaven] was like the last effort of despairing pioneers to break new country. The country had broken them.

It was too easy to die for what was good or beautiful, for home or children or a civilization – it needed a God to die for the half-hearted and the corrupt.

In 1921, T. S. Eliot, praising Donne and the other Metaphysical poets, had commended their ability to reconcile disparates. 'When a poet's mind is perfectly equipped for its work, it is constantly amalgamating disparate experience . . . . .' Greene's prose often seeks to achieve this effect. The rapid, terse association of thought and feeling, of idea and image, is a characteristic of Greene's mature work. 'The orchestra began to play: he felt the music as a movement in his belly: the violins wailed in his guts.' 'The yellow eyeballs stared up at him like a stranger's, flecked with red. It was as if this body had cast him off, disowned him – "I know you not." ' At its frequent best, Greene's prose is never inert; ruthlessly, it shuns the easy platitude, the convenient cliché, the waffling digression. He has the knack of the *mot juste*, the tellingly evocative word or phrase. The girls at Roedean play hockey on 'cropped expensive turf'; a tiny green snake 'hissed away into the grass like a match-flame'; the shadow of a palm-tree 'pointed at him like a zareba of sabres'; 'the huts leapt up in the lightning and stood there shaking – then disappeared in the rumbling darkness'. When Pinkie kisses Rose's hand, 'the fingers were rough on his skin and tasted a little of soap'. As in Jacobean drama, so (often) in Greene's novels: more truths in the texture than in the plot; a more searching fidelity to human experience in the captured details than in the paraphrasable story.

8 Critical accounts

Darkest Greeneland: Brighton Rock

Brighton Rock is not the best of Greene's novels (*The Power and the Glory* deserves that accolade), but it is probably the most striking, provocative and extreme; it is corrosively negative, grotesquely nightmarish, cynically black-comical. It is a thriller, a detective-novel and a moral-cum-theological paradox. It offers realism, expressionism and satiric stylisation. And it is hauntingly memorable rather than convincing.

The realism of the setting is easily verifiable. Greene evokes Brighton of 1936–37 with sharp accuracy. Today at Brighton you can still follow precisely Hale's route along the sea-front to his death under the Palace Pier, or Pinkie's route to the race-course, through that subway beneath the track, and back down to Whitehawk. The pub where Hale meets Ida is clearly Dr Brighton's, alias the Star and Garter: as late as 1980 the layout of the bars was the same, and it still sold Bass ale. Nearby remains the Old Ship Hotel; further to the west are the Metropole and the Norfolk. That girls' public school behind the wrought-iron gates on the coast is Roedean. If you stand at the entrance to the Palace Pier and face north, the view is much the same as Spicer's from that point: the Royal Albion Hotel, Old Steine, 'the pale green domes of the Pavilion float[ing] above the dusty trees' (p. 118). Admittedly, Sherry's dance-hall on West Street has been superseded by a slot-machine arcade; and the coastal hotel where Pinkie has his last drink, the Peacehaven Hotel, was demolished in the 1980s. The Palace Pier still overshadows shops selling Brighton Rock; and the steps beside it, where Ida Arnold left Hale, still lead down from Madeira Drive to the public lavatory. The chapel in which Rose was consoled by the wheezing priest is St John's, in Kemp Town.

In the novel, Ida bets (at odds of 10–1) on the horse called Black Boy. It wins, so she has enough money to devote time to the pursuit of Pinkie. When, decades ago, I did some research for Norman Sherry's biography of Greene, I found that Black Boy had a counterpart in a horse called Blue Boy which won the Balcombe Stakes at 10–1 in June 1936. The original of the 'Cosmopolitan' Hotel where Colleoni has his base was evidently the Bedford: Emperor Napoléon III and Empress Eugénie ('some polony') stayed there, as Colleoni reports. Rose's restaurant, 'Snow's', at the corner of West Street and Kings Road, corresponds to Sweeting's. Hale's job as 'Kolley Kibber', rewarding holiday-makers who identified him, was based on that of the *News Chronicle*'s 'Lobby Lud'. One surprising difference from reality, I found, was that the race-course fracas which provided the basis for the attack on Pinkie and Spicer in Part Four of the novel had taken place not at Brighton but at Lewes: Greene had transferred the fracas in the interests of narrative unity. The London gang, 'the Hoxton Mob', which attacked two local men at the Lewes race-course on 8 June 1935, in actuality used not razors but a hatchet, a jemmy, an iron bar and half a billiard-cue. Having been ambushed by the police, sixteen members of the Hoxton Mob were tried for malicious wounding and 'riotous assembly'. All were jailed, the ringleaders being sentenced to five years' penal servitude; the combined prison sentences amounted to more than forty-three years. (*The Times*, 30 July 1936, p. 11, gave prominence to this outcome.) In the novel, Colleoni's gang gets away: it serves Greene's purposes to suggest that this interloper's power will continue to increase. One historic Colleoni was a fifteenth-century Italian 'soldier of fortune'. Greene also knew of Darby Sabini, a successful race-course racketeer with a suite at Brighton's Grand Hotel. He was believed to have Mafia connections; his gang, based in London, was an alliance of Italians and Jews, their favoured weapon being the razor. Like Colleoni's, Sabini's gang controlled slot-machines in addition to 'protecting' bookmakers, and was said to enjoy a cooperative relationship with various police officers. Frater and Solomon, the bookmakers attacked at Lewes by the Hoxton Mob, were linked with Sabini. According to James Morton's account in *Gangland* (1992, p. 22), the Mob was seeking revenge, for one of their men had had his throat cut by Sabini's gang at Liverpool Street Station: a source for the death of Kite.

One peculiarity of Pinkie may have a factual basis: in 1936 the Brighton *Evening Argus* reported that a local gang-leader was only seventeen: Pinkie's age. The kidnapping and killing of Hale had real-life precedent: in 1928 Ernest Friend Smith was kidnapped from Madeira Drive, on the sea-front, and mortally wounded. Then in 1934 the 'trunk murders' (a female torso and a female body were found in trunks) gave Brighton the sobriquet 'The Queen of Slaughtering Places'. Thus, in reality, Brighton was associated not only with the seaside pleasures of holiday-makers from the city but also with rackets and violent crime.

In the novel, Rose's parents live at Nelson Place. There is still a Nelson Place in Brighton. It is now a block of council flats erected near the site of the street which bore that name: a street demolished during the slum-clearances observed by Pinkie. His home was in Paradise Piece, we are told. That name might seem to be a heavily ironic invention by Greene; but, not far from Nelson Place, a Paradise Street, also in the working-class district of eastern Brighton, had been knocked down as part of an earlier programme of urban reconstruction. Today, as in the 1930s, Brighton offers a conjunction of festivity and squalor, affluence and poverty.

Of course, the more one traces factual precedents and historic bases for *Brighton Rock*, the more one sees how Greene has allowed his Brighton to be annexed by Greeneland. In 1909 D.H. Lawrence visited the area. This is how he, looking westward along the coast from Rottingdean, described the sunset:

> The downs are all like a cloth when two people are shaking it unevenly – and full of shadows and lights – and on the sunny side there are cowslips out. I have watched the sun swim and go – I was terrified to see the swimming sun sink so quickly and deliberately behind the round hill where the windmill stands up stately but a bit ridiculous. Then Brighton in the red fusing light looked like a wonderful imagined place, and the lights on the sea just played about, and me, I played with them, and the wind ruffled the water back, and right up in the sky were two ruddy clouds flung together, and they were perfect, like two lovers at last met in a kiss, now they have met in the winds, and his head was hid in the tossed glitter and beauty of her hair that the wind shook, and his naked body flung towards her. It was fine.
>
> (*The Letters of D. H. Lawrence*, 1979, I, p. 127)

Lawrence revels in exuberant empathy. His description moves from the domestic to the ecstatic: sun, sea, lights, winds and clouds combine in play, and the play becomes wildly amatory. In contrast, here is Greene:

> The sun slid off the sea and like a cuttle fish shot into the sky the stain of agonies and endurances . . . . .
> An old man went stooping down the shore, very slowly, turning the stones, picking among the dry seaweed for cigarette ends, scraps of food. The gulls which had stood like candles down the beach rose and cried under the promenade. The old man found a boot and stowed it in his sack and a gull

Nelson Place, Brighton, in 1935.

dropped from the Parade and swept through the iron nave of
the Palace Pier, white and purposeful in the obscurity:
half-vulture and half-dove. In the end one always had to learn.

(pp. 187–8)

Greene's emphasis is on the poverty and squalor amid the
pleasure-resort's vulgar opulence. The sky's purple connotes the
blood of martyrdom; and here the very gulls become ambiguous:
half predatory, half symbols of peace. What, in the end, 'one
always had to learn' is, in Pinkie's case, the act of copulation
from which he recoils; but the passage also suggests that one
always had to learn the base realities of life; innocence must give
way to sour experience.

Later, when Ida is waiting to copulate with Phil Corkery, we
are told: 'She bore the same relation to passion as a peepshow';
she is 'just a great big blossoming surprise'. And this is the view:

Outside the window the sea ebbed, scraping the shingle,
exposing a boot, a piece of rusty iron, and the old man
stooped, searching between the stones. The sun dropped
behind the Hove houses and dusk came . . . . . A gull swooped
screaming down to a dead crab beaten and broken against the
iron foundation of the pier. It was the time of near-darkness
and of the evening mist from the Channel and of love.

(p. 211)

Again, the refuse on the beach, the searching beachcomber, a
gull. And the 'love' mentioned here is, in this context,
predominantly lust. Again, in contrast to Lawrence's ecstatic
romanticism, a sourly depressive romantic realism: it mourns a
fallen world and a defiled beauty.

At the novel's opening, the bright sunny glitter and bustle of
the sea-front were evoked; towards the end, Pinkie's car will
struggle though the dank drizzly gloom toward the blighted
coastal plain of Peacehaven. And the name 'Peacehaven' proves
bitterly ironic: the name of a drab speculative building-site of
cheap bungalows set out in a monotonous grid-pattern; the
location not of peace but of ugliness and, for Pinkie, torment
and violence. The liturgical *dona nobis pacem* echoes ironically
through the narrative.

In *Brighton Rock*, as Greene told his agent, the central
thematic tension is between the ethical and the religious
outlooks. The concepts of 'right and wrong' are challenged by
the concepts of 'Good and Evil'. Charles 'Fred' Hale is murdered
by Pinkie and his gang, though the inquest wrongly adduces a

171

verdict of death by natural causes. (He has a heart-attack as they try to choke him by means – it is hinted – of a stick of rock forced down the throat.) Ida Arnold, a Londoner who had befriended Hale, is suspicious of the circumstances and investigates. Endeavouring to protect Rose from Pinkie, she pursues him, saves Rose from suicide, and brings about the destruction of Pinkie. Ida feels that a good job has been well done: a double killer has been punished. In her view, 'right' has prevailed over 'wrong'. Against her secular ethic, however, the text invokes the religious frame of reference. And here the novel's appalling paradox is generated. Pinkie, the killer of Hale (and later of Spicer), has had a Roman Catholic indoctrination and is still, in his perverse way, a believer; thus, for all his evil, and indeed largely because of his sense of evil, he inhabits the religious dimension.

> 'These atheists, they don't know nothing. Of course there's Hell. Flames and damnation,' he said with his eyes on the dark shifting water and the lightning and the lamps going out above the black struts of the Palace Pier, 'torments.'
> 'And Heaven too,' Rose said with anxiety, while the rain fell interminably on.
> 'Oh, maybe,' the Boy said, 'maybe.'
>
> (p. 71)

In the characterisation of Pinkie, Greene seems to be conducting a taxing literary experiment: to see how far the reader's pity can be won for a person who seems to be irredeemably evil and monstrously callous. The ruthless cunning of this teenage gangster is starkly depicted: his sadistic quality is carried to almost ludicrous extremes. 'She loves me . . . . . she loves me not', he says, tearing the wings and legs off a fly. He wields a razor, carries a vitriol bottle, and jests crudely over his victims. He is a Judas to Spicer, his accomplice, and even to Rose, who is determinedly loyal to him even though she knows his wickedness. Yet, in various ways, Greene ingeniously seeks to win a degree of pity for him.

First, Ida's world of secular right and wrong is made to seem superficial. She has a blowsy appeal, a resilient courage, a hearty optimism; but she belongs to the world of carnality and vulgarity. Pinkie, in his warped Catholicism (partly Manichæism, almost Satanism) is half-way to belief in God. He is attuned to the transcendental, to an eternity – albeit of hell-fires. (' "*Credo in unum Satan[a]m*," the Boy said.') In contrast, his victim, Hale, after cremation at a (satirised) half-secular Anglican service witnessed by Ida, merely becomes 'part of the smoke nuisance over London'. In a superbly sardonic paragraph we are told:

> She came out of the crematorium, and there from the twin towers above her head fumed the very last of Fred, a thin stream of grey smoke from the ovens. People passing up the flowery suburban road looked up and noted the smoke; it had been a busy day at the furnaces. Fred dropped in indistinguishable grey ash on the pink blossoms: he became part of the smoke nuisance over London, and Ida wept.
>
> (p. 47)

Pinkie, the former choir-boy, resembles a priest *manqué*, being initially virginal; he recoils from alcohol, and intermittently feels nostalgia for the Mass and the choir. 'When I was a boy, I swore I'd be a priest':

> 'What's wrong with being a priest?' the Boy said. 'They know what's what. They keep away' – his whole mouth and jaw loosened: he might have been going to weep; he beat out wildly with his hands towards the window – Woman Found Drowned, two-valve, *Married Passion*, the horror – 'from this.'
>
> (p. 240)

The events unfold around the time of Pentecost; and in this case, it is Pinkie, a diabolical apostle, who receives the 'gift of tongues' (p. 240). He has at least elicited the selfless love of Rose, the naïve young Catholic; Ida's love-life, in contrast, is a matter of brief hedonistic encounters. Pinkie, furthermore, retains the notion that he might one day, *in extremis*, repent and gain salvation: he repeatedly half-recalls William Camden's lines 'Betwixt the stirrup and the ground, / Mercy I asked, mercy I found.' His death – as he, vitriol burning his face, throws himself from the cliff-top into the sea – may seem designed to rule out any last-minute penitence: taken by surprise, he commits suicide blindly, in agony. Nevertheless, after his death, when Rose visits her Catholic church, the priest tells her: 'You can't conceive, my child, nor can I or anyone – the . . . appalling . . . strangeness of the mercy of God.'

Thus, briefly, the text raises the truly appalling possibility that such an utter villain as Pinkie may be granted eternal salvation and heavenly bliss. Rose is doubly consoled, thinking she may be pregnant and may raise, as the priest says, 'a saint – to pray for his father'. But she then proceeds towards the 'worst horror of all': the gramophone disc on which Pinkie has recorded the words 'God damn you, you little bitch, why can't you go back home for ever and let me be?' It is one of the cruellest endings in literature. (In the film it was mitigated. Rose plays a record on which he declares: 'What you want me to say is, I love you'; and the needle then sticks in a crack, so that the phrase 'I love you' is repeated, while the camera pans up to a crucifix on the wall, and exultant music swells. We do not see whether she ever moves the needle forward to the subsequent words, 'Here's the truth: I hate you, you little slut'.)

Greene offers not only a religious case to challenge a simple hostile verdict against Pinkie but also a secular case of the kind that would appeal to liberals and socialists. 'His actions', said Greene later, 'arose out of the conditions to which he had been born' (*OM*, p. 159). One world for the rich, another for the poor: along the coast at Roedean, the daughters of affluence play hockey in their verdant enclave; but the novel stresses that Pinkie's early years were blighted by conditions in the slum. In the squalid setting of Paradise Piece, he shared the room in which, every Saturday night, his parents brutally copulated; hence, partly, his puritanical recoil from sexuality. Like the sixteen-year-old Rose, he has known the drabness and the squalor of the Carlton Hill area of Brighton. Ranged against the two shabby young people are the rich and powerful and (according to the first British edition of the novel) the Jews. There's no room at the inn for Pinkie and Rose; or, at least, no room at the Cosmopolitan, where they are refused accommodation on their wedding night. The luxurious Cosmopolitan is the stronghold of Jews, it seems; particularly of the affluent gangster from London, Colleoni. He is at home there, in his luxurious suite; his henchmen are Jews; well-dressed Jewesses ('little bitches') sit at ease, sneering at the shabby local boy. The Cosmopolitan is true to its name: it has a Louis Seize Writing Room, a Pompadour Boudoir, an American Bar – the aliens are invading Brighton.

In the battle to control the protection-racket in betting at Brighton, Colleoni (who already controls automatic machines) is bound to win. The forces of law and order purport to be neutral, but side with Colleoni. The local police advise Pinkie to give way to the greater rogue – 'He's got the alibis'. And Colleoni is buying his way to even greater power: he is set to become a Conservative MP. '[H]e'll go in for politics one day. The Conservatives think a lot of him – he's got contacts' (p. 231). Consequently, with his 'old Semitic face',

> he looked as a man might look who owned the whole world, the whole visible world that is, the cash registers and

Richard Attenborough and Carol Marsh as Pinkie and Rose, in the film
Brighton Rock

policemen and prostitutes, Parliament and the laws which say
'this is Right and this is Wrong'.

(p. 88)

Perhaps the most insidious part of the special pleading on
behalf of Pinkie is implicit in the narrator's descriptions. Pinkie's
disgust at life seems largely to be shared by the narrator in his
repeated observations of the tawdriness, the sleaziness, the
drabness of the world. 'Why, this is Hell, nor are we out of it',
says Prewitt, misquoting the words of Mephostophilis in
Marlowe's *Doctor Faustus*; and the narrator gives potent support
to that near-Manichæan sense of the hellish lurking beneath the
superficial pleasures and distractions of Brighton.

Expressionist art is characterised by the use of distortions
which evoke a deranged or unbalanced state of mind. The
accumulation of pessimistically skewed descriptive set-pieces gives
Brighton Rock a distinctly expressionist heightening. When Pinkie
returns to his home area, Paradise Piece, this is the scene:

[T]here he was, on the top of the hill, in the thick of the
bombardment – a flapping gutter, [glassless] windows, an iron
bedstead in a front garden the size of a table-top. Half
Paradise Piece had been torn up as if by bomb-bursts; the
children played about the steep slope of rubble . . . . . His
home was gone: a flat place among the rubble may have
marked its hearth; the room at the bend of the stairs where
the Saturday night exercise had taken place was now just air.
He wondered with horror whether it all had to be built again
for him; it looked better as air . . . . .
The children were scouting among the rubble with pistols
from Woolworth's; a group of girls surlily watched. A child
with its leg in an iron brace limped blindly into him; he
pushed it off; someone said in a high treble: 'Stick 'em up.'
They took his mind back and he hated them for it; it was like
the dreadful appeal of innocence, but *there* was not innocence;
you had to go back a long way further before you got
innocence; innocence was a slobbering mouth, a toothless
gum pulling at the teats; perhaps not even that; innocence was
the ugly cry of birth.

(pp. 202–3. I correct 'glass' to the 'glassless' of
other editions; in 1970 it became 'cracked'.)

At Nelson Place, where Rose's parents live, the front door's pane
is broken; the passage stinks 'like a lavatory'; the staircase is
carpeted with old newspapers reporting rape and murder; the

parents, sitting amid unwashed dishes by an unlighted stove, agree to the marriage – at a price. Effectively, Rose is sold to Pinkie for fifteen guineas. (Judas required thirty pieces of silver for his act of betrayal.)

The novel's title refers not only to the sticks of rock at the site of Hale's death but also, by a conceited simile, to human nature. Ida Arnold says to Rose:

> 'Look at me. I've never changed. It's like those sticks of rock: bite it all the way down, you'll still read Brighton. That's human nature.' . . . . .
> 'Confession . . . repentance,' Rose whispered.
> 'That's just religion,' the woman said. 'Believe me. It's the world we got to deal with.'
>
> (p. 288)

Human nature: reassuringly consistent, in Ida's view; tainted with original sin, according to the Catholic view. Confession and repentance may briefly cleanse that taint; for the world at large, the corruption remains. After his secular, and therefore sinful, marriage to Rose, Pinkie finds that he is capable of faint tenderness towards her; he feels 'the prowling pressure of pity'; in the car, driving towards death, he even has to ward off an 'enormous emotion' which beats on him 'like something trying to get in; the pressure of gigantic wings against the glass. *Dona nobis pacem*' (p. 349).

In *The Revenger's Tragedy* (*c.*1607), the central figure is Vindice, an avenger who becomes part of the corruption he excoriates. He moves amid a debased world, denouncing sexual vice and invoking the purity of death. Pinkie is a modern Vindice, part of what he detests; a deranged puritan who, looking at Spicer, notes the stink of whisky, the eruption around the mouth, the corn on the yellowed foot; and who, when Sylvie awaits him in the back of a car, recoils retching in nausea: 'I'd rather hang.'

Like a Jacobean revenge drama, a piece of Swiftian satire or a lurid expressionist film, *Brighton Rock* is a minor masterpiece in a highly stylised mode. It is a well-paced melodramatic thriller with metaphysical ambitions; a vivid, intense, bizarre, satirical crime-novel. Considered in an appropriate context of stylised literary works, it succeeds; considered primarily as realism, it is repeatedly flawed. Pinkie is a conspicuously artificial creation, a vile thesis rather than a credible character. When he says that his phone number is 666 (the number of the beast or devil in St John's Revelation, 13: 18), or when he declares '*Credo in unum Satan[a]m*', the text approaches self-parody. It certainly does so

177

here: ' "You were wonderful," she said, loving him among the lavatory smells, but her praise was poison: it marked her possession of him . . . . .' (p. 207). The narrator's contemptuous treatment of the secular marriage at the Registrar's Office is predictable. (Such marriages had been one of Thomas Hardy's targets in *Jude the Obscure*.) The dismissal of 'the great middle law-abiding class' as superstitious, superficial and unloving (p. 110) is so sweeping as to be self-refuting. Some comic details are effective: 'This is *real* country', says Sylvie at a road-house, 'they use their own eggs in the gin slings.' The denouement depends on coincidental meetings, lucky timings and unlikely sightings. Through the garish and blighted landscapes move grotesque, caricatural and pathetic characters, manipulated by a narrator who is a connoisseur of nastiness. *Brighton Rock* remains a memorable exploration of darkest Greeneland and of the appalling paradox of the virtue of evil.

Mastery: The Power and the Glory

Sources

The sources of this great novel may be considered under two headings, 'Mexican material' and 'accounts of saints'.

MEXICAN MATERIAL. *The Lawless Roads*, the account of Greene's journey through Mexico in spring 1938, describes the general situation and the regions which were to be depicted in *The Power and the Glory*.

One model for the whisky-priest was evidently Father Miguel Pro Juárez, a 35-year-old Jesuit who had landed at Veracruz in July 1926. Shortly afterwards, President Calles closed the churches and made the administering of the sacraments a criminal offence. Pro continued to give communion clandestinely, travelling around to elude the police. Eventually he was caught and was executed by firing squad on 23 November 1927. By the time Greene arrived in Mexico, the worst of the persecution of Catholics was over; under President Lázaro Cárdenas the Church was again tolerated in most regions. In the state of Tabasco, however, churches were destroyed by the local dictator, Garrido Canabal. Here priests had been hunted down and shot. The cathedral at Villahermosa had been demolished; its site was now a cement playground with metal swings 'like gallows': this playground features in the novel (on p. 26 of the 1940 edition).

Another model for the whisky-priest was a priest in Chiapas, who was so drunk at a boy's christening that he baptized him with a girl's name, Brigitta. In *The Power and the Glory*, Brigitta is the name of the hero's illegitimate child; and the episode of the mis-naming is cited on p. 30.

In the state of Tabasco, all alcoholic drink except beer was banned; this rule of near-prohibition adds to the hero's anguish. Greene met an ailing dentist at Frontera who was too poor to return to his homeland; the devaluation of the peso had reduced his savings. Evidently, he was a model for Mr Tench. The author's encounter with a loathsome *mestizo* who had two prominent yellow fangs generated the novel's Judas-figure. Near Palenque, Greene met a courteously hospitable brother and sister, both Lutherans: models for the Lehrs.

Greene experienced fully the discomfort of long journeys on a mule, the oppressiveness of the heat and the insects, the squalor of rural lodgings. He registered the hopelessness of impoverished people denied religious consolation. 'Even if it were all untrue and there were no God, surely life was happier with the enormous supernatural promise', he reflected. At times, like the whisky-priest, he felt he was a pariah. Though he was often disgusted by the oppression and squalor that he witnessed, at least there, he claimed, one could feel closer to religious realities than would be possible in the USA.

ACCOUNTS OF SAINTS. There is another kind of source-material that lies behind *The Power and the Glory*: literary or cinematic works dealing with martyrdom and sainthood. Joan of Arc was canonised in 1920, Sir Thomas More in 1935. Greene reviewed with disgust a German film, *Joan of Arc* (*Das Mädchen Johanna*, 1935), which seemed to him to be Nazi propaganda glorifying the treacherous Charles VII and belittling the martyr. On the other hand, he admired T. S. Eliot's work and praised *Murder in the Cathedral*, which had been successfully performed at Canterbury in 1935 and was later filmed: this verse-drama depicted Archbishop Thomas Becket's defiance of secular authority. St Thomas's martyrdom had previously been dramatised by Tennyson and would later be treated by Anouilh. Another renowned modern work about the making of a saint was Shaw's *Saint Joan*, 1923. (In the mid-1950s, Greene would write the film-script for Otto Preminger's film based on Shaw's play. This was released in 1957. Another acclaimed drama of martyrdom, Robert Bolt's *A Man for All Seasons*, about Sir Thomas More, would be staged in 1960 and subsequently filmed.)

In the 1920s and 1930s, priests had been persecuted not only in Mexico. During the Spanish Civil War, many priests were shot by communist and anarchist forces. In the Soviet Union, religious orders were persecuted by the Stalinist state. In Hitler's Germany and Mussolini's Italy, the relationship between the Churches and authority was fraught and complicated. In Germany, numerous priests (both Protestant and Catholic) who spoke out against Nazism were sent to concentration camps. Pope Pius XI denounced Nazism in the encyclical *Mit brennender Sorge* (1937). Greene remarked: 'Perhaps the only body in the world to-day which consistently – and sometimes successfully – opposes the totalitarian State is the Catholic Church' (*The Lawless Roads*, pp. 91–2).

In short, the prospect of martyrdom was, for priests in various parts of the world, a looming reality during the time when Greene, the Catholic convert, was making his way as a novelist. In *The Power and the Glory* he dramatised martyrdom in a memorably effective way: one that related the subject to the large ideological debates of the century, so that the plight of the whisky-priest became relevant to many people. Whether in Nazi Germany, the USSR or in numerous other lands, conscientious opposition to an oppressive state was a matter of life and death.

Structure and themes

The Power and the Glory is far more realistic, persuasive, subtle and humane than was *Brighton Rock*, but it still uses the basic suspense-generating plot-device of the pursuit of a law-breaker by an agent of justice, and it still aspires to the condition of moral and theological paradox.

The epigraph from Dryden establishes the theme of pursuit: 'Th'inclosure narrow'd; the sagacious power / Of hounds and death drew nearer every hour.' The priest who is the hero of the tale is trapped in a highly dangerous situation. His duty is to serve his flock, the Catholic community in his Mexican state. There any active priest may be arrested and shot. He also has a duty to stay alive so as to continue his service of God. So he is divided between a duty to remain and a duty to escape. From the first chapter, the tension is established. The priest reaches a port where waits a steamboat on which he might escape; but, though he is disguised, he is sought by a sick woman who needs to confess her sins. Reluctantly, bitterly, he goes to her; and, as he does so, he hears the steamboat leaving.

The priest's opponent is a fanatically dedicated and intelligently resourceful Marxist lieutenant, aided by soldiers and the police. In the situation, inevitably, our sympathies lie with the underdog, the fugitive who has odds stacked against him. Suspense mounts as the priest narrowly eludes recognition, first in his home village, and secondly when arrested in the capital; and he is dogged by a Judas-figure, the lying *mestizo* who seeks a reward for his capture. Another fugitive is Calver, a North American robber and killer whose route overlaps the hero's. At last the priest reaches the border and safety; but here, with cruel irony, the *mestizo* appears with a plea from the robber, who has been mortally wounded by the police. Although he knows that almost certainly an ambush awaits, the priest returns, tends Calver, is captured and, after a long dialogue with the lieutenant, is executed by a firing squad.

This is a novel about the making of a holy martyr, possibly of a saint. One obvious paradox is that the hero, this candidate for canonisation, regards himself as a failure. He repeatedly upbraids himself for his sins and inadequacies. The catalogue, admittedly, is quite full: he is a semi-alcoholic; he has fathered an illegitimate child; in the past, when life was easy, he was complacent; and now, when life is hard, his apparent courage can be construed – by him at least – as the sin of pride. He tells the lieutenant eventually that he expects damnation for himself:

'Pride's the worst thing of all. I thought I was a fine fellow to have stayed when the others had gone. And then I thought I was so grand I could make up my own rules. I gave up fasting, daily Mass. I neglected my prayers – and one day because I was drunk and lonely – well, you know how it was, I got a child. It was all pride. Just pride because I'd stayed. I wasn't any use, but I stayed.'

(pp. 246–7)

On the morning of his execution:

He felt only an immense disappointment because he had to go to God empty-handed, with nothing done at all . . . . . He knew now that at the end there was only one thing that counted – to be a saint.

(p. 264)

As *Murder in the Cathedral* had emphasised, the martyr has to do the right thing for the right reason. If a person were to say, 'I wish to be martyred so as to become a saint', that person would be expressing the sin of pride and would therefore not deserve to become a saint. Thomas, in the play, achieves the right combination of passivity and activity: inner submission to the will of God; a due humility. The more Greene's whisky-priest upbraids himself for his failings, the more he, too, expresses the virtue of humility. An immense irony invests his regret that 'he had to go to God empty-handed'. Althoough he does not know it, he has repeatedly changed people's lives for the better. Indeed, *The Power and the Glory* has an extensive covert plot on this theme.

A covert plot is one which is not seen by the reader as a coherent sequence at the first reading of the work. The reader sees elements of it, but not the entirety. Only at a second or subsequent reading is the plot-sequence likely to emerge as a clear, coordinated entity. A second reading of *The Power and the Glory* shows how the most seemingly disparate elements of the plot are coordinated by the changes for the better effected by the priest's presence. Tench, Luis, Coral Fellows, some of the villagers, Calver, even the lieutenant: all have been touched by grace.

At the outset, the priest meets Tench, who has long been separated from his wife and son. The priest enquires after them; and, when he has gone, Tench is moved to write to her to try to re-establish their relationship. In a deft irony, it is Tench who eventually inflicts the pains of dentistry on the police chief who approved the ruthless pursuit of the priest; the pains are protracted because the dentist watches the execution. A harsher irony is that when Tench's wife does reply, it is to offer him a divorce (she has been led astray by Buchmanites of the Oxford Group).

The realism of Greene's narrative is made the more persuasive by its lengthy contrastive 'quotations' from a work of Catholic propaganda or hagiography. A Catholic mother reads to her children the story of a recent martyr, Father Juan, who tended his flock but was captured and shot. The story she reads stresses *ad nauseam* the supposed virtues, the sweet saintly nature, of this priest. Understandably, her son, Luis, shows signs of rebellion against this indoctrination: he expresses boredom and scepticism. For him, a more convincing hero is the Marxist lieutenant: he is delighted to be allowed to touch the officer's revolver, and the lieutenant feels proud that he is winning young adherents. But, after meeting the whisky-priest, and after hearing of his execution, Luis turns in resentment against the officer, and spits on his revolver-butt. The novel ends as the boy kisses the hand of a new priest who clandestinely arrives to take the place of the martyr. We do not hear the new priest's name: it is the continuity of the sacred office that counts. We recall that just before the knock at the door from the newcomer, Luis had dreamt that the dead whisky-priest 'winked at him – an unmistakable flicker of the eyelid, just like that': a sign of complicity, a hint of resurrection, a glint of victory for the faith.

The death of the gangster, Calver, is finely rendered in sharp, ironic, and eventually moving detail. The priest leans over his 'stale and nauseating smell'; Calver's hand, struggling towards the shoulder-holster, stops at the heart, so that 'he imitated the prudish attitude of a female statue: one hand over the breast and one upon the stomach'; and eventually 'the whole body gave up the effort, the ghost, everything'. He has been used as the bait in the ambush; nevertheless, in his dying moments he tries to help the priest by offering him a knife. 'O merciful God, after all he was thinking of me', prays the priest; and, though he does so 'without conviction', a kind of altruism was there in Calver's action.

One irony of the situation is that Calver's victims include Coral Fellows, who had sheltered the priest. In addition to a large-scale covert plot concerning the priest's transformative power, there is a briefer covert plot concerning Coral's death. That death is never directly described. When the priest revisits the Fellows' homestead, he finds it deserted save for a broken-backed starving dog; a disaster has befallen the place. Near the end of the novel, we find that Coral's parents are on their way back to England; they try not to talk about her death, but the topic obtrudes; and chance references ('That scoundrel'; 'running away and leaving *her*'; 'It wasn't my fault. If you'd been at home . . . . .') enable us retrospectively to infer what has happened. While Captain Fellows was away from his homestead, Calver arrived there. Mrs Fellows, a depressive hypochondriac, always fearful of death, fled from the intruder. Coral, ever brave and responsible, tried to drive Calver away. We know that she had warded off the lieutenant long ago, threatening to set the dog on him; but on this occasion, it appears, Calver maimed the dog and shot Coral.

Coral's parents appear to have no religious belief; and she had said that she lost her faith 'at the age of ten'. She, however, had met both the lieutenant and the priest, and sided with the priest, taking him food and drink and resenting his persecution; it appears that he may have restored her faith. After her death, on the eve of his execution, the priest has a strange dream. In a cathedral, he feels detached from the Mass until Coral appears and fills his glass with wine ('She said, "I got it from my father's room" '); and the cleric and congregation then tap a message in Morse code which Coral interprets as 'News'. Evidently good news: the priest wakes 'with a huge feeling of hope'. Well, it's only a dream; but it hints that Coral, after death, has become an intermediary who can offer the priest a glimpse of his salvation to come. Perhaps, like Beatrice with Dante, she may guide this pilgrim heavenwards. The tragedy of the priest may be part of a new divine comedy.

One of Greene's later tales is 'The Last Word'. It describes a future era when atheistic totalitarianism has prevailed and the last Pope is kept alive only as a figure of scorn. Eventually, he is taken before the arch-dictator (a general) and shot. Yet, even as he pulls the trigger, the dictator reflects, '[I]s it possible that what this man believed may be true?', and we realise that the message of faith has, after all, been transmitted to posterity.

In *The Power and the Glory*, Greene has established an elegant dialectical contrast between the whisky-priest and the atheistic lieutenant. Both are idealists; both work hard for their ideals; both are concerned about the poor and the children. And both are ideologically opposed. The lieutenant is in some ways priest-like:

> There was something of a priest in his intent observant walk – a theologian going back over the errors of the past to destroy them again.
>   He reached his own lodging . . . . . In the light of a candle it looked as comfortless as a prison or a monastic cell.
>   . . . . . He was a mystic, too, and what he had experienced was vacancy – a complete certainty in the existence of a dying, cooling world, of human beings who had evolved from animals for no purpose at all. He knew.
>
> (p. 26)

During their meetings, some fellow-feeling is established. Eventually, experiencing increasing sympathy with and respect for the priest, the lieutenant seeks (illegally and unavailingly) to fetch a confessor for him: here the cowardice of Padre José, the married ex-priest, contrasts neatly with the courage of the whisky-priest. Next, the lieutenant brings him (again illegally) a bottle of brandy. 'You're a good man', the priest had told him earlier; 'You aren't a bad fellow', the lieutenant tells him now. After the execution, the officer finds that 'the dynamic love which used to move his trigger-finger felt flat and dead': perhaps that atheistic commitment will return; perhaps, like the general in 'The Last Word', the lieutenant has been inflected towards religious belief.

And many other people, whom the priest has helped, have been strengthened in their faith because of him: notably the people of his home village (with the striking exception, it seems, of his precociously depraved daughter) and perhaps some of his fellow-sufferers in jail. Even the Judas-figure grudgingly observes, 'You may be a saint for all I know', and seeks his blessing. The priest's execution takes place not, as is customary, in a public place (the cemetery), but in a private yard; for otherwise, we are told, 'There might have been a demonstration': a popular protest against the authorities.

Thus the narrative in which a representative of the Church is apparently defeated is one of covert victory for the faith. Abandonment has not, after all, been total. In Mexico, in Orizaba, Greene felt that 'it was like Galilee between the Crucifixion and the Resurrection' (*Lawless Roads*, p. 121). After Christ's crucifixion, the disciples felt abandoned on the journey to Emmaus; but Christ was present and accompanied them unrecognised. At the outset of Greene's *The Power and the Glory*, abandonment is repeatedly stressed. '[A] little additional pain was hardly noticeable in the huge abandonment', thinks Tench; 'the ship had kept to timetable: he was abandoned', thinks the priest. When Luis's parents consider the plight of the proscribed Church, his father says: 'We have been abandoned here'. Father José imagines that, to a watcher far away, this world 'would roll heavily in space under its fog like a burning and abandoned ship'; he envisages 'the whole abandoned star'. Sometimes the priest's own sense of abandonment brings to mind Christ's words on the cross: 'My God, my God, why hast thou forsaken me?' Greene, in his travels through those regions of Mexico where the Catholic Church had been prohibited, had experienced a sense of nightmarish vacancy; and he had recalled Newman's words about the 'aboriginal calamity' of a human race 'discarded' from God's presence. As *The Power and the Glory* unfolds, however, and as irony dovetails with irony, plot-detail with plot-detail, so the overt and covert plotting of the narrative imply a covert plot in the world; and that veiled master-plot is the divine ordinance whereby the apparent defeat of faith is merely a test for the faithful and the ground of new victories for divine grace.

If the priest is anonymous, so is his adversary, the lieutenant. Both have dialectically representative roles. Both are concerned with a world in which children must grow up. Jesus said: 'Suffer the little children to come unto me' (Mark 10: 14). This is the lieutenant's feeling, too.

> [I]t was for these he was fighting. He would eliminate from their childhood everything which had made him miserable, all that was poor, superstitious and corrupt . . . . . He was quite prepared to make a massacre for their sakes.
>
> (p. 69)

The priest considers the bad example he is setting the young:

> [H]e was the only priest the children could remember. It was

> from him they would take their ideas of the faith. But it was
> from him too they took God – in their mouths . . . . . Wasn't it
> his duty to stay . . . . . even if they were corrupted by his
> example?

> (pp. 80–1)

Children, present or absent, living or dead, abound in the novel:
Tench's dead son; the girl on the steamer; the boy who detains
the priest; Luis and his sisters; the children of the priest's village,
including his apparently corrupt daughter; Coral Fellows; the
Indian woman's three-year-old boy; a dying eleven-year-old girl
who supposedly saw Christ. In a dream, the priest sees a small
girl amid a group of Children of Mary, and feels that there is a
threat to her. Looking down at Brigitta, the lieutenant says: 'This
child is worth more than the Pope in Rome.'

By his detailed depiction of numerous children, Greene gives
substance to the thematic discussion of the needs and the
futurity of the younger generation; to the ideological battle for
hearts and minds. The lieutenant tries to make a better secular
world for children *now*; the priest predictably stresses a better
afterlife, offering this consolation to the poor villagers:

> 'The police watching you, the soldiers gathering taxes, the
> beating you always get from the jefe because you are too poor
> to pay, smallpox and fever, hunger . . . that is all part of
> heaven – the preparation. Perhaps without them, who can tell,
> you wouldn't enjoy heaven so much . . . . . Your children do
> not die in heaven.'

> (p. 86)

Both the secular state and the Catholic Church have their modes
of corruption; the priest and the lieutenant are, it seems,
dedicated exceptions to a general rule. Their values overlap and
are not totally opposed; but the plotting, partly by winning our
sympathies for an underdog, and partly by its hints of an
afterlife, tilts the balance in favour of the priest. He intermittently resembles Christ; but, if he is a saint in the making, at
least he is a scruffy and semi-alcoholic saint who, while a
prisoner, retches as he empties pails of urine and excrement into
a cesspool.

Preaching to the converted?

The large sales of *The Power and the Glory*, the high critical praise
accorded it, and (in the experience of teachers) the responses of

students from a variety of religious and irreligious backgrounds, show that *The Power and the Glory* has a remarkably wide appeal: it seems to be enjoyed almost as much by sceptics as by believers.

One reason for this is that Greene pre-empts the sceptic: he lets the lieutenant and others voice familiar hostile arguments (e.g. that priests line their own pockets while promising pie in the sky to the poor). The Lehrs criticise the priest from a Lutheran standpoint. Some Catholics (Luis's mother, María and a woman in jail) criticise him for being a disgrace to the faith. He himself is his own severest critic, noting his own pride, lust and cowardice; and he also comments bitterly on prosperous, complacent areas of the Church's hierarchy: he has known them at first hand. In addition, the priest moves among the poorest of the poor, sharing their squalor and wretchedness. Stinking, rotten-teethed, avid for brandy, he makes a credibly, flawed and sympathetic victim.

Thus an atheistic reader might as readily suspend disbelief in the religious premises of this text as when reading, say, Donne's or Hopkins's religious sonnets. Even a relatively inflexible atheist could still read the novel as a poignant study of a priest's delusion; though this would be a peculiarly self-denying ordinance, since it would entail a failure to relish numerous textual ironies. Just as we make 'historical allowances' for changes in style and vocabulary in the course of time, so we, often without realising it, make similar allowances for changes in value and ideology. In any case, atheism (like Catholicism) is based on empirically unverifiable metaphysical premises.

Another reason for the appeal of *The Power and the Glory* is that although the territory traversed is Greeneland, it is now a Greeneland within which there is scope for sympathy, compassion, and even joy. Since his hero must express the Christian virtues of love, charity and compassion, Greene has to mitigate that near-Manichæan harshness of rendition of the world which, in such earlier texts as *Stamboul Train* and *Brighton Rock*, came all too easily to his depressive imagination. If young Brigitta exudes depravity, there is a balance in the depiction of Coral. 'Hate was just a failure of imagination', reflects the priest; the novel works hard to encourage an extension of imagination. The wretchedness of the villagers in the forest; the squalor of the prisoners in the jail; the mourning of the Indian woman with her murdered child: all these are evoked by an eye which seeks to discriminate and understand, rather than to glare with fascinated disgust and contempt.

Technique

As we would expect, the Mexican setting is rendered with superb descriptive richness and resourcefulness; Greene's Mexican journey has provided him with a wealth of specific detail, tellingly incorporated. The integration of plot with setting is admirable. In other works by Greene, a flaw often lay in the plot-structure; here, partly because of the basic simplicity of the pursuit format, the plot unfolds with a logic that seems to stem fully from the situation and the characterisation rather than from imposed coincidences or interventions. *The Power and the Glory* gives an impression of deftly contrasted and coordinated scenes, all contributing, with gathering momentum, to the dénouement. The style is richly and lucidly effective. For example, contrasted with the conventional noble martyrdom of Father Juan (described in the propagandist clichés of the Catholic booklet) is the realism of the whisky-priest's execution as observed by Tench:

> A small man came out of a side door: he was held up by two policemen, but you could tell that he was doing his best – it was only that his legs were not fully under his control. They paddled him across to the opposite wall . . . . .
> He was trying to say something: what was the phrase they were always supposed to use? That was routine too, but perhaps his mouth was too dry, because nothing came out except a word that sounded more like 'Excuse'. The crash of the rifles shook Mr. Tench: they seemed to vibrate inside his own guts: he felt rather sick and shut his eyes.

> (p. 273)

Realistic, vivid, lucid and poignant. By such means, Greene's novel becomes not 'a Catholic novel' but a catholic novel, 'catholic' meaning 'comprehensive, relevant to all people'. It becomes a commentary on the inhumanity of man to man, on the price in human terms exacted by ideological abstractions, and on the cruelty that perennially results from the failure of the sympathetic imagination.

Collaborative excellence: the film, The Third Man

The film, *The Third Man*, was an immense success with critics and with the general public when it appeared in 1949. It has endured well; sometimes it is shown again in 'art cinemas' or on television, and a video has been issued. Those of us who saw it when it first appeared will recall its exceptional power and originality among films of that time. Greene's tale 'The Third Man', its basis, is a proficient thriller, but the film is a screen classic, and numerous people contributed to its success: Greene as writer, the producers, the director, the actors major and minor. The cast was dominated by Orson Welles, for whom the role of Harry Lime, the charismatic villain, was ideal. Joseph Cotten, Welles's acting partner since the Mercury Theatre days (he had appeared with Welles in *Citizen Kane* and *The Magnificent Ambersons*) played Holly Martins; Alida Valli was Lime's lover, Anna; Trevor Howard the British officer. A crucial contributor at the outset was Sir Alexander Korda, head of London Films (the distributor), who in the past had been derided by Greene. He and David O. Selznick were the main backers. The director was Carol Reed, who had successfully directed the adaptation of Greene's 'The Basement Room'. At this time, Reed was at the peak of his powers as an imaginative and technically daring film-maker; he had learnt lessons from Orson Welles's work, particularly *Citizen Kane*, and had won prizes at Cannes for *An Outcast of the Islands* and *The Fallen Idol*. Welles himself contributed some memorably cynical dialogue:

> 'In Italy for thirty years under the Borgias, they had murder, warfare, terror, bloodshed; but they produced Michelangelo, Leonardo da Vinci and the Renaissance. In Switzerland they had brotherly love, five hundred years of democracy and peace, and what did that produce? The cuckoo-clock.'

Greene says that the story began as a single paragraph about the apparent resurrection of a man thought dead and buried. Korda wanted a film dealing with the post-war occupation of Vienna, which was controlled by a combination of British, French, American and Russian military authorities. Greene then prepared a story, which eventually appeared in the volume *'The Third Man' and 'The Fallen Idol'*. Numerous changes were introduced during discussions between Reed and Greene. The author remarks: 'The film, in fact, is better than the story because it is in this case the finished state of the story.'

In the original version, Rollo Martins seeks to unravel the mystery of the apparent death of Harry Lime in Vienna; both men are English; their friendship began twenty years previously, at school. Martins gradually discovers that Lime has faked his death to elude pursuit by the British authorities; he also learns that Lime is a racketeer who, by selling adulterated penicillin,

Joseph Cotten and Orson Welles in The Third Man

has caused death and insanity among hospital patients, many of them children. Reluctantly, Martins agrees to help the British forces capture Lime; there is a pursuit, and Martins shoots and kills his former friend. In the meantime, he has fallen in love with Lime's mistress, Anna. She remains, for a while, resolutely loyal to Lime; but, at the end of the story, she is seen arm-in-arm with Martins.

So, although the setting of the tale was contemporaneous (occupied Vienna in the aftermath of war), the basis of the plot would have been familiar to Greene's readers. For example, as in *The Man Within,* a close friendship between two males culminates in betrayal and death; as in *Rumour at Nightfall,* after the death of one of the friends, the loving woman turns to the survivor; as in *England Made Me,* the moral justification of treachery to an associate is compromised by desire for the friend's mistress.

Under contractual arrangements with David Selznick, Joseph Cotten and Alida Valli had to be signed as stars. Welles was recruited. Thus the two central male characters became American instead of English (which would make the film more marketable in the USA). A residual sign of the original story is that Lime uses, oddly, the patronising English public-school term 'old boy' when addressing Martins. Cotten, as we have seen, insisted that Martins's first name be changed from Rollo, 'which to his American ear apparently involved homosexuality'; so it became Holly. In California, Selznick had declared 'It's just buggery, boys', on reading the script: in his crude way he had registered the fact that Martins's hero-worshipping attitude to Lime is a form of love-relationship. (A homophile theme ran through various works by Greene and would eventually, in *The Return of A. J. Raffles*, be turned into farcical comedy.) Since the main characters were now clearly from the USA, a Rumanian character was substituted for Cooler, an American in the original version.

The film added more action (in the form of chases) to the plot, enlarged the role of Anna Schmidt, and made Martins's reluctance to betray Lime more protracted. Visually, Reed's stylish direction constantly accentuated both the drama and the ironies of the original. One poignant irony of the tale had been the contrast between the legendary Vienna of fame and song and the devastated, bleak, gutted Vienna in the aftermath of war. Vienna, traditionally, evokes images of the hedonistic capital, culturally rich, the city of crowded ballrooms, elegant dancers, the waltz music of Strauss; of ornate and opulent high civilisation. In the tale, the city, having been battered and devastated by the wartime bombing, is now a cold, blighted location of rationing, shortages, austerity, black-marketeering; it is patrolled by the military forces of the four occupying nations. The film immensely augmented this irony of devastated Vienna: shot after shot showed ruins, gutted buildings, heaps of rubble; it made a powerful commentary on war, and particularly on the indiscriminate havoc wreaked by modern warfare. It also accentuated the irony of the charismatic villain. In one way, Lime's corruption was given some vindication by the setting. If he regards humans as dispensable, all around is evidence of the brutal manner in which war has dispensed with them. In another way, his corruption is condemned by the setting, for he operates in a city whose destruction testifies to the cataclysmic evil of a historic charismatic villain, Adolf Hitler.

In personality and acting style, Welles was ideal for the role of Lime. He readily conveyed an engaging boyish charm, a sophisticated *bonhomie*, a debonair corruption, a ruthless egotism. In one scene, he takes Martins on a ride in the Great Wheel in the barren fairground, where he both threatens his old friend and tempts him with a share in his racket. Looking down on diminished people far below, he says:

'Would you really feel any pity if one of those dots stopped moving – for ever? If I offered you twenty thousand pounds

191

for every dot that stops, would you really, old man, tell me to keep my money? Or would you calculate how many dots you could afford to spare? Free of income tax, old man.'

It's a debased modern counterpart of the biblical temptation-scene (Matthew 4: 8–9) in which Satan takes Christ to a mountain-top and offers him power over the world. Lime argues that as governments treat the governed with contempt, so he in turn does so: he follows his own 'Five-Year Plan'.

The tale's scenic locations in wintry Vienna had included the vast cemetery (the setting at the opening and the close); the fair-ground wheel; and the sewers through which Lime flees and where, appropriately, he dies. The film version gave striking memorability to these locations. The chase through the vast sewers of Vienna was exuberantly directed: the echoing shouts and voices, the tunnels of the bewildering subterranean labyrinth, dark shadows and sudden floodlights, the cascades of water from higher levels into the noisy torrent of the central river: all these were sharply evoked. Eventually, as the wounded Lime is trapped, his fingers reach unavailingly up towards freedom through the pattern of a manhole cover; seen from above ground, his fingers implore the air like short-lived delicate tendrils.

Reed's direction gave, for the time, an exceptionally realistic air to the film. Numerous shots were clearly taken on the spot, in ravaged Vienna: there was an unusually high ratio of location scenes to staged interior scenes. Authenticity was increased by a readiness to let denizens of Vienna speak German, instead of the inflected English normally used by foreign characters in British films. The sense of ominous drama was heightened by the nervous shifts in camera-angles, now looking down from an immense height, now moving at gutter-level; now focusing microscopically on a telling detail of facial expression, now taking in a panorama of ruined buildings and empty streets. From the expressionist cinema, Reed had learnt to use, intermittently, a canted camera, giving a disorientating tilt to the scene filmed; other scenes were strikingly framed. Imaginative, fluent and deft, the direction constantly accentuated, and often surpassed, the dramatic qualities of the original.

In *'The Third Man' and 'The Fallen Idol'* (1950, p. 5), Greene said: 'One of the very few major disputes between Carol Reed and myself concerned the ending, and he has been proved triumphantly right.' In the tale, the narrator, the British officer, observes Martins leaving Lime's funeral:

I watched him striding off on his overgrown legs after the girl. He caught her up and they walked side by side. I don't think he said a word to her: it was like the end of a story except that before they turned out of my sight her hand was through his arm . . . . .

(*'The Third Man' and 'The Fallen Idol'*, p. 141)

Instead of this rather conventional romantic ending, the film offered a closing shot which became famed in the annals of cinema for visual daring and for its ruthless defiance of cinematic convention. The screen shows a monotonous vista, a symmetrical perspective: a long straight road diminishing away from us, lined with lopped trees from which a few leaves drift. In the far distance is Anna, a small solitary figure walking towards the camera. Martins waits for her, leaning on a cart in the left middle distance. (There is characteristically ambiguous background music by Anton Karas's zither, a bittersweet melody.) Slowly, steadily, without hesitation, without glancing at the man, Anna walks down this immense dreary vista towards us; eventually, she simply walks offscreen to the right of the camera. The camera remains unmoved: Martins lights a cigarette and throws away the match; he remains a small figure in the long avenue of trees. A few leaves drift down. The film ends. In this hypnotically static camera-shot in which the individuals were perfectly framed and diminished by the roadway and the trees, Reed expressed an elegant revolt against the tyranny of the conventional happy ending, the tyranny of the last-scene embrace of hero and heroine. This woman, for once, would shun the man's tacit offer. The bleakness of the final stress on isolation was partly offset and partly compounded by the unflinching aestheticism of that long, steady camera-shot. It was compounded by the immobile perspective; it was offset by the formal beauty of patterning.

Inevitably, time has exposed some flaws in the film. The lighting of one or two of the nocturnal scenes now appears too theatrical; shadows loom too large. The zither-playing, which on the whole is admirably appropriate, sometimes provides too exclamatory an accompaniment to the drama. Anna's confrontation with Martins at the railway station (which had no counterpart in the tale) seems contrivedly melodramatic. Nevertheless, the film was a landmark in British film-making; the intelligent intensity of the direction and the exuberantly bold camera-work makes so many subsequent films seem relatively flaccid and inert in method. Here some of Greene's major themes and preoccupations found brilliant cinematic expression.

These included: the blighted setting – a world rendered hellish, largely by human agency; man's inhumanity to man; the devious interaction of loyalty and treachery; charismatic corruption – the appeal and the destructive force of dedicated villainy; the interaction of the political and the personal; the loneliness of the uprooted; the price exacted in human terms by international and ideological confict. And they included some traditionally exciting plot-stuff: the mystery of a figure who seems to have risen from the dead; the hero who knowingly enters ambush; the pursuit and the hunting-down of a figure seen as poignant in defeat. Greene said that the chase through the sewers might have derived from Rider Haggard: Allan Quatermain's entry to the city of Milosis through the underground river. Another association, as we have noted, is Conradian: the 'river of darkness' whereby Marlow encounters Kurtz. Like Conrad, Greene sought to reconcile the claims of narrative excitement with those of thematic complexity. With the help of Korda and Selznick, of Welles and the other actors, and, above all, of Carol Reed, the film of *The Third Man* brought the drama and the atmosphere of Greeneland before a huge public, interlocking (with fine visual imagery and sensitive acting) the romantic and the realistic, the perennial and the historically topical.

9 Conclusion: Greene's place in literary history

Greene did not claim to stand in the first rank of authors; he recognised the superiority of (for instance) Conrad and James. He could not rival Conrad's Olympian wisdom, his beauty of description, or his searching technical innovations. He lacked James's civilised delicacies and elaborate subtleties. Nevertheless, Greene's range was immense, and he succeeded in gaining both critical acclaim and a vast international readership. He produced novels, tales, plays, poems, film-scripts, critical and political essays, autobiographical works, travel books, biographical studies. They vary greatly in quality. Some of his works were slight or casual; others are intense, complex, and seem likely to endure. He could combine the grippingly readable and the revealingly intelligent. He is one of those writers who offer a distinctive vision or world-view: just as we speak of the Dickensian world or the Kafkaesque, so Greeneland is his characteristic imaginative terrain. Of course, as we have seen, he could be an astute critic of Greeneland, too. The dark vision of the earlier works gives way to the comedy of many later ones, just as the intensely religious preoccupation of some of his most famous novels gives way to works more secular or sceptical in basis.

In those writings, which spanned seventy years, he became one of the finest literary commentators on religious, cultural and political tensions in the twentieth century. He offered searching analyses of the tensions between the religious and the secular outlooks, and between political commitment and political scepticism. Paradoxes preoccupied him: the paradox of the sanctified sinner, for example; the concept of faith without belief; the knowledge of loyalty which entails treachery; the possible reconciliation of communism with Catholicism.

His works portray the stresses of modern life in numerous geographical regions: Europe, Africa, Asia, Central and South America. He was a literary citizen of the world, seeking to build imaginative bridges between continents. He displayed energy and courage in his quests. Certainly there were flaws in his judgement: we have noted the anti-Semitism of various early works, his glamorisation of some modes of corruption, his marked animosity towards North American influences, and an inclination to hero-worship which led him to flatter some dictators. Whether as an adulterer, as a practical joker, or as an agent of the SIS, Greene was experienced in modes of duplicity. As a patron of brothels, strip-clubs and opium-dens, he promoted the corruption he depicted. On the other hand, he repeatedly spoke up for the person or cause that seemed to be the underdog in a given situation; he displayed courage in opposing complacencies of orthodoxy, and a bold frankness in exposing the problems of belief and the stresses of sexual desire. In many respects, he was his own best critic: not only in his critical comments, often severe, on his writings and personal characteristics, but also implicitly, as a later work counter-balanced a bias in an earlier work, or as some of his later declared beliefs contradicted his earlier ones. In his life and his writings, he epitomised so many large-scale problems and divisions in twentieth-century culture and ideology.

Much of his fictional work is characterised by lucid intelligence, descriptive verve, and deftly perceptive analyses of characters and situations. The Brighton of *Brighton Rock*, the Mexico of *The Power and the Glory*, the Congo of *A Burnt-Out Case*, the Saigon of *The Quiet American*: he imprints them unforgettably on the imagination; and in each case he depicts vividly the downtrodden who suffer in a world of injustice and inequality. There are some traditional romantic qualities in his work: sympathy for the rebel or outcast, distrust of the mind-forg'd manacles, and scorn directed towards the materially successful and dominative. There is romanticism, too, in his depictions of the sometimes-fatal intensities of sexual love. So much of his darker writing is impelled by the romantic sense of the lost Eden; by the appalled yet fascinated recognition that the world has repeatedly been sullied and blighted by erring and egoistic humans. Again, he portrays with knowledgeable sympathy such individuals as Czinner in *Stamboul Train* or Dr Colin in *A Burnt-Out Case*, who strive, against heavy odds, to make the world a better place.

Greene's work appeared in newspapers and magazines, on radio and television, in the theatre and the cinema. He was an astute publicist, a resourceful entertainer and an indefatigable moral historian. One of his greatest positive qualities was the exploratory energy implicit partly in his travels, partly in that love of literature which he conveyed so well in critical essays, and partly in the love of language which irradiates his best novels and tales. The distinctive linguistic intelligence and humane sensitivity which characterise so much of his work, and which are most fully evident in *The Power and the Glory*, should ensure that Graham Greene's wide and appreciative readership will endure for many years to come.

Part Three
Reference Section

Gazetteer

Most of the areas in which Greene travelled are mentioned in the autobiographical volumes, *A Sort of Life*, *Ways of Escape* and *Reflections*. Paul Hogarth's book, *Graham Greene Country*, offers pictures of (and comments on) various regions.

AMSTERDAM. The setting of an adulterous liaison in *The Complaisant Lover*.

ANTIBES. The coastal resort in the South of France where Greene lived in his later years; the setting of 'May We Borrow Your Husband?', 'Beauty' and 'Chagrin in Three Parts'.

ARGENTINA. The region around Posadas (northern Corrientes), on the fluvial border with Paraguay, is the location of *The Honorary Consul*.

BELFAST. Wartime Belfast is described in 'Convoy to West Africa'; Greene's encounter there with the hostile housekeeper of a 'nice young priest' provided material for Act II, scene ii, of *The Potting Shed*.

BERKHAMSTED (Hertfordshire). This is where the young Greene lived. Its canal, railway bridge, common and remnants of a castle appear in numerous works, including *It's a Battlefield* (Chap. 4), 'The Innocent', 'The Other Side of the Border', 'Doctor Crombie', *The Human Factor* and *The Captain and the Enemy*.

BRIGHTON. 'No city before the war, not London, Paris or Oxford, had such a hold on my affections' (*WE*, p. 78). This colourful town is seen not only in *Brighton Rock* but also in *Travels with My Aunt*, and is recalled in *Carving a Statue*. Many of the features that Greene mentions (such as the Clock Tower, the Palace Pier, the Royal Albion Hotel, the gardens of Old Steine) remain. Dr Brighton's pub (the Star and Garter) has, sadly, been modernised, but the Cricketers (on the edge of the Lanes) has so far retained its Edwardian character, recalled fondly by Greene. The annual Brighton Festival sometimes includes conducted tours entitled 'Graham Greene's Brighton'.

CAPRI. Greene owned the Villa Rosaio in Anacapri, and numerous characters of Capri are described in the memoirs of Dottoressa Elizabeth Moor (*An Impossible Woman*), which Greene edited. She was one of the sources of Aunt Augusta in *Travels with My Aunt*. The veteran author and paedophile, Norman Douglas, was another of Greene's friends there; he and Capri are affectionately commemorated in the essay 'Norman Douglas', which says: 'Nepenthe [in Douglas's *South Wind*] had not been Capri, but Capri over half a century has striven with occasional success to be Nepenthe' (*CE*, p. 363). Eventually Greene was made an honorary citizen of Anacapri.

CHIPPING CAMPDEN. The market town in rural Gloucestershire where Graham and Vivien lived in the early years of their marriage. Its characters are described in 'Death in the Cotswolds' (*R*) and Chap. 11 of *A Sort of Life*.

CONGO. The Belgian Congo is the setting of his 'Congo Journal' and *A Burnt-Out Case*. In 1959 he spent a few weeks at the *léproserie* at Yonda: 'A garden city of 800 patients[;] . . . . . all here are contagious cases' (*IS*, p. 16). His diligent research informs the account of the leper colony in *A Burnt-Out Case*.

CUBA. *Our Man in Havana* is set in the Batista era and depicts Cuba as a police state mitigated by decadent, sleazy entertainments. 'The Marxist Heretic' (in *Collected Essays*), 'Return to Cuba' and 'Shadow and Sunlight in Cuba' (both in *Reflections*) offer predominantly flattering accounts of Fidel Castro and his Marxist dictatorship.

DUBLIN. 'Impressions of Dublin' (*R*) describes the atmosphere of the city in 1923, in the aftermath of the Civil War.

HAITI. Greene visited Haiti in 1963. The hideously tyrannical regime of Dr Duvalier is reported in Chap. 8 of *Ways of Escape* and in 'Papa Doc' (*R*), and is depicted in *The Comedians*. Duvalier's 'Department of Foreign Affairs' responded with the pamphlet *Graham Greene démasqué*, which accuses Greene of sadism and 'negrophobia'. (See *WE*, Chap. 8.)

JAMAICA, particularly Kingston: the location of 'Cheap in August'.

KENYA. Greene toured Kenya during the Mau Mau insurgency, a tense time recalled in the tale 'Church Militant' and in *Ways of*

Escape, Chap. 6. 'British justice was not a sufficient gift to the Kikuyu people to win them for the future.'

LEWES and the South Downs of Sussex. Described evocatively in 'A Walk on the Sussex Downs' (*R*, pp. 17–18) and *The Man Within.*

LIBERIA. The African country traversed by Graham and Barbara Greene. Their ordeals are described in his *Journey without Maps* and her *Land Benighted.* It provides the location of 'A Chance for Mr Lever'.

LONDON. Greene's employment by Gabbitas & Thring of Sackville Street and subsequently by *The Times* is remembered in *A Sort of Life*, Chaps 9 and 10. 'In *It's a Battlefield* the Assistant Commissioner's journey from Piccadilly to Wormwood Scrubs had to be followed street by street', recalled Greene. That novel provides many sharp cameos of London districts in the early 1930s. Greene knew intimately the pubs and clubs round Tottenham Court Road and Soho: they are cited and recalled in numerous works (even in 'The Third Man'). The Gower Street area, where he was a warden in the Blitz and worked for the Ministry of Information, is recalled in 'Men at Work', *The Ministry of Fear* and *The End of the Affair.* His journal of the Blitz is quoted in *Ways of Escape*, Chap. 4. Clapham Common, where his Queen Anne house at 14 North Side was bombed, features in *The Ministry of Fear, The End of the Affair* and, obliquely, in 'The Destructors'. Belgravia, with its imposing houses, square and plane trees, is the setting of 'The Basement Room' (and therefore of the film *The Fallen Idol* and the tale 'The Fallen Idol'). In *Journey without Maps*, Kensington Gardens is the location of an encounter with a perverted Old Etonian. 'A Little Place off the Edgware Road' is a horror story. Piccadilly is the location of 'Jubilee'. Albany (once the residence of Lord Melbourne in Piccadilly) is a setting of *The Return of A. J. Raffles.* In the 1950s Greene rented a flat in Albany and once smoked opium there with Catherine Walston. Previously he had rented a flat at 5, St James's Street, next to hers at number 6.

MALAYA. Greene's experiences during the emergency there are described in *Ways of Escape*, Chap. 6.

MEXICO. The border crossing on the Rio Grande (Laredo, Texas, and Nuevo Laredo, Mexico) is the setting of 'Across the Border'. Greene's journey through Tabasco and Chiapas is recorded in

The Lawless Roads and exploited in *The Power and the Glory*. The port of Frontera becomes 'Obregón' in the novel; the fictional capital is based on Villahermosa, humid capital of Tabasco. Veracruz is the location of 'The Lottery Ticket'.

MONTE CARLO. The appropriate setting of a novella of gambling, *Loser Takes All*. In 1955 Greene stayed at the Hôtel de Paris ('chargeable as an expense to my income tax') while pursuing research at the Casino.

MOSCOW. The bleak destination of Castle in *The Human Factor*. In Moscow in 1987, Greene declared to Mikhail Gorbachev: 'There is no longer a barrier between Roman Catholics and Communism' (*R*, p. 317).

NOTTINGHAM. Recalled in *Stamboul Train*, *A Gun for Sale* (as Nottwich), *The Confidential Agent*, *The Potting Shed* and Chap. 9 of *A Sort of Life*.

OXFORD. See 'Harkaway's Oxford', 'Anthony à Wood' and 'Inside Oxford' (*CE*). Greene's college, Balliol, is the location of *The Great Jowett* and appears in 'When Greek Meets Greek'.

PANAMA. Greene's involvement in Panamanian politics and, particularly, his friendship with General Torrijos and his henchman Chuchu are described in 'The Country with Five Frontiers' and *Getting to Know the General*. Panama is the setting of the second half of *The Captain and the Enemy*.

PARAGUAY. Discussed in 'The Worm inside the Lotus Blossom' (*R*). Asunción and its locality feature in *Travels with My Aunt* and *The Honorary Consul*.

PARIS. The tale 'Brother' is set in the Faubourg du Temple; 'Strike in Paris' (1934, *R*) reports the background. 'Two Gentle People' opens in the Parc Monceau.

PEACEHAVEN. In the 1930s this was a dreary, largely unfinished township (begun in 1922), mainly of cheap bungalows arranged on a grid pattern, speculatively built on a windswept coastal plateau north of the cliffs between Brighton and Newhaven. The location mocks the haven of divine peace invoked by '*dona nobis pacem*'. In *Brighton Rock*, after driving there with Rose, Pinkie leaps to his death at Telscombe Cliffs, contiguously to the west of Peacehaven.

SIERRA LEONE. Greene visited Freetown in 1935 and worked there as an agent for MI6 during the Second World War. His 'brighter schemes' for collecting information included 'a brothel to be opened in Bissau for visitors from Senegal'. His house there, evidently of a Greeneland design, was infested by rats, spiders, ants and flies; it backed on to an area of scrub-land used as a public lavatory. Freetown is the setting of *The Heart of the Matter* and features in 'The Other Side of the Border' and, briefly, in 'Convoy to West Africa'. His return at Christmas 1967 is described in 'The Soupsweet Land' (*CE*): 'I felt the guilt of a beach-comber *manqué*: I had failed at failure.'

SPAIN. *Rumour at Nightfall* is set in Spain in the late nineteenth century, but Greene said: 'I knew next to nothing of Spain where the story takes place (at sixteen I had spent one day between Vigo and Coruña)' (*WE*, p. 19). The Spanish Civil War provides the political background to *The Confidential Agent*.

STOCKHOLM. Greene visited Stockholm with his brother Hugh in 1933 to research *England Made Me*. The young woman who slapped his face by the lakeside there was transformed into Loo, the tourist from Coventry who slaps Anthony Farrant. Between 1955 and 1959, Greene was a lover of the Swedish actress Anita Björk, and bought a house for her near Stockholm.

TRIER. This ancient city on the Mosel River on the western border of Germany is the birthplace of Karl Marx and the location of *The Name of Action*.

VIENNA. The city in the late 1940s, devastated by war, is the setting of *The Third Man*.

VIETNAM. In the 1950s Greene made several tours of this war-torn land: they are described in *Ways of Escape*, Chap. 6, and in *Reflections*, pp. 160–88. The fictional outcome was *The Quiet American*. Greene's interview with Ho Chi Minh in Hanoi is reported in 'The Man as Pure as Lucifer' (*CE*, pp. 402–4). Under communist rule, Saigon, now Ho Chi Minh City, has lost its brothels and opium-dens; the French perfumeries on the leafy rue Catinat have been replaced by jewellery shops; the Roman Catholic cathedral at the top of the street is still a 'hideous pink'. The Place Garnier (where the bomb explodes in *The Quiet American*) now, as Lam Son Square, houses the building of the People's Committee, a fast-food shop called Planet Saigon, and the Queen Bee Karaoke Restaurant. Fowler might be disappointed.

Biographical list

ANITA BJÖRK (born 1923). Swedish actress, acclaimed for her role as the vivaciously seductive heroine in the film of *Miss Julie* (1951), directed by Alf Sjöberg. After her husband's suicide, Greene was her lover in the 1950s.

MARJORIE BOWEN (pseudonym of G. M. V. Campbell, 1886–1952). Prolific writer of historical novels and children's stories. In 'The Lost Childhood', Greene claims that when (around the age of fourteen) he read her novel *The Viper of Milan* (1906), it inspired him to become a fiction-writer. 'It was as if I had been supplied once and for all with a subject.' This story of double treachery taught him that 'human nature is not black and white but black and grey'; and its echoes can be found extensively in Greene's work. The betrayed betrayer is a recurrent character. (Eventually, *Travels with My Aunt* would jocularly feature a character called Visconti, described as a 'viper'.)

ROBERT BROWNING (1812–89). Greene admired his poetry, particularly its portrayals of devious, ruthless, ambiguous and sensual characters. 'Bishop Blougram's Apology' contains a passage about 'the dangerous edge' (commending duplicity and ambiguity) which, Greene said, could serve as the epigraph for all his novels, and offers the notion that 'faith means perpetual unbelief'.

LIONEL CARTER (1904–71). Greene, tormented by Carter at Berkhamsted School, associated him with Visconti in *The Viper of Milan*, 'with his beauty, his patience, and his genius for evil'. (See 'The Lost Childhood'.) The schoolday tormentor is fictionalised as 'Webber' in 'Prologue to Pilgrimage': see *Life* I, pp. 74–81.

FIDEL CASTRO (born 1926). Marxist dictator of Cuba who gained power in 1959 by overthrowing the corrupt regime of Fulgencio Batista. Greene met and admired him: see 'The Marxist Heretic' (*CE*), and 'Lines on the Liberation of Cuba', 'Return to Cuba' and 'Shadow and Sunlight in Cuba' (*R*).

YVONNE CLOETTA (born *c.* 1930). A married Frenchwoman who became Greene's lover (his 'Happy, Healthy Kitten') during the last thirty years of his life, particularly during his residence at Antibes. *Travels with My Aunt* is dedicated to 'H. H. K.'. He wrote *J'Accuse* in defence of her daughter, Martine.

CLAUD COCKBURN (1904–88). Friend of Greene's at Berkhamsted and Oxford. The two men went begging, disguised as organ-grinders, and later visited the Rhineland. See Greene's 'Barrel-organing' (*R*) and *A Sort of Life*, pp. 136–41. Cockburn became a communist, worked for the Spanish Republicans' counter-espionage agency, edited *The Week* (1933–46), was a correspondent for the *Daily Worker* (1935–46) and a contributor to the *New Statesman*. He also gained fame as a humorous writer for *Punch* and *Private Eye*.

JOSEPH CONRAD (1857–1924). Polish-born seaman who, having settled in England, became an acclaimed writer of novels, tales and essays (though he was less successful as a playwright). Greene greatly admired and frequently cited him, though he felt that some Conradian works (particularly *The Arrow of Gold*) had influenced adversely his own earliest writings. *It's a Battlefield* is extensively indebted to *The Secret Agent*. Like Conrad, Greene took popular forms of fiction and gave them new subtlety and intensity. See 'Congo Journal' (*IS*); *Ways of Escape*, Chap 1; 'Remembering Mr. Jones' and 'The Domestic Background' (*Collected Essays*); and the citations in *Reflections*. In 1937, echoing Conrad's 'A Familiar Preface', Greene wrote (*R*, p. 67): 'The poetic cinema . . . . . can be built up on a few very simple ideas, as simple as the ideas behind the poetic fictions of Conrad: the love of peace, of country, a feeling for fidelity . . . . .'

R. B. CUNNINGHAME GRAHAM (1852–1936). Aristocratic Scottish traveller, adventurer, pioneer socialist and Scottish Nationalist; author of numerous tales, essays, biographies and histories. Greene met him in 1929 and 1933; both men were published by Heinemann. In *Reflections*, Greene recalls Cunninghame Graham's *A Vanished Arcadia*, which deals sympathetically with the Jesuit missions in Paraguay (claiming that they represented a primitive form of communism). The whisky-priest of *The Power and the Glory* may be a relative of the tobacco-priest in Cunninghame Graham's tale 'A Jesuit'. His sympathy with the underdog led Cunninghame Graham not only to vigorous championship of left-wing and nationalist causes but also to defend some activities of Roman Catholics. His adventurous life has various affinities with Greene's.

J. W. DUNNE (1875–1949). Aircraft designer and author of the widely read *An Experiment with Time* (1927) and *The Serial Universe* (1934). His theories of precognitive dreams and temporal overlaps influenced various writers, notably John Buchan and J. B. Priestley. Greene endorsed Dunne's ideas and was encouraged by them not only to note his own apparently precognitive experiences but also to incorporate prophetic dreams in his novels. *The Bear Fell Free* is strongly influenced by the theory of serial time.

T. S. ELIOT (1888–1965). His poems considerably influenced Greene's writings: *The Waste Land* showed how glimpses of Heaven, Hell and Purgatory might intersect a debased modern world; 'The Hollow Men' provided an apt epigraph to *The Name of Action*; and the essay 'Baudelaire' epitomised some of Greene's most paradoxical preoccupations. (The novelist met Eliot several times.)

FORD MADOX FORD (previously Ford Madox Hueffer; 1873–1939). A Roman Catholic, he collaborated wtih Conrad on *The Inheritors* and *Romance*. His own novels, particularly *The Good Soldier*, were highly regarded by Greene, who arranged for Bodley Head to reprint a series of them. The essay 'Ford Madox Ford' is a warmly appreciative review of the man and his works: Greene said that Ford was 'the best literary editor England has ever had'. Ford praised *It's a Battlefield* at a time when Greene needed encouragement.

DOROTHY GLOVER (pen-names 'Dorothy Craigie' and 'David Craigie'; 1901–71). Greene's lover from the late 1930s until the mid-1940s; in letters he referred to her as 'M. G.' ('My Girl'). She illustrated his four books for children, and with him she amassed the collection catalogued as *Victorian Detective Fiction* (1966). During the Blitz, she worked as a fire-warden alongside Greene (see *WE*, Chap. 4) and he shared her flat at Gower Mews, which features in *The Confidential Agent*.

BARBARA GREENE (later Countess Strachwitz; 1907–91). A cousin of Graham Greene's who accompanied him on the arduous tour of Liberia in 1935, described in her book *Land Benighted* (1938).

CHARLES HENRY GREENE (1865–1942). Graham's father. He joined Berkhamsted School as assistant master in 1889, became second master in 1896 and was headmaster from 1910 to 1927, after which he retired to Crowborough. He married Marion Raymond (a cousin), daughter of the Reverend Carleton Greene, in 1895. See *The Old School*, final chapter, and *A Sort of Life*, Chaps 1–3.

ELISABETH GREENE (later Elisabeth Dennys; born 1914). Graham's younger sister. She joined the Secret Intelligence Service and married a colleague, Rodney Dennys, who held various important posts in that service. In 1941 she recruited Graham as a full-time agent; he officially left MI6 in 1944, after gaining experience to be used in *The Heart of the Matter*, *Our Man in Havana* and *The Human Factor*.

HERBERT GREENE (1892–*c*.1960). Graham's oldest brother, 'the black sheep of the family'; engaged in espionage, was unsuccessful in various jobs, and became an alcoholic. A source of the 'Anthony Farrant' type of character in Graham Greene's novels.

SIR HUGH CARLETON GREENE (1910–87). Graham's younger brother. A journalist in the 1930s, he eventually became Director-General of the BBC. From 1971 to 1978 he was also Chairman of Greene, King and Sons, brewers of the excellent Abbot Ale; and, at the publishers The Bodley Head, he was Chairman from 1969 to 1981 and Honorary President from 1981 to 1987. He co-edited with Graham *The Spy's Bedside Book* (1957) and *Victorian Villainies* (1984).

SIR WILLIAM GRAHAM GREENE (1857–1950). Graham's uncle. He served the Admiralty for thirty-six years (being Permanent Secretary from 1911 to 1917) and helped to establish the Naval Intelligence service. His home was Harston House in Cambridgeshire, a location used repeatedly in Greene's novels and tales, notably *The Ministry of Fear* and 'Under the Garden' (a tale in which Sir William's gardener, Ernest Northrop, makes a brief appearance).

VIVIEN GREENE (Vivienne Dayrell-Browning; born 1904). She was a Roman Catholic convert, a fact which led Graham Greene to conversion before he married her in 1927. They had two children. Long afterwards, she remarked: 'I had the hard part when we were young and poor. All the mistresses had the good times.' In 1995 *The Times* described her as 'the world's leading dolls' house expert': her collection is housed in the Rotunda Museum at Oxford.

SIR HENRY RIDER HAGGARD (1856–1925). Author of romantic adventure-novels: notably *King Solomon's Mines* (1885), which Jim in *The Captain and the Enemy* has read four times, and *Allan Quatermain* (1887), which Greene associated with 'The Third Man'. Greene retained his early enthusiasm for Haggard's work, and reflected that his own travels in Africa might have been prompted by *King Solomon's Mines*. (See 'The Lost Childhood' and 'Rider Haggard's Secret' in *CE*.)

HENRY JAMES (1843–1916). Dedicated and subtle American-born fiction-writer who settled in England and became a British subject in 1915. Greene argued that religious values pervade his work. 'Hell and Purgatory: James came very close to a direct statement of his belief in both of these.' James's *The Turn of the Screw* probably influenced 'The Basement Room'. *The Wings of the Dove* tinged Greene's love for Catherine Walston: he called her 'Kate Croy'. Numerous pieces in *Collected Essays* discuss James; see also 'The Young Henry James' in *Reflections*.

BENJAMIN JOWETT (1817–93). Master of Balliol College, Oxford. Greene's radio play *The Great Jowett* (1939, published 1981) commends him for introducing liberal reforms (he makes Balliol 'a college where a poor man could be happy') and for founding the University's Drama Society and Indian Institute.

SIR ALEXANDER KORDA (1893–1956). Hungarian-born movie mogul; head of London Films (which served as a cover for British espionage abroad). Greene, as film critic, repeatedly sniped at him; but Korda befriended Greene, employed him as a script-writer, and took him on voyages in the yacht *Elsewhere*. Korda was the original of Herbert Dreuther in *Loser Takes All*, and, said Greene, 'even provided me with the plot'. *Ways of Escape* (Chap. 7) includes an affectionate tribute to 'Alex, a man whom I loved'.

FRANÇOIS MAURIAC (1885–1970). French Catholic novelist, story-writer, dramatist and critic, awarded the Nobel Prize in 1952. When praising his works (in the essay 'François Mauriac'), Greene says that the actions of his characters 'are less important than the force, whether God or Devil, that compels them'; and he quotes with approval passages containing the following aphorisms: 'The patience of vice is infinite'; 'God is the good temptation to which many men finally succumb' (*CE*, pp. 119, 120). See also the comments in *CCE*, pp. 160–1.

CHARLES PÉGUY (1875–1914). French poet, essaysist and heterodox Catholic. His essay 'Un nouveau théologien, M. Fernand Laudet' (1911) provided the epigraph of *The Heart of the Matter*. Impressed by the life of Villon, Péguy alleged that the experts on Christianity are the sinner and the saint: indeed, basically they are the same: 'en principe c'est le même homme'.

J. B. PRIESTLEY (1894–1984). Prolific and popular author of novels (notably *The Good Companions*, 1929, and *Angel Pavement*, 1930) and plays (notably *An Inspector Calls*, 1947). Greene, in several novels, made sniping references to him; Priestley threatened a libel action for his portrayal as Savory in *Stamboul Train*. Priestley's wartime broadcasts helped to sustain national morale, and in 'A Lost Leader' (1940) Greene extolled him as 'a great man', 'second only in importance to Mr. Churchill'. Priestley became a director of The Bodley Head in 1957, Greene in 1958; each rented a flat in Albany.

SIR HERBERT READ (1893–1968). Poet, critic, novelist and autobiographer, recalled affectionately by Greene (*WE*, pp. 39–44): 'T. S. Eliot and Herbert Read were the two great figures of my young manhood.' As a literary critic for *Night and Day*, Read worked alongside Greene, who said that he would put his sole novel, *The Green Child* (1935), 'among the great poems of this century'.

SIR CAROL REED (1906–76). English film director whose films include *The Stars Look Down* (1939), *Odd Man Out* (1946), *An Outcast of the Islands* (1951) and three based on Greene's works: *The Fallen Idol* (1948), *The Third Man* (1949) and *Our Man in Havana* (1959). Of these, *The Fallen Idol* is excellent, *The Third Man* outstanding, and *Our Man in Havana* disappointing.

JOCELYN RICKARDS (born 1924). Australian-born painter and theatrical designer. In the 1950s, Greene was one of her lovers; others included A. J. Ayer, the philosopher, and John Osborne, the dramatist.

WILLIAM SHAKESPEARE (1564–1616). His writings pervasively influenced Greene's: for example, the title of *The Name of Action* quotes *Hamlet*, and so does Prewitt in *Brighton Rock*. *The Name of Action* sometimes recalls *Measure for Measure*, and *Pericles* provides thematic and comic material for *England Made Me*. In *British Dramatists*, Greene praises Shakespeare's precision; but in 'The Virtue of Disloyalty' (*R*) he complains that though Shakespeare is 'the greatest of all poets', he is the 'one supreme poet of conservatism'.

GENERAL OMAR TORRIJOS (Omar Torrijos Herrera; 1929–81). Seized power in Panama by means of a military coup in 1968, and curtailed civil liberties (some opponents were tortured and killed). He instituted various social reforms, and was flattered by Greene in *Getting to Know the General*. Torrijos died in a plane crash, which may have suggested the ending of *The Captain and the Enemy*.

CATHERINE WALSTON (later Lady Walston; 1916–78). Wife of Henry (later Lord) Walston, the wealthy landowner. She was beautiful, vivacious and sexually bold. Evelyn Waugh's *Diaries* (1976, p. 702) described her thus in 1948: 'Fine big eyes and mouth, unaffected to the verge of insanity, unvain, no ostentation – simple friendliness and generosity and childish curiosity . . . . . Her bedside littered with books of devotion.' Greene, her godfather when she became a Catholic convert, was one of her lovers between 1946 and the early 1960s; he hoped to marry her. His collection of poems, *After Two Years*, was privately printed for Catherine, and his relationship with her provides the basis of *The End of the Affair*. The American edition of that novel is dedicated 'To Catherine with love'; the British and American editions of *The Living Room* are dedicated (slightly more emphatically) 'To Catherine with Love'.

EVELYN WAUGH (1903–66). Catholic convert (1930) and novelist acclaimed for the satiric works *Vile Bodies* (1930), *Black Mischief* (1932), *A Handful of Dust* (1934) and *Scoop* (1938). He also wrote biographies of Edmund Campion and Ronald Knox. A friend and correspondent of Greene's, he nevertheless criticised the theology of *The Heart of the Matter* and declined to review *A Burnt-Out Case*. His *Diaries* (1976, p. 779) say of the latter novel: 'It is the first time Graham has come out as specifically faithless – pray God it is a mood, but it strikes deeper and colder . . . . . What is more – no, less – Graham's skill is fading.'

MALCOLM WILLIAMSON (born 1931). Australian composer who converted Greene's *Our Man in Havana* into an opera (1963) which Greene enjoyed: '[S]ome people were very unkind to it, quite wrongly I thought. It had some good tunes – must have had if I enjoyed it.' (*Sunday Times*, 5 March 1978, p. 37.)

Bibliography, further reading, and list of films

Bibliographies

J. DON VANN: *Graham Greene: A Checklist of Criticism* (n.p.: Kent State University Press, 1970).

R. A. WOBBE: *Graham Greene: A Bibliography and Guide to Research* (New York and London: Garland, 1979).

A. F. CASSIS: *Graham Greene: An Annotated Bibliography of Criticism* (Metuchen, N.J., and London: Scarecrow Press, 1981).

First British editions of Greene's works

Babbling April (Oxford: Blackwell, 1925).

The Man Within (London: Heinemann, 1929).

The Name of Action (London: Heinemann, 1930; subsequently suppressed by Greene, who excluded it from the Uniform Edition, the Collected Edition, and the Penguin series of his works).

Rumour at Nightfall (London: Heinemann, 1931; subsequently suppressed by Greene).

Stamboul Train (London: Heinemann, 1932).

It's a Battlefield (London: Heinemann, 1934).

England Made Me: A Novel (London: Heinemann, 1935).

The Bear Fell Free (London: Grayson and Grayson, 1935)

The Basement Room and Other Stories (London: Cresset Press, 1935).

Journey without Maps (London: Heinemann, 1936).

A Gun for Sale (London: Heinemann, 1936).

Brighton Rock: A Novel (London: Heinemann, 1938).

The Lawless Roads (London: Longmans, Green, 1939).

The Confidential Agent: An Entertainment (London: Heinemann, 1939).

The Power and the Glory (London: Heinemann, 1940).

British Dramatists (London: Collins, 1942).

The Ministry of Fear: An Entertainment (London: Heinemann, 1943).

The Little Train (London: Eyre & Spottiswoode, 1946).

Nineteen Stories (London: Heinemann, 1947).

The Heart of the Matter (London: Heinemann, 1948).

'The Third Man' and 'The Fallen Idol' (London: Heinemann, 1950).

The Little Fire Engine (London: Parrish, 1950).

The Lost Childhood and Other Essays (London: Eyre & Spottiswoode, 1951).

The End of the Affair (London: Heinemann, 1951).

The Little Horse Bus (London: Parrish, 1952).

The Living Room (London: Heinemann, 1953).

The Little Steamroller (London: Parrish, 1953).

Twenty-One Stories (London: Heinemann, 1954).

Loser Takes All (London: Heinemann, 1955).

The Quiet American (London: Heinemann, 1955).

The Potting Shed (London: Heinemann, 1958).

Our Man in Havana (London: Heinemann, 1958).

The Complaisant Lover (London: Heinemann, 1959).

A Visit to Morin (London: Heinemann, 1960).

A Burnt-Out Case (London: Heinemann, 1961).

In Search of a Character: Two African Journals (London: Bodley Head, 1961).

A Sense of Reality (London: Bodley Head, 1963).

Carving a Statue (London: Bodley Head, 1964).

The Comedians (London: Bodley Head, 1966).

'May We Borrow Your Husband?' and Other Comedies of the Sexual Life (London: Bodley Head, 1967).

The Third Man. A Film by Graham Greene and Carol Reed (London: Lorrimer, 1969).

Collected Essays (London: Bodley Head, 1969).

Travels with My Aunt (London: Bodley Head, 1969).

A Sort of Life (London: Bodley Head, 1971).

Collected Stories (London: Bodley Head and Heinemann, 1972).

The Pleasure-Dome: The Collected Film Criticism 1935–1940, ed. John Russell Taylor (London: Secker & Warburg, 1972).

The Honorary Consul (London: Bodley Head, 1973).

Lord Rochester's Monkey (London: Bodley Head, 1974).

The Return of A. J. Raffles (London: Bodley Head, 1975).

The Human Factor (London: Bodley Head, 1978).

Doctor Fischer of Geneva or The Bomb Party (London: Bodley Head, 1980).

Ways of Escape (London: Bodley Head, 1980).

The Great Jowett (London: Bodley Head, 1981).

Monsignor Quixote (London: Bodley Head, 1982).

J'Accuse: The Dark Side of Nice (London: Bodley Head, 1982).

'Yes and No' and 'For Whom the Bell Chimes' (London: Bodley Head, 1983).

Getting to Know the General (London: Bodley Head, 1984).

The Tenth Man (London: Bodley Head and Anthony Blond, 1985).

The Captain and the Enemy (London: Reinhardt, 1988).

Yours, Etc. (London: Reinhardt, 1989).

The Last Word and Other Stories (London: Reinhardt, 1990).

Reflections (London: Reinhardt, 1990).

A World of My Own: A Dream Diary (London: Reinhardt, 1992).

The Graham Greene Film Reader: Mornings in the Dark, ed. David Parkinson (Manchester: Carcanet Press, 1993).

Under the Garden (London: Penguin, 1995).

Related works

Why Do I Write? An Exchange of Views between Elizabeth Bowen, Graham Greene & V. S. Pritchett (London: Percival Marshall, 1948).

Essais Catholiques (Paris: Editions du Seuil, 1953).

Introductions to Three Novels (Stockholm: Norstadt & Söners, 1962).

Victorian Detective Fiction, ed. Eric Osborne (London: Bodley Head, 1966).

The Other Man: Conversations with Graham Greene, ed. Marie-Françoise Allain (London: Bodley Head, 1983).

Reference Section

PAUL HOGARTH: *Graham Greene Country* (London: Pavilion Books, 1986).

Works edited by Graham Greene

The Old School: Essays by Divers Hands (London: Jonathan Cape, 1934).

The Best of Saki (London: British Publishers' Guild, 1950).

The Spy's Bedside Book (co-editor: Hugh Greene. London: Hart-Davis, 1957).

An Impossible Woman: The Memories of Dottoressa Moor of Capri (London: Bodley Head, 1975).

Victorian Villainies (co-editor: Hugh Greene. Harmondsworth: Viking, 1984).

Biographies

NORMAN SHERRY: *The Life of Graham Greene: Volume One: 1904–1939* (London: Cape, 1989).

NORMAN SHERRY: *The Life of Graham Greene: Volume Two: 1939–1955* (London: Cape, 1994).

MICHAEL SHELDEN: *Graham Greene: The Man Within* (London: Heinemann, 1994).

ANTHONY MOCKLER: *Graham Greene: Three Lives* (Arbroath: Hunter Mackay, 1994).

Criticism

DEREK TRAVERSI: 'Graham Greene', *Twentieth Century* 149 (1951), pp. 231–40, 319–28.

P. H. NEWBY: *The Novel, 1945–1950* (London: Longman, 1951).

KENNETH ALLOTT and MIRIAM FARRIS: *The Art of Graham Greene* (London: Hamilton, 1951; New York: Russell & Russell, 1983).

RICHARD HOGGART: 'The Force of Caricature', *Essays in Criticism* 3 (October 1953), pp. 447–62.

ARNOLD KETTLE: 'Graham Greene' in *An Introduction to the English Novel*, Vol. 2 [1953] (London: Hutchinson, 1972).

KARL PATTEN: 'The Structure of *The Power and the Glory*', *Modern Fiction Studies* 3 (Autumn 1957), pp. 225–34.

MORTON DAWEN ZABEL: 'Graham Greene: The Best and the Worst' in *Craft and Character* (London: Gollancz, 1957).

V. S. PRITCHETT: 'The World of Graham Greene', *New Statesman*, 4 January 1958, pp. 17–18.

DAVID PRYCE-JONES: *Graham Greene* (Edinburgh: Oliver and Boyd, 1963).

DAVID LODGE: *Graham Greene* (New York and London: Columbia University Press, 1966).

Graham Greene: Some Critical Considerations, ed. Robert O. Evans (Lexington: University of Kentucky Press, 1967).

ANTHONY BURGESS: 'The Greene and the Red: Politics in the Novels of Graham Greene' in *Urgent Copy: Literary Studies* (London: Cape, 1968).

Graham Greene: A Collection of Critical Essays, ed. Samuel Hynes (New York: Prentice-Hall, 1973).

GENE D. PHILLIPS, S.J.: *Graham Greene: The Films of His Fiction* (New York and London: Teachers' College Press, 1974).

H. J. DONAGHY: *Graham Greene: An Introduction to His Writings* (Amsterdam: Rodopi, 1983).

QUENTIN FALK: *Travels in Greeneland: The Cinema of Graham Greene* (London: Quartet, 1984).

ROGER SHARROCK: *Saints, Sinners and Comedians: The Novels of Graham Greene* (Tunbridge Wells: Burns and Oates, 1984).

GRAHAME SMITH: *The Achievement of Graham Greene* (Brighton: Harvester, 1986).

A. A. DeVITIS: *Graham Greene* [1964] (revised edition; Boston: Twayne, 1986).

PAUL O'PREY: *A Reader's Guide to Graham Greene* (London: Thames & Hudson, 1988).

VALENTINE CUNNINGHAM: *British Writers of the Thirties* (Oxford: Oxford University Press, 1989).

Graham Greene: A Revaluation: New Essays, ed. Jeffrey Meyers (Basingstoke: Macmillan, 1990).

ANDREA FREUD LOEWENSTEIN: *Loathsome Jews and Engulfing Women* (New York and London: New York University Press, 1993).

Films of Greene's works

Orient Express. Director: Paul Martin. Cast included Heather Angel and Norman Foster. (USA, 1934.)

The Green Cockatoo. Dir.: William Cameron Menzies. John Mills, Rene Ray, Robert Newton. Based on story and scenario by Greene. (GB, 1937.)

This Gun for Hire. Dir.: Frank Tuttle. Veronica Lake, Alan Ladd. (USA, 1942.)

Went the Day Well? (US title: *Forty-Eight Hours*). Dir.: Alberto Cavalcanti. Leslie Banks, Elizabeth Allan. Based on 'The Lieutenant Died Last'. (GB, 1942.)

The Ministry of Fear. Dir.: Fritz Lang. Ray Milland, Marjorie Reynolds. (USA, 1943.)

The Confidential Agent. Dir.: Herman Shumlin. Charles Boyer, Lauren Bacall. (USA, 1945.)

The Man Within (US title: *The Smugglers*). Dir.: Bernard Knowles. Richard Attenborough, Joan Greenwood, Michael Redgrave, Jean Kent. (GB, 1947.)

The Fugitive. Dir.: John Ford. Henry Fonda, Dolores del Rio, Pedro Armendariz. Based on *The Power and the Glory*. (USA, 1947.)

Brighton Rock (US title: *Young Scarface*). Dir.: John Boulting. Richard Attenborough, Carol Marsh, Hermione Baddeley. (GB, 1947.)

The Fallen Idol. Dir.: Carol Reed. Ralph Richardson, Michèle Morgan, Sonia Dresdel, Bobby Henrey. Based on 'The Basement Room'. (GB, 1948.)

The Third Man. Dir.: Carol Reed. Joseph Cotten, Orson Welles, Alida Valli, Trevor Howard. (GB, 1949.)

The Heart of the Matter. Dir.: G. M. O'Ferrall. Trevor Howard, Elizabeth Allan, Maria Schell, Peter Finch. (GB, 1953.)

The End of the Affair. Dir.: Edward Dmytryk. Deborah Kerr, Van Johnson, Peter Cushing, John Mills. (GB, 1955.)

Loser Takes All. Dir.: Ken Annakin. Robert Morley, Rossano Brazzi, Glynis Johns. (GB, 1956.)

Across the Bridge. Dir.: Ken Annakin. Rod Steiger, Bill Nagy. Based on Greene's tale. (GB, 1957.)

Short Cut to Hell. Dir.: James Cagney. Robet Ivers, Georgeann Johnson, William Bishop. Based on *A Gun for Sale*. (USA, 1957.)

The Quiet American. Dir.: Joseph L. Mankiewicz. Audie Murphy, Michael Redgrave, Georgia Moll. (USA, 1957.)

Our Man in Havana. Dir.: Carol Reed. Alec Guinness, Noël Coward, Ralph Richardson, Maureen O'Hara. (GB, 1959.)

The Comedians. Dir.: Peter Glenville. Richard Burton, Elizabeth Taylor, Peter Ustinov, Alex Guinness. (USA, Bermuda, France, 1967.)

Travels with My Aunt. Dir.: George Cukor. Maggie Smith, Alec McCowan. (USA, 1972.)

England Made Me. Dir.: Peter Duffell. Peter Finch, Michael York, Hildegaard Neil. (GB, 1972.)

The Human Factor. Dir.: Otto Preminger. Nicol Williamson, Iman, Ann Todd, Derek Jacobi. (GB, 1979.)

A Shocking Accident. Dir.: James Scott. Rupert Everett, Jenny Seagrove. Based on Greene's tale. (GB, 1982.)

The Honorary Consul (US title: *Beyond the Limit*). Dir.: John Mackenzie. Richard Gere, Michael Caine. (USA, 1983.)

Loser Takes All (US title: *Strike It Rich*). Dir.: James Scott. Robert Lindsay, Molly Ringwald, John Gielgud. (USA, 1990.)

(Adaptations for television are listed in *The Graham Greene Film Reader*.)

General Index

Index to Greene's Works